HYPERMEDIA LEARNING ENVIRONMENTS
Instructional Design and Integration

Edited by:

Piet A. M. Kommers

University of Twente, The Netherlands

Scott Grabinger

University of Colorado at Denver

Joanna C. Dunlap

University of Colorado at Denver

LEA LAWRENCE ERLBAUM ASSOCIATES, PUBLISHERS
1996   Mahwah, New Jersey

Lawrence Erlbaum Associates, Inc., Publishers
10 Industrial Avenue
Mahwah, New Jersey 07430

Library of Congress Cataloging-in-Publication Data

Hypermedia learning environments : instructional design and
   integration / edited by Piet A.M. Kommers, Scott Grabinger, Joanna
   C. Dunlap.
      p.   cm.
   Includes bibliographical references and index.
   ISBN 0-8058-1828-6 (alk. paper). -- ISBN 0-8058-1829-4 (pbk. :
alk. paper)
   1. Interactive multimedia. 2. Hypertext systems. 3. Computer
-assisted instruction. 4. Instructional systems--Design.
I. Kommers, Piet A. M. II. Grabinger, R. Scott, 1950-   .
III. Dunlap, Joanna C.
LB1028.55.H96 1996
371.3'34--dc20   96-8898

Books published by Lawrence Erlbaum Associates are printed
on acid-free paper, and their bindings are chosen
for strength and durability.

Printed in the United States of America

10 9 8 7 6 5 4 3 2

HYPERMEDIA LEARNING ENVIRONMENTS
Instructional Design and Integration

TABLE OF CONTENTS

Preface...ix
    Purpose ix
    Goals x
    Audience..xi
    Content and Parts...xi
    Limitations...xi
    How to Use this Book..xi
    Acknowledgments..xii
    Software Examples xii
    Contributors xii

Part I: Hypermedia and Multimedia Concepts

1. Definitions...1
    Piet A. M. Kommers

New Media: Are they Essential to Learning and Teaching....................1
Definitions 2
The Family of New Media 9
References 11

2. Multimedia Environments 13
    Piet A. M. Kommers

Hypermedia as Information Resources for Learning................................15
Three Metaphors underlying Hypermedia.................................20
Learning Through CD-ROM-based Hypermedia.........................25
Conclusion...31
References..32

3. Research on the Use of Hypermedia.....................................33
    Piet A. M. Kommers

Multimedia in the Landscape of Teaching and Learning.......................34
Didactic, Physical, and Epistemic Navigation in Hypertext.....................39
Research Line 1: Can hypertext essentially assist in complex mental tasks,
        such as learning and knowledge acquisition? 41
Research Line 2: Which is the best way of interacting between users and a
        hypertext system?...52

Research Line 3: What user interfaces are appropriate for navigation and
  collaboration in hypertext?...56
Research Line 4: Which Is the right granularity to represent knowledge beyond
  the level of associative links?...64
Conclusion...67
References...68

Part II: Developing Hypermedia and Multimedia Applications

4. Nodes and Organization **79**
  Joanna C. Dunlap and Scott Grabinger

Node Characteristics 79
Guidelines...81
Conclusion...87

5. Links **89**
  Scott Grabinger and Joanna C. Dunlap

Characteristics of Links 89
Kinds of Links: Contextual Links.......................................94
Kinds of Links: Support Links..99
Guidelines...107
Conclusion...114

6. Human-Computer Interface Design **115**
  Rose Marra

HCI Definition...116
Basic HCI Principles 117
Production Bias 121
Assimilation Bias 124
Intuitiveness...127
Computer as Tool 129
Conclusion...134
References 134

7. Screen Design **137**
  Scott Grabinger

Legibility..138
Aesthetic Quality Guidelines 141
Basic Typography Guidelines...144
Macrolevel Design Guidelines..150
Microlevel Design Guidelines 153
Conclusion...155
References 155

8. User Support Strategies **157**
  Joanna C. Dunlap

Orienting Users to the Application 158
Facilitating Navigation 161
Feedback to Keep Users Informed 165
General User Support 168
Conclusion...171

9. Evolution and Maintenance **173**
   Rose Marra

Definitions 173
Rationale for Evolution and Maintenance 174
Creating Procedures 176
Guidelines 178
Conclusion 184
References 185

10. Formative Evaluation **187**
   Martin Tessmer

Front-end and Formative Evaluation Purposes 187
Multimedia Evaluation Needs 188
Front-end Evaluation Questions 189
Formative Evaluation Questions 196
Evaluating the Multimedia Experience and Outcomes 205
Conclusion 206
References 207

Part III: Rich Environments for Active Learning

11. Encourage Student Responsibility **211**
   Scott Grabinger and Joanna C. Dunlap

REALs 212
Guidelines 213
Conclusion 222
References 223

12. Make Learning Meaningful **227**
   Joanna C. Dunlap and Scott Grabinger

Generative Learning 228
Anchored Instruction 229
Cooperative Learning and Generativity 229
Guidelines 230
Conclusion 238
References 238

13. Active Knowledge Construction **239**
   Joanna C. Dunlap and Scott Grabinger

Guidelines 240
Conclusion 253
References 253

14. Learner Assessment **255**
   Thomas A. Cyr

Tests versus Assessment 255
Basic Premises 258
Assessment Guidelines 259
Lifelong Learning Competencies and Assessment 265
Conclusion 268
References 270

Index **273**

PREFACE

> *New technologies in Education and Training will be accepted quite easily, as long as the actual process of teaching and learning is not touched.*

Purpose   The preceding hasty, skeptical remark was the trigger for a thorough overview of hypermedia and multimedia for all who like to see more specific benefits and worked-out examples based on practical experiences in real school settings. During a large-scale implementation experiment in the Netherlands, we heaved sighs resembling the skeptic slogan above. It appeared that during the first confrontation with multimedia, teachers said, "We're going to whoop it up." Some weeks later, however, it seemed as though they preferred to use the new tools to amplify their traditional way of teaching. One idea was to use the hypertext approach to deliver multiple choice questions in which statements are followed by alternative explanations. Students click the hot spot covering the correct alternative to proceed through the program. In itself there is no objection to this testing technique, however it bypasses the central didactic potential in multimedia — providing optimal flexibility for the learner and stimulating the learner to construct private concepts rather than reproducing given explanations.

   Our school observations convinced us that it is not sufficient to launch new learning media. New approaches to learning seem to sink away in cosmetic features rather than penetrate to the arena of didactic thinking and innovative imagination. Teachers need strong, generic examples showing how to use media in lessons, and they also need examples for adapting the new ideas to their own setting.

Writing this book was necessary and challenging because we saw the enthusiasm of teachers, program developers, and students working with new learning tools. Its final impact on learning and teaching practices will be felt immediately. Maybe it will still take few decades for its view to be adopted, but the longer it takes, the more profound the adoption will be.

An equivalent delayed acceptance of an essential new view on teaching and learning was displayed in the late 1960s and 1970s in Europe: the notion of goal-directed instruction based on behaviorist theories, instrumental learning, and programmed instruction. Before that time, the European tradition in school learning was one of a pedagogical climate, socio-cultural transfer and maturation. Instructional science coming from military training and job training brought a cybernetic element in our view on learning. Learning preferably takes place when the teacher and the environment systematically presents new knowledge and skills to the learner, and reinforces correct reactions of the learner.

This very aspiration to anticipate, arrange, and control individual learning processes is the basic opponent of today's idea of exploratory learning with multimedia, which aims to arouse the student's curiosity by giving him or her full freedom and responsibility for *how* things should be learned. Multimedia are inherently focusing open and exploratory learning events, rather than being canned teaching dialogues in the famous tradition of so-called programmed instruction.

> ...*the drudgery of teaching and learning the barest inchoate of knowledge.*
> R. W. Hamilton,
> *Popular Education, vi., 1846. 135.*

This desperate citation reflects a disparaging view on elementary stages in learning. The pretension of this book, however, contrasts with this 19th century fragment. We intend to explicate learning environments as creative stages in the design of students' knowledge.

Goals Three goals are pursued in this book. First, we discuss the concepts of hypermedia, multimedia, and hypertext, and review pertinent research lines. Second, we provide guidelines and suggestions for developing multimedia applications. Finally, we place technology within a broader context of education and training through a discussion of rich environments for active learning (REALs).

Audience This book aims at novice practitioners — people who teach about or develop multimedia and hypermedia applications. It examines carefully the main components and issues in developing applications. It provides suggestions and heuristics for sound, fundamental design processes. Although it provides a conceptual framework for the application of technology in Part III, it is not a research-based or theoretical book. Faculty who teach classes related to computer-based application and multimedia design can use this as a guiding text for their students. Producers of applications will find this text useful as a reference.

Content and Parts *Part I.* The body of this book presents a landscape of practical experiences and experiments from the University of Colorado at Denver and The University of Twente in The Netherlands. The first part, written by Piet Kommers from Twente, defines the areas of hypermedia and multimedia and looks back on multimedia prototypes under experimentation in four classes of secondary education. He concludes his part with a chapter that reviews research from the area of hypertext and hypermedia.

Part II. The second part is based on the experiences of developers of computer-based applications at the University of Colorado at Denver. Chapters 4 through 10 cover issues crucial to the development and design of applications including nodes, links, human-computer interface design, screen design, user support, program maintenance, and formative evaluation. We present the synthesis of our experience, teaching, and research in the form of guidelines for development.

Part III. The third part takes a broader look at education and multimedia, describing a context within which technology may be used. This context is called rich environments for active learning (REALs). The discussion covers the fundamental characteristics of student-centered environments focusing on developing student responsibility, making learning meaningful, promoting overt knowledge-construction, and learner assessment.

Limitations This text takes a development focus. It is not a technical or how-to manual on working with video, sound, digitized graphics, or computer code. There are other highly technical books that do that kind of work. This book helps you to set up and manage the process of developing a multimedia application. Finally, the text takes a unique approach to the idea of media. We view media as delivery systems. If video is required, use it. If sound will help your application, use it. The fundamental development guidelines here are usually *not* media specific. Media work only within the strategies for which they are used.

HOW TO USE THIS BOOK

This book is for teachers, trainers, and curriculum and courseware designers who want to use the new spectrum of multimedia tools. Besides seeing the examples we give in Parts II and III, it is essential to orient yourself in the rationale behind multimedia, exploratory learning, and knowledge representation presented in Part I. In principle, we believe that reading the book in its current order is quite effective for readers who need both practical and theoretical support. However, the book is intended as a reference and may be read to satisfy specific needs. If you are primarily interested in practical examples that can be applied in your current teaching practice and development work, it might be good to go directly to Part II. It may encourage you to return to Part I later.

If you are primarily interested in the more generic ideas behind multimedia in education, it would be better to start with Part I, which should be sufficient for starting your imagination to create your own multimedia sessions in your classroom. Reading Part II is then a comparison between your own and our interpretation of the potential of multimedia.

ACKNOWLEDGMENTS

The authors wish to express gratitude to several people instrumental in the publication of this text. We thank David H. Jonassen (The Pennsylvania State University) for early comments in the conceptualization of this manuscript and its prospectus. He was also instrumental in bringing the Twente and Denver collaborators together. We thank Thomas Duffy (Indiana University) for encouraging the Denver authors over several rough spots. Several classes at the University of Colorado at Denver also deserve thanks for providing formative feedback on several iterations of most of the chapters. Scott Heath and Dr. Daniel Ambruso (The Transfusion Medicine Group) permitted us to copy screens from their programs for examples. Susan and Kevin McKenney did a wonderful job in editing parts of the manuscript. A Ph.D. seminar of CU-Denver students: Gloria Gyure, Michael Batty, Janell Sueltz, Vicky Wood, Bob Davis, David Ackerman, Richard Morse, Karen Myers, and Robert Thompson offered comments on one of the later drafts. Finally, we express our undying gratitude to Rionda Osman-Jouchoux for formatting and producing the camera ready copy.

SOFTWARE EXAMPLES

The book contains numerous illustrations, most from several HyperCard (equipment required: Macintosh, System 7, 4 megabytes of RAM, HyperCard 2.0 or later) programs. The programs *Desert Shield, InfoAgent,* and *Instructional Technology in Teacher Education ITiTE)* are available for downloading from the Lawrence Erlbaum web site:

http://www.erlbaum.com/

CONTRIBUTORS

Thomas A. Cyr   Dr. Tom Cyr is an instructional designer/researcher at the University of Colorado at Denver. He wrote chapter 14 on learner assessment. He was a classroom teacher and school project director involved with classroom technology. He recently completed his Ph.D. in information and learning technologies with an emphasis in assessment issues. He can be reached via his e-mail address: tacyr@ouray.cudenver.edu.

Joni Dunlap   Dr. Joanna C. Dunlap is Director of Distance Learning at Regis University in Denver and an honorarium professor at the University of Colorado at Denver and a consultant in the areas of constructivist training environments, problem-based learning, collaborative problem-solving, and hypermedia instructional design. She recently completed her doctorate at the University of Colorado at Denver with an emphasis on rich environments for active learning (student-centered learning environments). Her research interests include the quality of thinking in students involved in problem-based learning and the development of life-long learning skills. She can be reached via her e-mail address: jcdunlap@carbon.cudenver.edu

Scott Grabinger   Dr. Scott Grabinger is program coordinator and associate professor of Information and Learning Technologies in the Division of Technology and Special Services at the University of Colorado at Denver. He teaches classes in multimedia design, instructional message design, and rich environments for active learning. His research interests include screen design for computer-based applications and the effects of REAL strategies on problem solving skills. He consults regularly with business and industry on training design, problem-based learning, and the design of CBT and electronic performance support systems. He is the author (with Brent G. Wilson and David H. Jonassen) of *Building Expert Systems for Training and Education* (Praeger). He can be reached via his e-mail address: sgrabing@carbon.cudenver.edu.

Piet Kommers   Dr. Piet Kommers is lecturer and researcher in the Department of Education at Twente University in the Netherlands. His specialties are hypermedia, knowledge representation, and concept mapping. He was director and scientific editor of NATO's Advanced Research Workshop on Cognitive Tools for Learning in 1991. Basing his work on Graph Theory and SGML metainformation, he defined information management procedures to be used for the design and the maintenance of technical documentation and CD-ROM-based encyclopedias for learning. He was executive manager in industrial hypermedia projects for Philips Electronics and Elsevier Publishers. His dissertation, Hypertext and the Acquisition of Knowledge, addressed the evoked learning effects of studying via hypertext. He is main editor of *Cognitive Tools for Learning* (Springer, 1991), *Document Management for Hypermedia Design* (Springer, 1996), and *Educational Technology in the former Soviet Union* (in press, 1996). He was visiting Professor and consultant in East China Normal University at Shanghai, the Gluskov Institute for Cybernetics at Kiev, and the University of Colorado at Denver. He can be reached via his e-mail address: kommers@edte.utwente.nl.

Rose Marra   Dr. Rose Marra recently received her Ph.D. from the University of Colorado at Denver. She studied the effect of semantic networks on the creation of expert systems. She holds a master's degree in computer science from the University of Kansas and has 8 years experience as a software engineer and technical writer for AT&T Bell Laboratories. She is currently employed as an instructional designer at the Applied Research Laboratories and the Leonhard Center for Engineering Education Innovation, both at the Pennsylvania State University. She may be reached via her e-mail address: rmm13@psu.edu

Martin Tessmer   Dr. Martin Tessmer is Professor of Instructional Design at the University of South Alabama. He completed his Ph.D. in instructional design at Florida State University (1982). Over the past 13 years he has worked as an instructional design consultant to postsecondary administration and faculty at four different institutions. He has participated in over a 100 design projects, ranging from faculty development to multimedia design. He is the author of *Planning and Conducting Formative Evaluations* (Kogan Page) *A Nonprogrammer's Guide to Designing Instruction for Microcomputers* (with David Jonassen & David Caverly; Libraries Unlimited), *Analysing the Instructional Setting (*with Duncan Harris; Kogan Page), and *A Handbook of Task Analysis Procedures* (with David Jonassen and Wallace Hannum; Praeger). He can be reached at his e-mail address: mtessmer@jaguar1.usouthal.edu

PART I

Hypermedia and Multimedia Concepts

CHAPTER 1

Definitions

Piet A. M. Kommers

Chapter Objectives The new members of the media family: hypertext, hypermedia, and multimedia have already won their place in popular journals, library indices, and television programs. However in the scope of education, training and instruction they need a fundamental characterization so that we as professionals can benefit from their potential and impact. My objectives for this chapter are to:

- provide you with definitions of multimedia, hypermedia, and hypertext;

- describe their relationships with new information carriers such as compact discs; and

- provide an overview of application areas adjacent to teaching and learning.

NEW MEDIA: ARE THEY ESSENTIAL TO LEARNING AND TEACHING

As employees in education, schooling, and training we are set in an ambivalent position. By tradition we know that media are only appliances in the didactic arena. At the same time, however, we know that citizens in the next century will be dependent on the media that surround them to perform their jobs, to communicate, and to expand their knowledge. This means that the integration of media with school life is no longer optional, but crucial in terms of content and way of working.

Teachers and educators are persistent in their personal styles of teaching and explaining to students. That is why they need media advocates who show simple and convincing examples of the ways that new gadgets such as hypertext and hypermedia can support learning processes.

Only once in many years does a new idea appear that penetrates the way we learn, teach, and structure our knowledge, and which gradually pervades the full spectrum of media. Hypermedia and multimedia applications represent such a pervasive idea. The following observations explain why:

- Hypermedia enable us to conquer the straitjacket of linear thought dictated by oral and written narration. Creating hypermedia allows us to anticipate the capricious and unpredictable way our colleagues and students will react to new information.

- Hypermedia allow many persons to contribute to the evolution of thoughts in written documents without affecting original formulations. As hypermedia promote different views on concepts and topics, it is appropriate for distributed documents spread along many different machines at remote locations.

It may be clear from the discussion so far that the hypermedia method has implications for creating and reading text as well. From an educational point of view it may be your direct response to say, "Okay, I see." Teachers and curriculum designers have to *write* learning material in a hypermedia format, and students have to *read* it in that format.

Reading this book, you will discover that the major benefit from the hypermedia approach may be that students are invited to elicit their ideas and prior concepts and externalize them with hypermedia tools. While doing so, they can employ hypermedia documents such as CD–ROM–based[1] encyclopedias or regular learning material. However, the key student activity is to articulate, externalize, and structure conceptual knowledge. The use of hypermedia fits in the notion of what we call *concept engineering*, an umbrella term for all the cognitive tools that facilitate necessary mental processes such as learning and subsequent problem solving, decision making, simulation, collaboration, and finally designing new constructs for work or private life.

Besides the two operational benefits of hypermedia — flexibility and virtuality — an even more essential perspective can be sketched for teachers, linguists, and so-called knowledge engineers. It is the notion that hypermedia, passing over the linear and basically episodic architecture in explanations and arguments, reinforce the multidimensional and subjective aspects of content matter and knowledge about that. This notion in itself is not new. However, bringing it into educational practice, it may help teachers to stimulate students to handle knowledge in a flexible way. It may also stimulate both teachers and students to reflect on and negotiate about diverse concept meanings essential to understanding reality.

DEFINITIONS

Media Media are the tools we use to store, process, and communicate information. Media imply physical devices, formats about how to write and read the information exactly and not to forget the organizations around these media enabling us to function in society.

Question: How do we choose a media format?

---

[1] CD-ROM is an acronym for Compact Disc–Read Only Memory. It is a compact disc which looks similar to a normal audio CD, but which stores all types of multimedia data that can be read by a computer.

Answer: Any convention about how to prepare and actually imprint information so that it can be read again in a reliable way determines the format (e.g., carvings in stone, clay, or wood; ink patterns on paper; rows of holes in paper; magnetic changes in metal on a flexible tape; optical or chemical structures; and many others still to be discovered).

An important property of media is that they are interconnected as in the following:

- The hot lines of your newspaper can also be seen on your TV screen as you activate Videotext, but also at your computer screen as you access a CD-ROM with the last few months of full-text newspaper contents.

- The satellite photographs with clouds and turbulence indications can also be displayed on your computer by connecting it to your short-wave receiver.

- Sending and receiving faxes can be done by your fax machine, but also by your modem card in the computer.

Besides media integration we see a quick shift from individual media usage to collaborative usage. For example, working or learning together on a new idea or product design via interconnected computer systems becomes the de facto way, replacing solitary, isolated creations on separated work stations.

- Media comprise not only the distribution characteristic of newspapers, videos, or computers, but also include the overall infrastructure. In a well-known illustration of Pieter Breughel's "The Wedding Banquet" (c. 1558), the dishes on the stretcher have been replaced by floppy discs, the bagpiper carries a pile of backup tapes, guests at the dining table work with teletypes and long source listings, a young boy sitting in the foreground does not eat bread, but has a cassette with computer data, etc. This caricature, as you can imagine, illustrates the delicate interdependency of humans' daily necessities, available infrastructure, level of schooling, and the types of tools and media we use today. It becomes immediately clear that technology needs the right aspirations and infrastructure before we as a society can benefit from it. We might try to imagine how these facilities could penetrate Breughel's era technically, but they would not function in that setting because life had different priorities at that time. Media are designed in specific cultural contexts. We must acknowledge, however, that cultural reality gradually changes by technical approaches such as these:

- Allowing ourselves to live 40 miles away from our work place occurred by the coming of fast transportation.

- Abandoning long travels every day becomes possible as media for telecommuting arrive.

It is good to be aware of the overall media impact when we think about hyper- and multimedia in learning settings. It will become clear to you that these novelties are not only guests in the classroom. The converse is true: Schools probably become guests in the media society quite soon. They then have to compete with new, maybe even more elegant and efficient ways of teaching and learning than we might imagine from our current school culture. Remember Ivan Illich's *Deschooling Society* from the early 1960s, asserting that schools as institutions will finally disappear as learning becomes an integrated part of work, entertainment, social contacts, family life and so forth. The potential of hyper- and multimedia can hardly be imagined without an awareness of this longer-term perspective.

Hypertext Hypertext is a method to create and access nonlinear text. Texts in hypermedia are small self-containing paragraphs. Essential words or groups of words (hot spots) in a paragraph refer to other paragraphs or to other words or groups of words in other paragraphs. The user is free to decide whether to create a link or not: Any semantic relation or mental association may be an argument for defining or tracing a hypermedia link. After clicking on a highlighted term, the user jumps via the link and will immediately see the requested explanation.

The terminology to indicate new types of computer programs became well known in a short period. The idea of hypertext appeared first when Vannevar Bush (1945) pointed to the ever-growing problem of investigators staggered by the enormous quantities of available information created by colleagues, which would cost researchers years and years to search for relevant ideas. Instead of card boxes with records indexed by a limited set of key words, Bush imagined that any word in these descriptions could point to all passages all over the document collection in which the same word appeared. Bush thought only about a personalized information base, called a *memex*, which stores all books, records, journals, annotations and communications of a person. The idea of interconnectedness is still the key issue in hypertext. We observe later that it is not a trivial problem to decide which words are relevant to include in the keyword list. Too many words obscure the meaningful links between text fragments and also introduce ambiguity: The same word usually has quite different meanings in different contexts. Creating only a few links simplifies the preparation of a hypertext system, but is not helpful for those users who ask for subtle semantic relations. We see a hypertext example in Figure 1.1.

Both screens in Figure 1.1 were created by Microsoft's help function in its spreadsheet program Excel. The underlined words are so-called hot spots and are highlighted by green color on the computer screen. Hot spots can launch the user to another text fragment that will tell more information about the term in the hot spot. In fact two types of hypermedia links can be distinguished:

1. From a hot spot to the header of another article that elaborates on the meaning and background of the launching hot spot.

2. From one hot spot to a hot spot in another article. This enables the reader to see a certain concept in another context.

Activating new paragraphs of information and again clicking on hot spots leads the user through a network of connected texts. The reader may sooner or later arrive back at a screen visited earlier. This is, for instance, the case as the user goes from *InfoWindow* (within the "File Page Setup" explanation) to *InfoWindow* (within the "File Print" explanation).

Fig. 1.1. Hypertext mechanism in Microsoft's "Help for Windows."

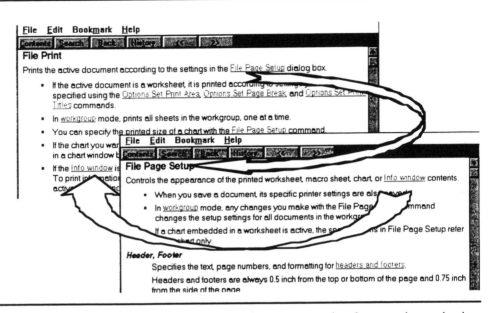

Hypermedia systems vary in their features to assist the user in navigating through larger hypermedia databases. One type of solution for complexities in navigation is to display maps of the connections between hot spots. Concept maps provide graphical overviews with nodes and links showing

- which nodes you already visited.

- via which links you could go back to earlier points.

- which hinterland is accessible behind available concept nodes.

- how distinct concepts are related via shorter or longer paths.

Multimedia Multimedia are those computer-based applications that allow the user to see and hear different types of information via one screen with audio support. The combination of more than one modality of information (e.g. text, pictures, video, animation, and sound fragments) on one screen with simultaneous control of one software application brings the user a bigger variety in information and realizes important elements for virtual reality.

Many learning settings had multimedia resources long before the name was invented. By having a video, a slide projector, an audio tape recorder, and computer screens or teletype keyboard printers one could claim the predicate, multimedia. The weakness of media combinations is in its complexity. To process more complex user actions such as taking previews and returning to earlier fragments, a central process control is needed. Another complexity is that information from different sources need to be synchronized. This implies one integrated computer device with facilities to capture, store, and display video sequences.

Traditional hybrid multimedia configurations were quite complex to build up, debug, and maintain, even for instructional designers with high skills and high aspirations in technology and instrumentation. Dedicated multimedia players such as CD-ROM and CD-interactive (CD-I) still have a short tradition, but are widespread and robust. They allow end users to consult multimedia in a standard way. Whereas CD-ROM intends to integrate multimedia in a computer environment (Macintosh or MS-Windows), CD-I seamlessly fits into the low-end consumer market and schools, using a normal television set with an easy handheld remote control.

Hypermedia Hypermedia are computer-based applications for consulting multimedia information resources. The accessing of new information is equivalent to the previously described hypermedia method: clicking on relevant areas in texts; pictures; and video, animation, and sound fragments. The hot spots in time-based fragments can be situated on a time scale, an oscillogram, or a scenario line.

Hypermedia give a better idea how to use multimedia resources. Whereas, the term "multimedia" indicates only that the variety in modalities of information is big, the term "hypermedia" implicitly advocates how to access information elements and how to crisscross in information space. The spatial metaphor is typical for the complexity that arises in creating and using hypermedia. Orientation and navigation are the costs that emerge from the desire to interconnect information elements and from the ambition to browse freely between semantic elements that you would normally find at different locations in books, different books, different libraries, and so forth. The tour through Microsoft's *Encarta* in chapter 2 gives you a flavor of the "hyper" approach: The system invites the user to go where his interest is going. Important notion in hypermedia is the appearance of hot spots. A hot spot is a marked-up word or group of words prompting the user to click or double-click. Activating a hot spot triggers a jump in information space. Normally you would need to skip large pieces of text, or books, go to other buildings, or even take a plane to another country. Hypermedia claim to help you trace semantic lines that you barely miss if you follow the author's rhetoric in a linear prescribed text. The ease of being launched from words to other contexts is attractive as the reader feels more free and experiences a low resistance in stepping away from a current passage, being confident about finding the way back.

As you get a taste of browsing, you will soon discover its price: Jumping away via hot spots often brings you into contexts that have little to do with either the previous fragment or your global interest. Here are some reasons that users might give for activating hot spots and taking the risk of being confronted with unexpected information:

1. I do not understand this word or this expression. Please explain its meaning to me now.

2. I know the meaning of this word. Tell me if my interpretation is Okay.

3. I like this passage. I like to know all details about it. Please give me more about this hot spot first of all.

4. I do not like this passage. Please bring me to related information that might be more interesting to me. I expect to come to the current passage later.

5. I do not like this topic. Please launch me to a totally different topic that might be more interesting to me.

These alternatives do not necessarily exclude each other. The order in which they are listed suggests a shift from zooming in (going more deep into details of a presented concept) to zooming out and finally jumping away from the topic or even the subject domain.

Hypermedia implicitly stimulate the user to digress to other information, even before the meaning and implications of the currently display have become clear. This digressive effect has been mentioned by several proponents of educational hypermedia as facilitating cognitive flexibility or stimulating versatility in mental perspective. We have registered positive didactic phenomenon stemming from this hypermedia tendency, but we are also aware that it needs a more profound analysis and fit to existing instructional situations before it really pays off in different practical settings. This is the scope for viewing hypermedia in the rest of this book.

Browsing and Navigation

Browsing and navigation concerns the way a user follows or creates a path along links between information nodes. Browsing through information occurs when the user clicks on hot spots or defines new hot spots and fills in subsequent nodes with information.

Browsing describes the detailed sequence of steps. Navigation characterizes the browsing pattern due to overall intentions of the user. As we explain in more detail later in this chapter, users can navigate depth-first versus breadth-first. Breadth-first navigation typically takes place because the reader does not want to miss excursions from the point where he or she started. Users inclined toward global facts will continue to jump away from their starting point, not worrying about how to return to previous nodes of interest. (Fig. 1.2). The breadth-first type of navigation can be seen in the upper part of the network, whereas the depth-first type is displayed in the lower left part.

A serialistic versus holistic style of learning occurs several times in the literature (Liu & Reed, 1994). However, it is not quite clear how to recognize it while observing users of hypermedia. A simple version of this theory would be that breadth-first learners are serialists because they tend to visit as many semantic aspects around a concept node as possible, whereas holists prefer to get a complete view on the whole subject in the hypermedia system, before they go into details. In our own research (Kommers, 1991) we found a slight difference between primary, secondary, and university students. Secondary school students tended more toward returning to previously visited nodes. Both primary and university students showed less tendency to backtrack. At all levels of schooling the tendency to go back became bigger as the hypersession proceeded. No relation became clear

Fig. 1.2. Navigation patterns.

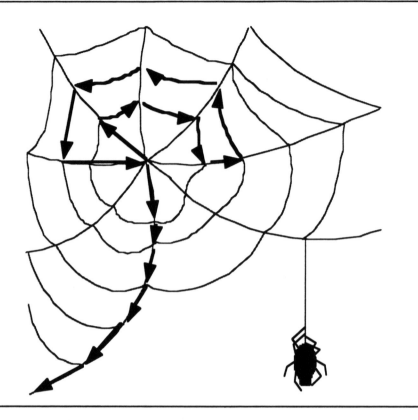

between the preferred navigation style and the amount of learning. In general we can say that the flexibility in browsing is beneficial for two reasons:

1. It allows learners to adapt reading sequences to their cognitive need for specific information. Linear text needs advanced skimming, selection, and jumping skills before readers can actually find their way.

2. Learners who face the hypermedia approach are urged to make sequencing decisions that stimulate a higher level of so-called metacognition: the consciousness about what and how one knows.

Before hypermedia training in classrooms takes place, teachers are advised to vitalize earlier learned study skills in the learners. Isolated browsing and navigation skills are likely to function only for a short time and will hardly transfer to a study approach later on (Brigham, 1994).

Navigational Support As you will experience yourself, browsing tendencies while traveling from one piece of information to another tends to distract your attention from the a priori goal from the start. Quite often users confess: "I discovered what I was looking for during my travel through the unknown." This adventure effect can be useful for those who have plenty of time and those who have no particular goal in mind. This is a rare situation though. Learners usually face a learning task that implies the confrontation and assimilation of certain concepts. It is therefore quite desirable that we add navigation tools for this purpose. These should allow learners to mold global routes, and protect them while they are crisscrossing through the tempting hot spots in the browsing phase (Swan, 1994). Chapters 2 and 5 of this book will go deeper into navigational support approaches such as concept mapping and techniques for zooming and filtering.

THE FAMILY OF NEW MEDIA

Hypertext and hypermedia both store and give access to information in a nonlinear way. The prefix "hype" indicates that something is "excessive," or "above and beyond." Like the terms "hyperspace" or "cyberspace," it projects extra dimensions such as virtuality and interconnectedness. Since the mid-1980s terms such as three-dimensional text and metatext have also been launched. Although the prefix "hyper" in fact obscures the key element, we expect its use to remain widespread.

Hypermedia inherited the hypertext mechanism as soon as the first commercial prototypes appeared (Fig. 1.3). Text, pictures, schemes, and tables; they all ask for progressive zooming techniques. The user decides which part of the current view needs more details, and the system responds by generating a new, magnified view in the desired direction. Before such advanced browsers as "fish-eye" and "network" tools were designed, three basic modes were there:

1. Clicking hot spots

2. Backtrack buttons or a repeated escape to revert to earlier nodes

3. Index lists allowing the reader to jump to nodes without intermediate steps.

Aside from problems with global navigation, multimedia made it clear that simple stepwise browsing was not adequate. It became obvious that users do not merely "travel through information." They intervene, arbitrate, mediate, negotiate, disrupt, and do many more things while taking note of new information. All of the generations of hypermedia systems designed so far have added navigation facilities that reflect other task elements of the user (Grabowski & Curtis, 1991). In fact, we might conclude that the hypermedia method has already become submissive to primary tasks the user must perform. The urgency of these primary tasks requires that hypermedia project different faces. For example, hypermedia can be used

1. As an authoring support tool

2. As encyclopedic search support

3. For software engineering

4. As a mock-up for database design

Fig. 1.3. Family nesting of new media.

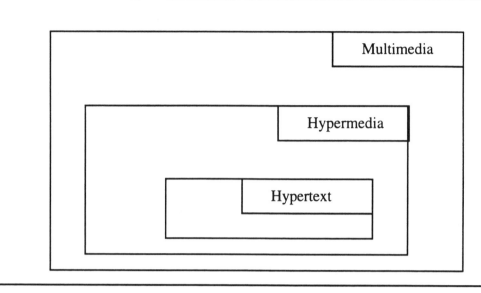

5. For shared workspaces and collaborative support

6. As a tool for teaching and learning

We will not go into detail about the first five faces of hypermedia applications. Those who are interested in one of them should consult one of the ACM Conference Proceedings on Hypertext. A particularly good one is that of Hypertext 91 at San Antonio, Texas. See also: R. M. Akscyn (1991).

The sixth application area is central in the rest of this book, which shows that the learning and teaching domain is quite diverse, even if we look at it from the hypermedia perspective. Your teaching interest may be close to one of the five mentioned application fields. This is a common finding in the design of new training media: Application-specific training brings more and more notions to the current state of the art in didactics. It is as if Ivan Illich's prediction already becomes tangible: Schools as learning institutes will disappear, as learning will become an inherent component of societal life.

Isolating its pure didactic component, then, is only sensible so far as it still brings in forgotten notions from the past. Chapter 2 expands on the growing deficit in traditional learning theories making them unable to comply with the potentials in new media.

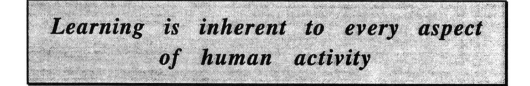

Learning is inherent to every aspect of human activity

REFERENCES

Akscyn, Robert M. (1991). The ACM Hypertext Compendium: Lessons in Hypertext Publishing. *Proceedings of ACM Hypertext '91. Technical Briefings.* New York: Association for Computing Machinery.

Brigham, F. J. (1994, February 25). *Hypermedia supports for student learning.* Indianapolis IN: Council for Exceptional Children, Indianapolis Federation.

Bush, V. (1945). As we may think. *Atlantic Monthly, 176*, 101-108.

Excel by Microsoft. (1987). *Microsoft Excel Reference Manual, Version 2.0 for IBM Personal System/2TM, IBM PS AT, and Compatibles.* Redmond WA: Microsoft Corporation.

Grabowski, B. L, & Curtis, R. (1991). Information, instruction, and learning: A hypermedia perspective. *Performance Improvement Quarterly, 4*(3), 2-12.

Illich, Ivan. (1970). *Deschooling society.* New York: Penguin Books.

Kommers, P. A. M. (1991). *Hypertext and the acquisition of knowledge.* Dissertation at the University of Twente, Enschede, The Netherlands.

Liu, M., & Reed, W. M. (1994). The relationship between the learning strategies and learning styles in a hypermedia environment. *Computers in Human Behavior, 10*(4), 419-434.

Microsoft Encarta. Redmond WA: Microsoft.

Swan, K. (1994). History, hypermedia, and criss-crossed landscapes. *Journal of Educational Multimedia and Hypermedia, 3*(2), 120-139.

CHAPTER 2

Multimedia Environments

Piet A. M. Kommers

Chapter Objectives This chapter helps you to step from the glossy slogans of hypermedia to its practical implications in realistic learning settings. It provides an overview of the potential impact of flexible information environments on human thinking and imagination. This chapter

- discusses the important links between information resources, hypermedia and learning

- describes three metaphors that underlie instructional uses of hypermedia and multimedia, and

- looks over the shoulder of a learner who browses through an electronic encyclopedia and concludes with a discussion about the necessary change in learning for the use of hypermedia environments.

We begin our examination of interactive multimedia by looking at the several ways in which it might be used. First, we start at the top floor, the "attic" so to speak (see the virtual building in Fig. 2.1), which hides three fundamental metaphoric relics that precede the many faces of fashionable hypermedia applications. The most reputable one is the so-called *resource* metaphor, acknowledging the fact that information assets are handed to the student. Less obvious are the *communication* and the *exploration* metaphors. They become more significant as teachers concede the need for vivid transactions between students and for mental excursions before learning reveals integrated and flexible knowledge.

Fig. 2.1. The Hypermedia/Multimedia Building.

The second level floor brings us to the potential impact of hypermedia systems on students in secondary school settings. To clarify how the benefits of the resource metaphor may work in practice, we will look over the shoulder of a secondary school student searching for the background of the Kurds and the reason why they experienced problems after the recent Persian Gulf War.

This floor also illustrates that in hypermedia environments the learner needs a far more active attitude than in reading a prefabricated expository text. The student needs to invest and explore new hypotheses, to see the consequences of accepting the new knowledge.

The ground floor of this chapter shows how adding the typical communication approach to hypermedia easily entails navigation assistance as known from the programmed instruction approach. It intimates the true hypermedia approach by dismissing the student from the task of controlling his or her own learning process.

Finally, the tour through the basement might be the most essential in the long run, because it exposes the idea that active learning is in fact a process of knowledge design by the student, rather than an undergoing of the teaching process. Effective teaching in this sense becomes more a process of facilitating the "extraction" of tacit knowledge from the student, rather than instruction of new information. Essential in this process of molding new concepts by the teacher, is the student's task of bringing him- or herself to new views and ideas.

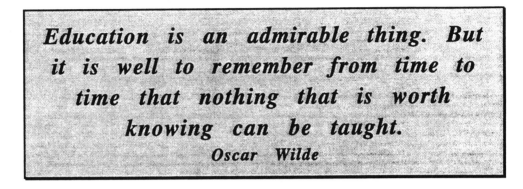

Education is an admirable thing. But it is well to remember from time to time that nothing that is worth knowing can be taught.
Oscar Wilde

HYPERMEDIA AS INFORMATION RESOURCES FOR LEARNING

Information resources are those data assets that you might need at a particular moment in learning, thinking, and designing new ideas. Information is a by-product of human mental effort, but it also becomes more important as a strategic input for mental tasks.

During the recent evolution of new media such as hypermedia, multimedia and telematic services, the impact of information resources changed quite quickly. Digitizing streams of data implies that visual and acoustic elements can be linked, combined, or filtered by a computer system. The major advantage of this flexibility is the freedom for users to control their access to information. Especially in case of learning situations this is an important quality because it increases the level of awareness, alertness, and motivation as can be seen in computer games. From a cognitive point of view this arranged flexibility is important because it allows students to adapt available information streams to their mental need at a certain moment (Lin, 1994). Experiments in project schools in the Netherlands showed that these benefits do not automatically appear as teachers allow hypermedia into their lessons. Two additional prerequisites emerged:

1. The arranged didactics and instruction by the teacher should anticipate hypermedia explorations by students before they benefit from this flexible information access.

2. Students should be trained in the use of hypermedia as a cognitive learning tool. This implies a higher level of metacognition (knowing what you know and how you learn).

In addition to these typical constraints in the field of learning, a general shift in the status of information took place: The problem of information deficiency in educational settings has been minimized in favor of information overload. Publishers until now played a crucial role in sanctifying the scope and perspectives in learning material. Books restrict the depth and breadth of background details, whereas optical data carriers such as CD-ROMs and especially telematic services allow virtual unlimited access to extensive remote assets. This change in the scale of information availability has brought a shift from an information supply market to an information demand market. In other words, those who offer information resources must bargain about prices and conditions rather than those who need information (Kommers, 1993).

The compactness of information on CDs has brought back the notion of encyclopedic orientation in learning and electronic task support environments in general.

To illustrate the lengthy tradition of technology used to manipulate books we might go back in the late Middle Ages when monks and noblemen permitted themselves to browse in Bible manuscripts and archives for several years. The idea behind the construction of the carousel containing 16 books was to switch smoothly between the different views of authors on the same topic (Fig. 2.2).

This 16th century book mill reminds us of a more generic element in our recent hypermedia aspiration: Try to assist users in finding specific combinations of textual elements from a wide domain of available books. The adventure in doing so may create exotic conclusions because authors do not always take into account the findings of other authors.

The book mill was the answer to a fast-growing number of clerical and secular libraries with handwritten and facsimile books, and to the desire for quick access to all relevant passages in all of these volumes.

Before the ingenious book mill was designed, monks and scholars had to walk along long rows of tables covered with the heavy Bibles as shown in Figure 2.3. Comparing and interrelating text passages especially need intensive book transport and put the reader at risk of being distracted by adjacent paragraphs. The book mill allowed the reader to turn the vertical wheel while the rod transmission inside controlled the book stands to prevent books falling down when they reached the back positions. The vertical position of the wheel made room for many of them to stand in a room.

The extensiveness and flexibility of reference information like present in the book mill already showed a clear demand for reducing the noise: Information that comes up as an answer to the query, however being not useful as a contribution to the desired answer.

Only the intersection between the actually retrieved documents and the relevant documents embodies the useful information (Fig. 2.4). Retrieval help systems in a classical approach should therefore reduce both noise and "silence." However, the arrival of hypermedia has brought along a renewed notion of the serendipity phenomenon. Serendip is the name of the former Sri Lanka. The *Oxford English Dictionary* on compact disc (1992) describes "serendipity" thus:

Fig. 2.2. Rotating reading table as a precursor to hypertext.

Fig 2.3. The early library concept.

Fig 2.4. The retrieval trade-off between silence and noise.

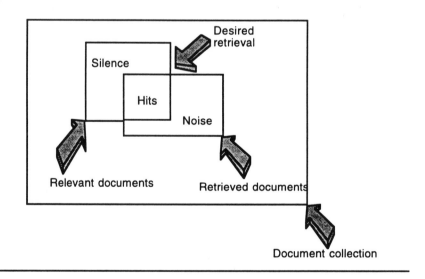

A word coined by Horace Walpole, who says (Let. to Mann, 28 Jan. 1754) that he had formed it upon the title of the fairy-tale "The Three Princes of Serendip," the heroes of which were always making discoveries, by accidents and sagacity, of things they were not in quest of. The faculty of making happy and unexpected discoveries by accident. Also, the fact or an instance of such a discovery. Formerly rare, this word and its derivatives have had wide currency in the 20th century.

The serendipity effect in hypermedia is that the user might miss an answer to his initial question, but find quite unrelated and unpredicted information that is much more relevant than a clear answer to the initial question. A famous example describes a man looking for the name of an ancestor. He does not find the name, but instead finds a letter mentioning that his family possessed a brilliant violin. The man starts searching the attic of his parents and finds a Guarneri del Gesu, which can be sold for $700,000. It is not too clear how the serendipity phenomenon looks if it operates in the cognitive sense while a person is learning and searching for conceptual information. It may tell us however that students need additional skills and intuition where to find valuable information assets for their learning. Also it might bring us to the conclusion that hypermedia- and traditional indexing systems still need additional tools in order to support study tasks.

The literature up until now has focused primarily on the value of freedom in the learning sequence, which makes the students more aware of gaps in their prior knowledge and of the concept entailments triggered by the explanation of abstract entities such as "democracy," "responsibility," or "power."

Hypermedia designers, however, detect a certain benefit for those users who are intrinsically motivated and who have a global interest about the way things are. Their products such as Microsoft's *Encarta* (1991) multimedia encyclopedia offers a special knowledge elicitation from the user that would rarely evolve in paper-based explorations. Before reflecting on metaphoric elements in hypermedia, it would be helpful to taste the typical divergent ways of thinking and that occur in creative tasks (Cates, 1994).

Imagine that you want to spend your summer holidays in London to observe the classical architecture from the 17th and 18th century as well as the remainders of the city innovation project in the late sixties. Confronted with the information about the London inner city we meet the new concept of "industrial monuments" and finally arrive in York (England) or even Antwerp (Belgium).

This flow of thought is a classical experience appearing at the start of plans and creative design stages as well: The final step to go and visit York is a product of interest transformations driven by new facts and perspectives that you did not meet before you formulated the initial interest. This example shows that information is more than a final destination in thinking or searching: It controls specific stages in mental evolution and may even overrule initial goals, methods, and perspectives. Means and ends swap their priorities.

THREE METAPHORS UNDERLYING HYPERMEDIA

The Resource Metaphor

The most prominent feature in hypermedia is the search facility in reference documents. Paper-based documents are restricted to text, tables, schematic line drawings, pictures, and index lists, whereas hypermedia allow sound and video sequences as well. Surpassing paper-based resources, hypermedia give full priority to the multiple dimensions in the meanings of expressed ideas. From a static point of view, the meaning of a passage ultimately needs all other passages that discuss the same topic from different views.

> *Titles distinguish the mediocre, embarrass the superior, and are disgraced by the inferior.*
> *George Bernard Shaw*

Homonyms represent well-known dilemmas to teachers and authors, because they frustrate the contract between the donator and the recipient, who both imply, "I mean what I say." Mentioning the same word for different meanings weakens this contract. However, the homonym phenomenon is only the tip of an iceberg. Textual, pictorial, and schematic explanations lead the recipient to facets of the concepts to be taught. For a more complete understanding the student needs alternative digressions, which can be seen as excursions or subroutines.

For example, before formally defining the concept of "turbulence," a teacher or a text author can start with an overview of domains in which this concept may occur: physical, electrical, chemical, astronomical, acoustical, and social areas, to name a few. Only certain key elements of these contexts can support the common element in the concept of "turbulence." Excursions introduce specific connotations of the same concept.

Also, if a concept is dispersed along different domains, it is obvious that learning needs more than one explanation sequence. Those who have taught physical concepts such as power, force, strength, capacity, velocity, or acceleration know by experience that many conversational tours with dedicated examples and comprehensive questions were necessary before average students could get a grip on them.

The elegance of hypermedia digressions also brings risks and costs:

1. First, is the peril of allowing students to see the same concept in different contexts. The reader who jumps to various contexts in which a certain concept plays a role does not necessarily get a valid and consistent view of the meaning of a concept. The general point of attention for the educational use of hypermedia is to make links as explicit as possible, and to make them

compatible with the learning goals at that moment. Hypermedia relations, in fact, should anticipate desired concept links in the student's mind.

2. Second, hypermedia confront students with a task of navigating through related passages instead of having one book prescribe a linear way to study, making it easier for students and teachers to plan, test, evaluate, and remediate. The underlying idea is that following a prescribed chapter sequence brings you from elementary to more complex issues, and thus helps you to master the subject. The hypertext principle, however, places the students at the helm. They must decide which direction to go in order to make the delicate connection between new and prior knowledge.

3. Third, the readability, portability, and fragility of computer-based information is still a drawback (Search, 1992). Alan Kay (1969), the first inventor of windowing and the use of the mouse, has been involved with high-quality screens for NASA space devices. He discovered that slight changes in the intensity of today's screens alert deep layers of the human brain, activating the orientation reflex, which is the first reaction if one detects a slight sign of danger. Kay claimed that learning from screens is a crime because it disturbs the learner's ability to assimilate new information (Kay & Goldberg, 1977). The subconsciously perceived flickering causes arousal and a stimulus to flee. He claims that we need screens with at least 6.3 million pixels. They will likely not be affordable for another 5 to 7 years.

The resource metaphor behind hypermedia amplifies the notion that we can isolate information in some form so that it represents *what* has to be learned. You can take it, take it with you, give it to someone else, copy it, and so forth. The introduction of interactive and distance media have reinforced many features of traditional, static information assets in the form of books, journals, libraries, and the like. Although this metaphorical backing has helped newcomers to adopt these new media, we expect them to be beneficial only at the first stage. Taking advantage of more advanced possibilities such as virtuality, distributedness, collaboration, and the potential to become mentally compatible, requires new approaches.

The tradition of laying out books, and adding indices, references, and content tables has been adopted quite well by the designers of hypertext and hypermedia systems. Still there are things for hypermedia design to adopt from book-design. The most important one is portability. Related to the physical appearance of a book is its identity and face, which helps students to remember where to find its information again.

Microsoft's Bookshelf (Microsoft Bookshelf for Windows on CD-ROM, 1991) on CD-ROM (Fig. 2.5) is a good example of trying to keep the appearance of book faces. The more anonymous bookshelf at the right might look more tidy, but it lacks cues for our memory. This practical example illustrates the delicacy of using the resource metaphor.

Fig. 2.5. Books representing the resource metaphor.

The Communication Metaphor

Complementary to the notion that information resources have to be present is the notion that students need interaction with other students and among students and teachers or students and experts. Computer-based training in the last 20 years also has worked from the idea that the system had to be programmed so that a dialogue could evolve between the machine and a learner. The tutoring model was a direct consequence of taking the Socratic teacher as an interrogator who gives new information, and puts questions, then tries to derive misconceptions from the student's answers and gives new information or new confronting questions to repair them.

Media itself are incapable of communicating. The introduction of interactive video launched the suggestion that user-controlled video programs would finally instigate communication between the medium and the user. The same thing happened with computer-based training programs, which pretend to maintain a dialogue with the learner: Any observation of user sessions, however, will soon show that the bandwidth of the communication is extremely narrow. A more realistic and even more vivid communication metaphor in media design is the so-called cooperative or collaborative facility such as telemedia. The idea is that social cognition and mental reflection precedes cognitive development and intellectual learning. Doise and Mugny (1985) in the Piagetian tradition found, contrary to their expectation, that children placed in situations where they needed social skills and negotiations about equally dividing lemonade in differently shaped glasses, developed the ability of the constancy principle earlier. The amount of liquid poured into different glasses stayed the same, even when this shape appeared less or more.

Conference and correspondence systems today such as the Internet promote a quicker and more vivid way to exchange ideas among students. The ability to practice a second language and at the same time become aware of intercultural differences is a de facto consequence. Co-authoring hypermedia, annotating, and taking different perspectives on written arguments do not need long-distance networks. Users access local networks within one classroom or one school building.

There is a substantial difference between the communication metaphor in the cases of tutoring CBT and the communication facilities between students. The latter supports true interpersonal interaction, whereas any suggestion of interaction between students and CBT is based on suggestion and wishful thinking. The fallacy of many CBT projects can be ascribed to an overestimation of the communicative power of predetermined dialogues (McGraw, 1994), which pretend to react on the student's answers, but soon show a narrow bandwidth and cause boring wait-and-see reactions at the student's side.

The Exploration Metaphor Computer simulation programs themselves are convincing for demonstrating their educational value. A good reason for confronting the student with a simulation rather than reality itself is that a simulation allows more drastic, flexible, and critical manipulations. Training an airplane pilot in the air does not allow dangerous operations because they may cause loss of life and enormous costs. Flying in a so-called link trainer makes it feasible and even desirable to elicit critical situations such as landing with a tail wind, landing with only one engine, or landing on the water.

Although the link trainer may not always give accurate predictions of the pilot's interventions as they would turn out in reality, these explorations at least give some experience and shape adequate reflexes that would rarely have been performed by airplane pilots restricted to training in the air.

The exploratory approach made possible in simulation settings has a broader history and can be generalized to hypertext and hypermedia as well. The origin of exploration is in the phenomenon of playing and learning by discovery. In playing it is essential that the learner imagines him- or herself in another situation and role. The table becomes a house, the pencil becomes a gun. The imagined operation often requires more facilities and attributes than those available. This is not totally a handicap; because it helps to bridge the gap between the actual and the target behavior repertoire. The microworld of the Crane Game (Fig. 2.6) will illustrate this point.

Crane Game Suppose a learner needs to get acquainted with the following prepositions:

OVER	UNDER	ABOVE
BESIDE	BEHIND	BEFORE

A teacher could instruct the learner by explaining the meanings of these words in examples, test questions, and so forth. However, from an exploratory point of view it is better to give the primitives to the learner, and let him or her work with them. Syntactic constructions can be made by dragging prepositions and operators to the command space. Operators in this case could be these:

Fig. 2.6. Crane Game.

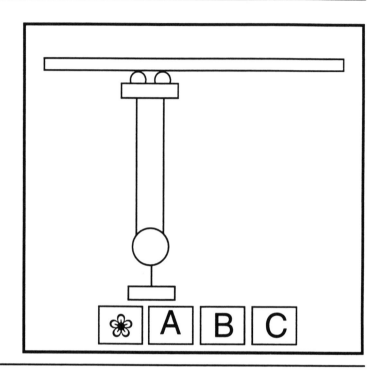

LIFT	MOVE	PUT
DROP	TAKE	TURN

The scenery on the screen contains blocks and objects ready to be manipulated by the learner. Command sentences could be the following:

- PUT A ON THE FLOWER
- LIFT BLOCK_B
- MOVE BLOCK_B ABOVE BLOCK_C
- etc.

Once the learner thinks the sentence is correct he or she pushes the evaluate button:

Important properties of the exploration approach are the low threshold for learners to perform actions and a natural way of displaying the consequences of the learner's construction so that existing misconceptions disappear. A well-known example of an exploratory learning environment is Papert's LOGO system intended for allowing young pupils to discover algorithmic concepts to control a turtle. (Papert, 1993).

The typical attitude of the student in an exploratory learning phase is "What if?" The typical attitude of the exploration tools is "Why not?"

LEARNING THROUGH CD-ROM-BASED HYPERMEDIA

Hypermedia are also strongly based on the idea of exploration. In accessing and creating information and links between parts of information, it is the user as learner who is the director. The information base is designed to be penetrated very easily. The learner who has a specific question should readily find an answer. Most interesting are the facilities for constructing desired knowledge from a diffuse interest by crisscrossing through the network of relations. The following is a typical browsing sequence performed by a student with access to Microsoft's *Encarta* (Fig. 2.7). The student is interested in the background of the Kurds as they came into a difficult position during and after the Gulf War._

The first step after starting *Encarta* is to choose "Encyclopedia Contents," then activate "Contents" and type in "Kurds" (Fig. 2.8). The screen that pops up then shows that the description of Kurds was found in the category "Anthropology" (Fig. 2.9). This explains why the aspect "Kurdish Folk Music" is explicitly prompted. A piece of their music can be called by clicking on the loudspeaker symbol. The text about Kurds contains words printed in red (here underlined) called hotspots. The observed student clicks on "Sunnites" (second hotspot in Fig. 2.10), persuaded to do so, perhaps, because the local description was found to be too short (e.g., orthodox Muslims, many of them living, etc.).

A second persuading factor may be the student's need to know more about Sunnites. A third argument could be the learner's desire to leave the search for information about Kurds and change the track to a religious aspect of people in the Middle East. A fourth argument could be the learner's interest for an actuality topic like for instance the Persian Gulf War at the time we experimented in our own teaching (Fig. 2.11). Already one year later the next explanation could be found in Encarta.

Once the student has clicked on "Sunnites," in Figure 2.10, the refresher window goes into detail explaining that the term "sunna" probably means "the middle of the road." The current category has changed from "anthropology" to "religions and religious groups." Going further into details of "sunna" would, for instance, bring this learner to an explanation of the "Koran," and a departure from

Fig. 2.7. *Encarta* presentation mode.

Fig. 2.8. Alphabetical entries.

Fig. 2.9. Kurds.

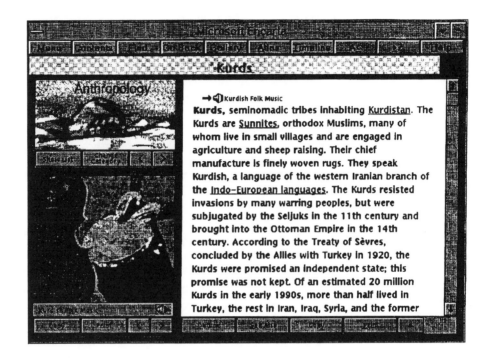

Fig. 2.10. Sunnites.

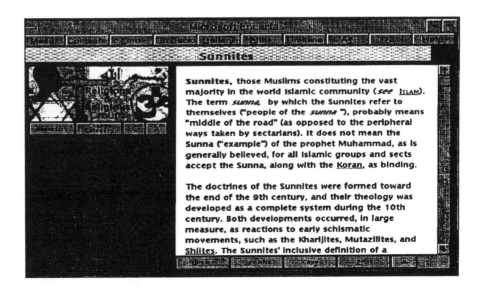

Fig. 2.11. Persian Gulf War explanatory text.

> **Persian Gulf War**
> Persian Gulf War, military struggle fought principally in Kuwait and Iraq during January and February 1991. The crisis began when President Saddam Hussein invaded and annexed Kuwait. Between August and November the United Nations Security Council passed a series of resolutions that culminated in the demand that Iraq withdraw unconditionally from Kuwait by January 15, 1991. By that time, some 500,000 allied ground, air, and naval forces — chiefly from the United States, Saudi Arabia, Great Britain, Egypt, Syria, and France — were arrayed against an Iraqi army estimated at that time to number 540,000 .
> . . .

the direct relation with the initial interest in "Kurds." Our observed learner selects "Go Back" from the menu bar and sees the first window about "Kurds" again. This backtracking element is crucial in hypertext browsing, because it shows the breadth-first approach, which normally goes together with content-driven explorations. Using this approach, the learner would click on another hotspot in the text about "Kurds," again making a one-step excursion to one of the explanatory details.

After scrolling the horizontal slidebar, it is easy for the learner to find the requested time period to be about A.D. 1,100. During the time trip, the learner sees intermediate episodes that show the vast changes in human culture during the leap in time.

The learner's initial point of interest was the background of the Kurds as they came into a difficult position during and after the Gulf War. The learner seems to be satisfied about a first view on "the Kurds" for the moment, and gives attention to the aspect of the "Gulf War" (Fig. 2.11). Requesting *Encarta*'s database for the "Gulf War" reveals a reference to the "Persian Gulf War" heading the paragraph at the side.

Scrolling the text on the "Kurds" gives no result: The learner now faces this choice: ask for an important element in the current paragraph on "Iraq," or go back to find a relation between the Kurds and the Gulf War in a more subtle way. Here are the procedures for both:

1. Requesting the explanation of "Iraq" delivers a long article with four passages (Fig. 2.12) that are relevant to the relation between Kurds and Gulf War. The remaining parts of the article on Iraq are omitted here.

2. However the learner chooses "Timeline" from the menu bar, following an interest in the subjugation of the Kurds by the Seljuks in the 11th century. The timeline appears, but alas it displays as its starting point 5 million B.C. The screen in Figure 2.13 shows the Sumerian civilization in Mesopotamia. Again we see the temptation for the learner to digress to different topics. Exploration

Fig. 2.12. Plain explanatory text.

Iraq

Population

About 75% of the population of Iraq is Arab. Kurds dwelling in the highlands of northern Iraq constitute about %15 to 20 of the population. Smaller groups include Turkomans, Yazidis, and Jews. In the rural areas of the country many of the people still live in tribal communities, leading a nomadic or seminomadic existence and keeping herds of camels, horses, and sheep.

Government

Iraq is governed under a provisional constitution adopted in 1968 and subsequently amended. In 1980 the Kurds, who make up about %15 to 20 of Iran's inhabitants, were given some autonomy and elected an executive council and a 50-member legislature.

War with Iran

In early 1974 heavy fighting erupted in northern Iraq between government forces and Kurdish nationalists, who rejected as inadequate a new Kurdish autonomy law based on the 1970 agreement. The Kurds, led by Mustafa al-Barzani (1904-1979), received arms and other supplies from Iran. After Iraq agreed in early 1975 to make major concessions to Iran in settling border disputes between the two countries, Iran halted aid to the Kurds, and the revolt was dealt a severe blow. In July 1979 President Bakr was succeeded by General Saddam Hussein, who immediately rounded up dozens of officials on charges of treason.

Tension between Iraq and the revolutionary regime in Iran increased during 1979, when unrest among Iranian Kurds spilled over into Iraq. Sectarian religious animosities exacerbated the differences.

Occupation of Kuwait

Meanwhile, the Baghdad government used its remaining military forces to suppress rebellions by Shiites in the south and Kurds in the north. An estimated 1 million Kurdish refugees fled into Turkey and Iran, and contingents of U.S., British, and French troops landed inside Iraq's northern border to set up refugee camps and protect another 500,000 or more Kurds from Iraqi government reprisals. In 1992, violence against the Kurds by Iraq and Turkey escalated. The stay of peacekeeping troops was extended to June.

Fig. 2.13. *Encarta* timeline mode

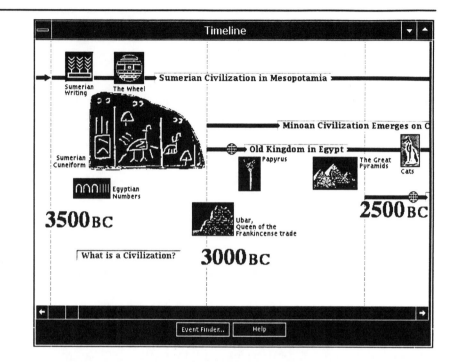

inherently brings the risks of such digression and distraction. Important, however, is the facility to comply with momentary interests as they pop up in the learner's mind after confrontations with new information.

Prominent in hypermedia learning is its potential to integrate previously isolated knowledge. (e.g., in this case the student might take a step of 3,600 years ahead and land at about A.D. 1,100 as displayed in Fig. 2.13.) Allowing the learner to digress to normally separated domains or topics might seem time consuming, but it might be crucial for complex learning processes later on.

Four passages in the article on Iraq contain expositions on the Kurds. The last one explicitly elaborates the Kurdish position during the Gulf War. However the three preceding passages on *population*, *government*, and *war with Iran* give crucial background information for understanding Iraq's attitude during and after the Gulf War. The learner concludes that the first attempt to bridge the information gap was successful.

The learner's second approach for finding more on the relation between the Kurds and the Gulf War is to request all available articles containing both "Kurds" and "Gulf War." The learner uses *Encarta*'s "Find" command. It reveals five topics, two of them have already been retrieved by the learner. Only the fourth one about Turkey contains relevant information about the Kurdish position right after the Gulf War. The learner concludes that the first attempt to see more about the relation between Kurds and Gulf War gives a broader view on the conflict between Kurds and Iraqis. The second attempt to place a free text search for all articles that mention both of them introduces more noise in terms of distracting peripheral aspects. However, it gives two of them in rather precise statements about the background with Iran and the acute problems for the Kurds right after the Gulf War, namely to those who fled to Turkey and ran into the arms of another enemy.

CONCLUSION

As shown, hypermedia explorations give essentially the same occasional learning effects that we saw in computer-based simulations, the Crane Game, and the LOGO system: Learners can play around and discover meaningful aspects that would be hidden away in a direct instruction approach.

The difference between hypermedia environments with exploratory tools such as simulations and the Crane Game is in the available tools. These urge the learner to make a delicate trade-off between requesting broad searches such as free-text retrieval with the risk for noise (undesired information that may deter the learner) and placing focused requests with the risk for silence (returning no matches at all, leading the learner to think the wanted information is not available).

The exploration approach in suggesting new subjects implies a more responsible attitude for the learner and requires teacher confidence that elaborating, integrating, and orienting for the learner will pay back in the long run. It also trains the learner to work more autonomously and stimulates a higher level of metaknowledge: knowing what you know, knowing how you learn, and knowing how to discuss your knowledge with the system, your classmates, and your teacher in particular.

REFERENCES

Cates, W. M. (1994). Designing hypermedia is hell: Metaphor's role in instructional design. In *Proceedings of selected research and development presentations*, Nashville TN: National Conference for the Association for Educational Communications and Technology.

Doise, W., & Mugny, G. (1985). *The Social Development of the Intellect. International Series in Experimental Social Psychology, Vol. 10.* (1st ed.)   Oxford: Pergamon. ISBN: 0080302092

Kay, A. (1969). The reactive engine. Doctoral dissertation, University of Utah.

Kay, A., & Goldberg, A. (1977). Personal Dynamic Media. *IEEE Computer, 10*(3), March 1977, 31-42.

Kommers, P. A. M. (1993). Scenarios for the development of educational hypermedia. *Educational and Training Technology International, 30*(3), 234-254.

Lin, X. (1994). Metacognition: Implications for research in hypermedia-based learning environments. In *Proceedings of selected research and development presentations*, Nashville, TN: National Conference of the Association for Educational Communications and Technology.

McGraw, K. L. (1994). Performance support systems: Integrating AI, hypermedia, and CBT to enhance user performance. *Journal of Artificial Intelligence in Education, 5*(1), 3-26.

Microsoft Bookshelf for Windows ™ on CD-ROM (1991). *CD-ROM Reference Library 1991 Edition*. User's Guide. Redmond WA: Microsoft.

Microsoft Encarta. CD-ROM.

Oxford English Dictionary. CD-ROM.

Papert, S. (1993). *Mindstorms: Children, Computers, and Powerful Ideas.* (2nd ed.) International Society for Technology.

Search, P. (1992). The art and science of hypermedia. In *Art, science, & visual literacy: selected readings*, Pittsburgh, PA: Annual Conference of the International Visual Literacy Association.

Wilde, O. (1856-1900). British poet and dramatist.

CHAPTER 3

Research on the Use of Hypermedia

Piet A. M. Kommers

> *But of the quarrel with others we make rhetoric. Out of the quarrel with ourselves we make poetry.*
> **William Butler Yeats**

Chapter Objectives   After introducing the trade-off between hypertext's inherent freedom for exploring and the reputable status of system control in traditional instruction, this chapter

- categorizes recent studies of the problem of hypertext navigation into four lines of research, and

- covers both the teachability, learnability, and quality aspects of hypermedia design.

The reported research on hypertext and interactive multimedia in this chapter is selected to give you confidence in adapting the hypermedia approach to your own situation and didactic habits. The selected research lines do not entirely cover the whole spectrum of questions about new media and learning. Their function is rather to help you in generalizing the ideas in the preceding chapters so that your approach may become more flexible and able to overcome impediments in the surf of everyday practice.

As you are probably not primarily a researcher, we prefer to give you a taste of potential impacts of hypermedia in school culture. Without this (slow) evolution

As you are probably not primarily a researcher, we prefer to give you a taste of potential impacts of hypermedia in school culture. Without this (slow) evolution in the subsoil of didactic notions and pedagogic conceptions, any media-driven innovations will finally be extinguished and bring disappointment for its crusaders.

MULTIMEDIA IN THE LANDSCAPE OF TEACHING AND LEARNING

Hypertext Like many products of advanced software engineering, hypertext has been accepted as a candidate for assisting the delicate process of teaching and learning. Hypertext as defined by Engelbart (1963) and Nelson (1967, 1981, 1980, 1988) essentially presents a new way of linking texts and the user interface to deal with vast resources of text. This facility enables teachers and students to create personalized text bases and (in combination with telematics and high-density storage systems) permits the consulting of previously unattainable information. A most obvious effect of hypertext is that it can contribute to the availability of information and merge its consumption and production.

Hypertext material can be downloaded from remote resources by the teacher or student. Students can explore new information without being restricted by the regular curriculum and can include documents from students or industries abroad. The inherent exploratory approach of browsing through hypertext can motivate users to link their own documents to the mental products of other people. In this the hypertext trend can best survive in combination with other telematic infrastructures and media for high-density storage (Hedberg, 1990).

This image of hypertext facilities in schools coincides with the commonly accepted phenomenon (sometimes threatening for teachers) of technological innovation being permanently present in the field of education. In the traditional situation (Fig. 3.1) the teacher controls the external knowledge bases. Paine (1989) put it dramatically when he concluded that the teacher will inevitably become a facilitator or a manager of the learning process (Fig. 3.2) rather than the mediator of all knowledge.

> It is literally his or her finger on the buttons. The shift required must be a model where the teacher steps to one side and allows the student direct access to knowledge, with the teacher facilitating and organizing that learning process. (p. 50)

Science, schooling, and the dynamics of the information society are highly dependent on each other. Computer technology can play a crucial role in this system. We are nevertheless aware that the availability of information (even when it is transmitted by computers) is only a tiny slice of mental power (Weizenbaum, 1976). Hypertext, as it initiates a general feeling about how to reflect and feed our thinking, imagination, and learning, is an evident example of the innovation process.

Fig. 3.1. Paine's control system for conventional teaching (Paine, 1989, p. 50).

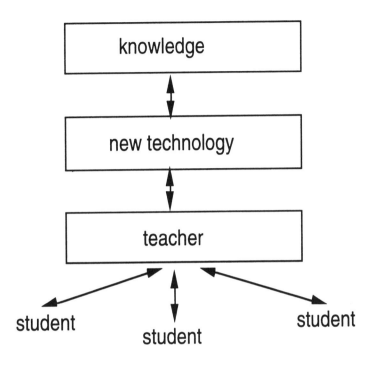

Fig. 3.2. Paine's desirable new teaching model (Paine, 1989, p. 50).

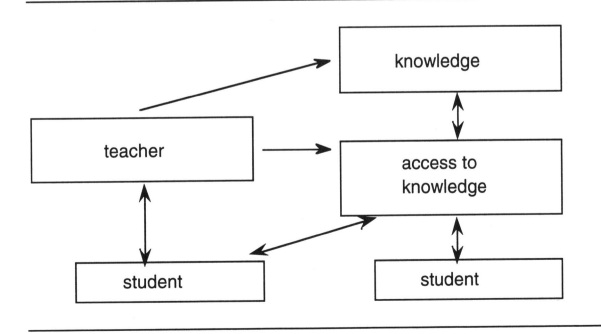

The new element in the wave of hypertext systems might be brushed aside as a synergism of slightly related pieces of information that bring up new associations as one browses around. However, hypertext motivates teachers and students to collaborate in creating alternative views on topics, which can be a powerful use of telemedia as can be seen in the electronic field trip project oncommunity archaeology between the Netherlands and British Columbia. (Sligte, 1989; Kersten, Nienhuis, Sligte, Timmer, & De Zeeuw, 1987). This project shows that the impact of electronic message systems goes far beyond the interaction between learning systems and the individual student.

To understand the impact of hypertext systems for education, we should take into account three global development effects:

1. There is a fast-growing need for collaborative working environments created by means of hypermedia and telematics. The current generation of hypertext is restricted to fast browsing and flexible linking. Most of the authoring processes in learning and working environments, however, need cooperative writing, planning, revision, and so forth. This poses the need for new hypertext systems, that support individual creative processes.

2. The multimedia trend toward using hypermedia methods for study and work has implications not only for the equipment presentation storage device we are going to use. Its impact will mainly manifest itself in the flexibility of our students' learning.

3. The process of teaching and learning will not remain unaffected by these new techniques. An important function of new generations of hypertext is the support they will give to externalizing the way we think about complex concept domains. The paradigm of knowledge engineering becomes essential for subject matter analysis (on the teacher side) as well as for cognitive tool use for learning (on the student side). Hypertext facilitates flexible techniques to make latent ideas more explicit as teachers and students gradually accept the opportunities of knowledge representation.

Free Exploration by Navigation

Like many underestimated problems, "the computer as a teacher" seemed to be attainable after many years of fundamental research on cognitive psychology, student modeling, and developments in man-machine interaction. However, basic problems, for instance, in the interpretation of meaning in human language, exhaustive task analysis, and machine learning are still unsolved. This results in the development of CBL[1] programs that are still only variations on programmed instruction.

In contrast, there is the exploration of open, user-controlled systems, which are less dominant and prescriptive in sequence control: They simply pass the responsibility of navigation to the student. Examples are simulation programs and hypertext (Stanton & Baber, 1994).

Cumming and Self (1989) made a compromise between system and learner control when they proposed collaborative learning, which does not have the aim

[1] CBL Computer-Based Learning

of instructing, but of engaging the learner in partnership. They give two reasons to reject tutoring strategies in CBL:

1. The difficulty (Clancey, 1987) or impossibility (Winograd & Flores, 1986) of capturing domain knowledge that is sufficiently rich so that a system is able to offer a learner a full and appropriate explanation in every situation

2. The need to stimulate meta-level skills in the learner: developing control strategies and abilities for allocating resources, making judgments, and taking initiatives in the target domain

The virtual contrast between intelligent tutoring systems (ITS) and the approach of microworlds (Papert, 1984) could possibly be reconciled by giving advice and comments instead of prescribing where to go next.

The discussion about the risks of free hypertext browsing can be clarified if we take Cumming and Self's plea for a collaboration model into account. Essentially this plea calls for the decoupling of the task level and the meta level at which the task performance is discussed. In other words, at one level there is the skill or knowledge to be learned; at another level there is reflection on the type of learning, planning, and mental awareness of one's actions. As an example, Cumming and Self give the analogy of someone being coached to play a violin concerto by a master pianist. In this case the teacher is focusing on the approach and interpretation of the music, rather than the exact movements to be made by the student.

If we apply the collaboration-model (between teacher and student) to the situation of hypertext, the student would remain autonomous in his or her explorations while the system evokes reflections from the student on his or her achievement at a more global procedural level (Myers & Anderson, 1994).

In the field of CBL we have already seen a similar distinction between "knowing what" and "knowing how." In the case of computer simulations it is generally recognized that effective learning needs more than the actual knowledge about the relations between the parameters in the model: Reflection on performed interventions during the previous period and an explanation framework to understand the mechanisms in the domain are important as well. Expert systems can be well equipped to explain how they arrive at certain conclusions, lacking the bandwidth of reliable predictions in a domain of surface knowledge.

Cumming and Self admit the need to accept the learner as an autonomous and self-responsible actor who retains scope for initiative. This reconciliation between two often-opposed extremes is quite valuable in the design of the navigation assistance needed in hypertext. Examples of how to give navigational advice (e.g. by displaying the centrality of the concept nodes) without taking away student initiative are implemented in TextVision; (Kommers, 1989; Kommers, Jonassen, & Mayes, 1992).

Two complementary opinions about the ideal locus of control in collaborative learning situations emerge in current literature:

1. Student control enhances the power of human learners by initiating metalearning and eliciting prior knowledge during the learning process.

2. We will soon need scenarios for mixed initiative collaborations. Both simulation and explorative information retrieval need some navigational assistance to prevent the student from being lost or trapped in misconceptions.

The central question to be solved in the case of hypertext systems is how to maintain the principle of student control and exploration while having a system that implicitly orients the student browsing through the hypertext information base? We can distinguish four approaches to solve this problem:

1. *Navigational device*: Provide the student with an orientation device, that shows the current position in the configuration of relations. The key discipline to be taught is student awareness of central versus peripheral information.

2. *Didactic embeddedness*: Specify the function of hypertext by creating a series of lessons. Each time the student uses the hypertext tool, he or she has a specific goal (e.g., summarizing prior knowledge in hypertext or retrieving specific information from the hypertext resources). In this way the student can be trained progressively to exploit all the hypertext utilities and to handle the freedom in the system. (See chapter 2).

3. *Cognitive modeling*: By installing learning templates that describe a restricted number of learning strategies, the system could coach the student in accordance with his or her preferred style of learning. For example, the work of Pask (1975, 1976, 1984) has reinforced the idea that serial and holistic describe two basic modalities for learning.

4. *Knowledge engineering*: Stimulate the student to express in more detail which type of relation exists between the linked concepts in the hypertext paragraph. Exploring several semantics by which the student can define the types of relations can finally demonstrate how far knowledge engineering can contribute to the process of learning from texts.

The first two approaches are worked out in this book. The functions of cognitive modeling and knowledge engineering techniques are not covered here.

The use of hypertext in learning situations is still in discussion. Research projects focus most on the user level of satisfaction rather than on providing process analysis about how the users of hypertext navigate and whether they acquire knowledge (Small & Grabowski, 1992).

> The dominant conception of the hypertext form is as a medium for information retrieval, rather than learning (Whalley, 1989, p. 61).

This critical remark reflects the actual state of present evidence and provokes a critical attitude towards the use of hypertext in educational settings. The hypothesis that users can usefully navigate through the many lines of association between paragraphs of text still has to be proved and should be translated into learning goals or cognitive benefits. McKnight, Richardson, and Dillon (1989a,

1989b) reminded us of Engelbart (1963), who claimed that word processors, which allowed cut-and-paste, undoing, and so forth, would provide an aid to creativity. Why should the claims for hypertext not be accurate also?

DIDACTIC, PHYSICAL, AND EPISTEMIC NAVIGATION IN HYPERTEXT

Among the landmarks of hypertext design, the work of Nelson in the period 1965 until 1987 took an important place as he explicated an ideological background for using literary machines and nonsequential writing. Nelson's work (1965, 1973, 1974) and initial ideas about storing and retrieving chunked text have been ignored for many years. It is interesting to see that the idea of hypertext has elicited quite a spectrum of research lines. These are announced here and worked out in the remaining part of this chapter.

- Can hypertext essentially assist in complex mental tasks, such as learning and knowledge acquisition?

- Which is the best way of interaction between users and a hypertext system?

- What are appropriate user interfaces for navigation and collaboration in hypertext?

- Which is the right granularity for representing knowledge beyond the level of associative links?

Before actually working out these four lines of research as they exist in current hypertext research programs, it is good to remember how Nelson perceived that the problems could be solved.

Rather than worrying about the way the user interface should present itself, Nelson started with deliberations relative to the second and third lines of research listed above. Instead of mentioning problems in which hypertext could be a solution, Nelson started with technical solutions such as Xanalogical storage as efficient ways for representing virtual links between fragments of text. The term Xanalogical (analog to Xanadu) stems from Nelson's (1987, p. 3) Xanadu hypertext system. In addition to that, Nelson generated solutions relative to research Line 4, namely how to map interlinked texts in a pool of interconnected communication networks, which he supposed would be present about 40 years from the time of his writing. Xanalogical storage refers to the Project of Xanadu that started in the fall of 1960. Its aspiration was to deliver a relatively small piece of software that could be run in each storage machine of an ever-growing network.

Documents are series of pointers in the changing web of data. Links are connections between documents that the user may follow. Nelson's (1987) work *Literary Machines* stressed the need of virtuality in designing interactive systems. Virtuality embodies conceptual structure and feel. It is a plea for an extended preliminary design: years of blackboard philosophizing. In fact Nelson touched on the necessary research in Lines 2 and 3 without mentioning the problems with user interfaces and the display of extended networks. Nelson followed the line of Bush (1945) and Engelbart (1963). He started by clearly defining why one should break away from sequential presentations such conventional linear text. Nelson argued:

- Linear text spoils the unity and structure of interconnection.

- Traditional sequential text can be explained because language, writing, printing, and even binding needs to be done in a sequence of time.

Nelson considered thought to be an interwoven system of ideas, none of its parts necessarily coming first. As he boldly stated it:

> The structure of ideas is never sequential, and indeed our thought processes are not very sequential either…. True, only a few thoughts at a time pass across the central screen of the mind, but as you consider a thing, your thoughts crisscross it constantly, reviewing first one connection, then another. Each new idea is compared with many parts of the whole picture, or with some mental visualization of the whole picture itself. (Nelson, 1987, pp. 0/1 to 2/3)

The third argument of Nelson is this:

- As linear text forces a single sequence for all readers, it may be appropriate for none.

Readers should be invited to create different pathways based on background, taste, and proper understanding. The only way to handle this is to write many books dealing with the same content, in order to approach it differently for all users. Advocates for text on paper will respond Nelson's argument by saying that readers can also jump between texts in books. Some books are prepared for multisequential reading by inclusion of references, tabulated pages, and so forth. However, Nelson was right when he said that computers are more adequate tools to assist in traversing dispersed fragments of text.

Most of Nelson's argumentation was about authoring rather than reading hypertext. Some of the reasons for this emphasis could be the immense problem of managing the many versions of text, the resistance to unlimited quotation, and the redundant publication of similar books on the same topic.

Nelson proposed two styles of hypertext organization. They are the classics in the field of cognition and text processing. It is appropriate to mention them because they mirror the psychological versus the computational approach:

- *Presentation and effect:* Adapted to the mental processes of the consumer of the text resource

- *Lines of structure:* Intended to reflect the basic structure of the contents of the information

Many problems about navigation in the network of hypertext relations and the epistemology of hypertext relations were not considered in Nelson's work. Neither did he describe types of links the author may use to join paragraphs of text. Nelson gave the metaphor of "virtual yellow stickers" alerting the user when to jump backwards or where to find annotations afterwards. Nelson's work left quite a set of relevant research questions to be answered by cognitive psychologists, user interface designers, and also educational designers.

RESEARCH LINE 1: CAN HYPERTEXT ESSENTIALLY ASSIST IN COMPLEX MENTAL TASKS, SUCH AS LEARNING AND KNOWLEDGE ACQUISITION?

The first research line investigates the total effect of hypertext as in the testing of a new car model. In such a test, for example, one would not scrutinize the principle of combustion engines in general, but focus on different types of functionality for the intended user.

Examples in the case of hypertext are experiments or field studies on the actual use of hypertext in learning situations, questioning the level of satisfaction, effectiveness, or both. Good examples are the studies of Leggett, Schnase, and Kacmar (1989) on using hypertext to learn Modula assembly language programming and hypertext itself) and Catano (1979) on teaching poetry. These give an impression of the possible impact of the new medium on education as a whole.

It is not difficult to foresee that there will be many cognitive tools (such as hypertext) in computer-based learning, but it is more demanding to predict how they will change the relation between teacher and students, between spare time and learning, and between publishing and knowledge engineering. Isaac Asimov (1974) said it thus:

> The important thing to forecast is not the automobile, but the parking problem;
> not the television, but the soap opera.

Media technologists should be the first to be aware of media consequences rather than the advocates of its technical potential. Despite the enthusiasm and perseverance of hypertext researchers in general, they are aware that the definite answer to the question in research Line 1 can and will be given within the next 5 to 20 years from the field of education itself. Both teachers and students can accept or reject the challenge to encapsulate hypertext in curricula (Lacey & Merseth, 1993).

Even more intriguing from the research perspective at this moment is the question of whether current hypertext approaches will survive against the instructional paradigms that depict learning as a process to be controlled by the teacher component. A second question asks whether we (educational technologists) can master the complexity of managing streams of information when participants are equally invited to enter their opinions into the hypertext database. The proponents of hypertext give the impression that they have more in mind than they can prove at this moment with the systems they defend.

To answer the question of research Line 1, recent literature was screened for supporting evidence that hypertext can indeed assist in learning situations. The many facets that contribute to an answer have been grouped into three clusters:

1. Hypertext in traditional classroom-learning

2. Learner control

3. Openness/closeness of educational hypertext systems

Hypertext in Traditional Classroom Learning

Leggett et al. (1989) describe an experimental evaluation of hypertext use at the university level. Three courses on programming and computer science were implemented in hypertext shells. The students had access to a local network of 30 workstations. The students could browse each other's work and were finally interviewed for their experiences. The findings of Leggett et al. (1989) from the experiments (based on the system HyperTIES [Schneiderman & Morariu, 1986; Schneiderman & Kearsley, 1989]) were consistent across all four semesters:

1. The students found books easier to read and more accessible than the hypertext tutorial.

2. The students were divided on which method, books or hypertext, was more enjoyable.

3. Disorientation was not a problem.

4. Accessing information by following links was well-liked.

5. The students felt that they understood the material presented in the hypertext tutorial.

Four major comments were detected:

1. Students wanted to annotate.

2. Students wanted a mouse-driven user interface.

3. Students wanted bookmark facilities.

4. Students wanted the tutorial integrated directly into the programming environment.

The findings of Leggett et al. (1989) in their latest experiment based on the system, Knowledge Management System (KMS), (Akscyn, McCracken, and Yoder, 1988) were reported after the class had been taught twice. Positive responses were:

1. The students liked being able to annotate each other's work at precisely the place of their choice.

2. The students enjoyed the capability of collateral display.

3. The students appreciated having space to jot things down while browsing.

4. Disorientation did not appear often.

5. Navigational access to information was well-liked.

6. The students felt that they understood the issues of computer-supported collaboration.

Negative responses were:

1. The students wanted better collaboration support when several are working in the same area of the hypertext (e.g., locking particular frames so that they cannot be overwritten by other users).

2. The students wanted a communication facility within KMS that is easy to use when they are working at distributed sites.

3. The students wanted to be able to link inside a frame.

4. The students wanted to personalize KMS functionality, the facility to define special utilities as they arise while they are working with the system.

5. The students wanted an easy bookmarking facility.

The overall conclusions of Leggett et al. (1989) are these:

- Simple access to literature goes easier by book material than by hypertext in computers.

- If disorientation occurs, it happens mostly in groups of younger students. Less mature groups want trails (paths) for finding their way back.

- There is a substantial need to personalize the hypertext material by adding bookmarks (see also Bernstein, 1988) and by integrating the system into the normal environment.

- Students like the spatial desktop metaphor of the front end, such as that present in KMS.

A more global (compared to the work of Leggett et al. [1989]) evaluation report has been published by Apple Classroom of Tomorrow (ACOT) in which Tierney (1989) summarizes "The Influence of HyperCard on Students' Thinking." The study examined a school project in which pairs of ACOT 10th graders chose a chapter from a biology textbook and developed a study guide using hypertext in the form of HyperCard. These were the results:

1. Readers tended to go beyond a regimented concern for facts and explored ideas and issues of interest.

2. Strategies for learning appeared less linear than traditional reading from text on paper. For example, students reading the hypertext stack were apt to pause to consider alternative explanations or check emerging understandings.

3. Readers referred more often to visual representations to clarify, enlarge, or check understandings.

4. Hypertext appeared to make ideas more accessible.

5. Hypertext appeared to have motivational qualities that the regular textbooks did not have.

Students and authors responded as follows:

1. Authors were more sensitive to the liberties readers might need, compared with authoring linear text.

2. Working with hypertext helped students and authors to expand their views of how hypertext stacks might be used.

3. Hypertext authors gave more considerations to the relationship between function and form, such as the role of visual representation to complement and expand the text explanation.

4. In contrast, hypertext also seemed to encourage students authors to consider form over content.

The findings by Tierney (1989) confirm many of the conceptually defined arguments in the literature explaining why hypertext can play a crucial role in the shift from learning by consumption to learning by exploration and construction. Anderson-Inman (1989) gave a representative phrase:

> One of the most important factors influencing whether or not studying will actually lead to knowledge acquisition is the degree to which students become actively involved in trying to make sense out of the material to be presented. This involvement might be in the form of frequent interaction and decision making with respect to the content being studied or it might be the reorganization in personally meaningful ways (p. 27).

The work of Rohwer (1984) and Weinstein & Mayer (1986) concluded that high (conceptual) levels of text interaction and text manipulation enhance active text processing and therefore lead to increased comprehension and retention.

The same is true for the headword-linking capability of hypertext, which allows the readers to choose a personally meaningful path through the system's content, a path not dedicated by the linear arrangement of a textbook; the issues and main characters in an event; or the chronology of historical, cultural periods, and so forth. The headword-linking capability enables a learner to access the content of a hypertext system much as a database is accessed by collecting text-based chunks of information and creating personal subdocuments and annotations.

Learner Control Two doubts about learning from hypertext relate to the inherent lack of facilities to promote self-monitoring during the study process and the missing features related to self-testing knowledge of the content. This brings us back to early discussion about discovery learning, guided discovery and the so-called need for system control (Bruner, 1970; Gal'perin & Leontev, 1972; Jacobs, 1992).

The actuality of the trade-off between guidance and learner control is obvious in many of the research reports on hypertext. For example, the designers of the ElectroText Authoring System are currently conducting research on the learning capabilities of secondary students within hypertext study environments and the extent to which some form of guidance may be needed (Anderson-Inman, 1989; Becker & Dwyer, 1994; Chung & Reigeluth, 1992; Shin, 1994).

Disorientation, confusion, and the lack of inherent coaching go with the free-dom to browse along and the openness for students to fill in their own lines of thought.

Learner Control From a Cognitive Point of View The notion of learner control has been discussed by Merrill (1980) at the level of cognitive processes in the learner: The importance of giving the learner control over both the conscious processing of the immediate material and the metaprocesses involved in learning how to learn. Merrill assumes that the quality of learning will be better in the learner-controlled condition because it will inevitably be more compatible with the learner's preexisting schemata and repertoire of learning skills. "The best possible model of the learner's state of knowledge is that residing in the learner" (Kibby & Mayes, 1989, pp. 164-172; Kibby & Kommers, 1988, p.5). "The enormous advantage to be gained by passing on instructional control to the learner is that the learner becomes active. That implies a greater depth and breadth of processing which in turn will lead to more durable memory." (Ausubel, 1963, pp. 55-63). However, the metacognitive hypothesis behind learner control is constrained by the fact that initial learning often needs to be guided by a teacher or an external system.

Learner Control From a Didactic Point of View Research findings regarding the effects of learner control as an adaptive strategy have been inconsistent, but more frequently negative than positive. (Tennyson, 1980; Tennyson & Buttrey, 1980).

Ross and Morisson (1989) reviewed the research studies on learner control and gave as an overall conclusion the finding that many students, especially low achievers, lack the knowledge and motivation to make appropriate decisions regarding such conditions as pacing, sequencing of content, use of learning aids, and amount of practice. They summarized eight situations in which learner control is likely to work out positively:

1. Learners are older and more mature.

2. Learners are more capable.

3. Higher-order skills are taught rather than factual information.

4. The learning content is more familiar.

5. The learner is provided with advice to make decisions and use strategies known to be effective.

6. Learner control is used consistently within a lesson.

7. The unsuccessful learners are immediately provided with system control.

8. If learner controlled sessions are evaluated and corrected afterward so that misconception and omissions can be remediated.

Previous studies by Ross and Morrison (1989) concluded that high achievers seem capable of using most forms of learner control effectively, whereas low achievers seem capable of controlling only presentation aspects such as how information is formatted or delivered.

However, despite the fact that low achievers probably will need external guidance with respect to the strategy of their studying and the questions they can expect in the test (Tennyson & Buttrey, 1980), there is research evidence showing that even low achievers profit from a certain amount of learner control. (Kinzie, 1988; Carrier & Williams, 1988). The trade-off between learner control and the risk of misconceptions about the task can hardly be made in general concerning navigational freedom for learners in hypertext.

Hypertext as a Learning Tool Opposed to Instructional Tool

Computer-assisted instruction (CAI) has frequently been promoted because it provides the possibility of keeping learning systematic and well controlled in order to avoid too-large steps for the student and to provide quick and adequate feedback.

The atmosphere in a hypertext and especially hypertext environment is quite different and has many characteristics of entertainment such as adventures and fantasy and elicits free association in the learner.

> Rather than trying to create a model of the learner, and seeking to prescribe his or her route through the subject matter, the role of the computer should be organizing and representing knowledge to give the user easy access and control (Megarry, 1988, p. 174).

This citation reflects the general opinion from hypertext proponents during the period of hypertext activity in the early 1990s. The aspiration is diametrically opposed to the search for Intelligent Computer Assisted Instruction (ICAI) as it shifts the attention from system to student control. Weyer (1988) gave six basic interaction facilities that enable the student to follow his or her cognitive interest within a hypertext situation:

Request	Present the system's interpretation.
Tell me	Give the facts but no embellishments.
Inform me	Provide facts plus background and other viewpoints.
Amuse me	Find interesting connections or perspectives.
Challenge	Make the learner find or create connections or insights.
Guide me	Suggest pathways but allow browsing.
Teach me	Provide step-by-step-guidance.

The main loop of interaction between student and learning environment starts from questioning the student: "What do you want to know, and how do you prefer to be confronted with the subject matter?"

ICAI attempts to have this task done by the system, whereas open learning systems capitalize on the level of metaknowledge in the learner: The best student representation is in the experience of the student himself.

Even if the domain of knowledge is highly structured and decomposed into prerequisite steps, most of the ICAI systems restrict the student model to a so-called overlay of expert behavior. In other words, the student's knowledge is regarded as a subset of those of the expert, and mistakes are not described in terms of misconceptions in the expert model. A convincing exception to this is the Buggy system, which detects bugs in simple procedural skills (Burton, 1982; McNamara & Pettitt, 1991).

In contrast, we are of the opinion that CAI demonstrators show a preference for skill learning instead of knowledge acquisition. Behaviorism, task analysis, and the cybernetic approach of early teaching devices, still often penetrate the design of authoring tools for CAI. Figure 3.3 shows the overall strategy in controlling learning dialogues by CAI.

Fig 3.3. Overall control structure for CAI based on system control.

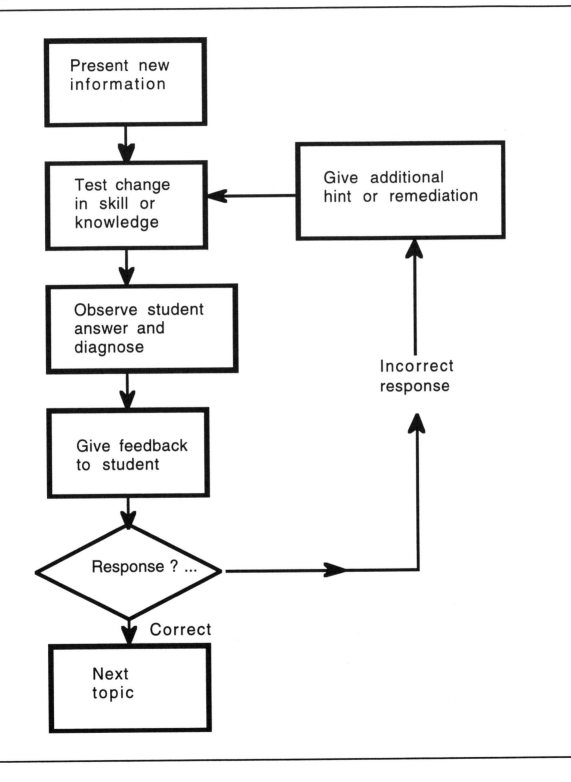

Cognitive psychology has been paying attention to the idiosyncrasy of knowledge integration in human memory. The more specific research into knowledge acquisition from textual information shows that learners incorporate new information into existing knowledge structures (Anderson, 1977; Goetz & Armbruster, 1980; Spiro, 1980; Symons & Pressley, 1993). In other words, what readers actually learn from textual information is controlled mainly by the activation of their prior knowledge. Bransford and Johnson (1973) and Frederiksen (1975, 1977a, 1977b) went even further when they described knowledge growth as a process of construction rather than acquisition. One of the consequences of this last insight is the elaboration technique:

> It allows the learner to learn at the level of complexity that is most appropriate and meaningful to him or her at any given state in the development of one's knowledge. (Reigeluth & Stein, 1983, p. 341).

Reigeluth (1979) gave the analogy between elaboration and a zoom lens. A person starts with a wide-angle view that allows him or her to see the major parts of the picture and the major relationships among those parts, but without any detail. (p. 340).

Student control is an important overall strategy in the work of Merrill (1980) and Reigeluth (1979), and refers to the freedom the learner has to take command of the selection and sequencing of content and procedures for addressing information. Reigeluth initially aimed to rest his theory on Ausubel's work (1963, 1966). He advocated that learning should start with general-level knowledge that subsumes the information to follow. The major part of knowledge acquisition could reflect successive differentiation theory in Ausubel's work.

Reigeluth's analogy between a student's adaptation to the level of detail and zooming has been utilized in TextVision-3D and Hypernet with respect to the dynamic display of hypertext networks (Kommers, Ferreira, and Jonker, 1989). The importance of elaboration theory within the current chapter however is its illustration of student control and its precursors in cognitive psychology.

Figure 3.4 stresses the contrast between the interaction sequence in system-controlled CAI and exploratory mixed-initiative dialogues.

A crucial element in the cycle is the phase of eliciting performance indicated in the hatched area of Figure 3.3. A good example of this is Seymour Papert's LOGO system (Papert, 1984). The student can explore geometric and algorithmic concepts by exploration and construction.

A significant difference between closed-loop learning (Fig. 3.3) and double-loop learning (Fig. 3.4) has been introduced by Klabbers (1988). Double-loop learning can occur in cases of exploratory learning events in which the student is aiming not only at an acknowledgment from the learning system. Exploration should essentially motivate the student to reflect on the problem approach.

Cognitive tools describe those computer-based learning programs that can be handed to the student as devices for thinking, learning, and knowledge acquisition. They are often precursors to new cognitive theories or vice versa.

Fig. 3.4. Overall control structure for exploratory learning.

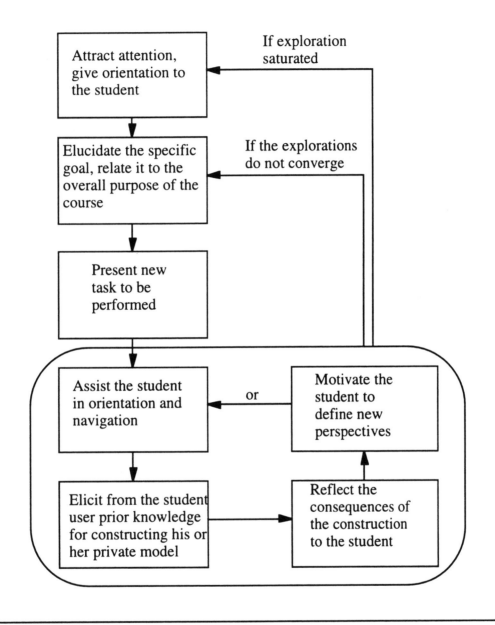

For example, Collins-Stevens (1982) proposed procedures for having a specific rule or theory applied by students or for letting them derive rules or theories from examples, which goes back to the very principles of discovery learning (Bruner, 1960, 1970, 1974), but also triggers the SCHOLAR CAI and WHY systems that make use of Socratic dialogue techniques.

Ausubel's (1963, 1966) expository approach, which concentrates on the technique of advance organizer, is fundamental to Schema Theory (Norman and Solso, 1973; Norman, 1983), Elaboration Theory (Reigeluth, 1979; Reigeluth & Stein, 1983), Structural Learning (Scandura, 1980) and Component Display Theory (Merrill, 1980; Merrill, Richards, Schmidt & Wood, 1977). Several of these theories have been operationalized in dedicated prototypes for ICAI and have again started a long sequence of epigones.

Most of these ICAI prototypes were designed to aid students in task-relevant, cognitive components of a performance such as revision in the writing of a composition or computation in the solution of physics problem, while leaving the performance open-ended and controlled by the learner (Kozma, 1987):

> They are designed to function by short-circuiting task-relevant, cognitive processes so as to reduce the cognitive load on the learner and free up cognitive resources that may be used for other, perhaps higher-level, cognitive processing. The tool does not teach the skill it activates, but once activated the skill can be used in learning. The learner can use these activated skills in the self-regulated acquisition of other skills or new declarative knowledge. A tool may also overtly display the processes they perform, thus providing the opportunity for some learners to internalize these processes (p. 21).

Kozma postulated that although experienced students have access to learning strategies such as giving rules and providing examples, younger pupils do not have access to them or do not make use of them. Rather than short-circuiting these learning activities by having the learning done for them, (like much CAI material does), cognitive tools evoke those necessary activities from the pupils themselves. Kozma mentions seven possible functions to be supplied by cognitive tools:

1. Supplementing limited working memory by making large amounts of information immediately available for the learner's use

2. Making relevant previously learned information available simultaneously with the acquisition of new information

3. Enabling learners to quickly retrieve previously learned information that is needed to help them in learning specific new information

4. Prompting the learner to structure, integrate, and interconnect new ideas with previous ones

5. Providing for self-testing and practice, thus increasing the retrievability of information

6. Enabling the learner to represent ideas both verbal and pictorial.

7. Providing for the easy movement, consolidation, and restructuring of information needed by students as their knowledge base grows

Examples of cognitive guiding questions are:

- What kind of image have I created from the text?

- What thoughts occur to me on the basis of the title?

- What do I understand from the text so far?

Kozma's approach is closely linked to cognitive research on proficient reader's behavior as performed by Baker and Brown (1984). Its application closely parallels the traditional approach of comprehensive reading and study skills. However, the potential of cognitive tools goes far ahead and will ultimately prove their value in the field of strategies for problem solving and knowledge elicitation.

This last, fast-developing didactic technique has been explored by Huntley (1989), who used a learning tool to construct graphical representations of a subject's structure, substructures, and relations. The most valuable three learning tool attributes are:

- The user can construct graphical networks.

- The software keeps links attached to nodes when nodes are moved.

- The user can attach textual information to detail cards.

In summary, instructional usage of computers has evolved through different stages from computer-assisted instruction to programming languages to computer literacy and finally to computers as open tools for learning activities (e.g., word processors, data bases, spread-sheets, graphics).

Advanced instrumentation now focuses on two additional types of software for learning:

- Intelligent tutoring systems
- Cognition enhancers

Hypertext and microworlds are the most obvious examples of the latter category. Their underlying concept is complementary to human cognition and the power of computers to perform algorithms, keep extensive short memory, infer from rules and data, manipulate symbols, and handle N-dimensions (see also the studies of Glass & Holyoak, 1986.)

Openness/ Closedness of Educational Hypertext Systems

Hypertext is a general tool that can be utilized in several ways. In addition to serving as an externalized associative memory for the student, it can be an alternative representational system for a large, shared data base (e.g. an integrated textbook series) and could encourage interdisciplinary group work by explicitly interconnecting similar ideas in different subjects.

Tchudi (1988) saw in a not-too-distant future, classrooms where a hypertext computer would be linked to the following:

- Topical bulletin boards on which young inquirers exchange messages, possibly even with scholars in a discipline

- Various communications and information sources such as stock market price indexes, statistical data on geography, economy, and so forth

- Libraries, in which students not only can look up call numbers and references, but also can insert optically scanned text in their own writings or retrieve information from encyclopedias, handbooks and manuals.

Open versus closed hypertext is the extent to which the system can or should be modifiable by the learner (or the learner's teacher). The content in exploratory hypertext systems is usually conceptualized and written by experts in the field being studied, and the systems are not designed to support additions to that content by the student, except in the form of reader's notes. Although this is understandable from the expert's point of view, the disadvantage is that the system cannot be updated or augmented with information by the teacher or the learner. The need to tune hypertext resources to this very situation becomes apparent as teachers prefer to articulate specific perspectives. Teacher generally agree that students should be able to differentiate between different views of the same facts.

CD-ROM and CD-I[2] will significantly speed up the availability of complete information resources in the learning situation, but will require a read/write procedure for the exchange of textual creations among groups of users. Nelson (1987) spoke about "where hypertext systems tend to be incompatible with the rest of the world, and thus throw away the power of interconnection and accessibility, in favor of publishing companies" (pp. 1-9).

In conclusion, crucial for hypertext is the pliability and plasticity of literature that should be open for alterations whenever and by whomever. CD-ROM-based hypertext resources essentially can be used without the need for modification, but should be combined with a flexible mechanism for virtually overruling the expert utterances. Besides the pliability of educational hypertext, we need the exchange of its resources between all kinds of groups at different locations.

RESEARCH LINE 2: WHICH IS THE BEST WAY OF INTERACTING BETWEEN USERS AND A HYPERTEXT SYSTEM?

The second research line studies isolated functions such as the flexibility of browsing, the effectiveness of navigation tools, or the amount of errors made by the users.

Again, the overall question is divided into three clusters:

1. Nielsen's benchmarks for hypertext user interfaces (UIFs); (Nielsen, & Lyngbaek, 1989).

2. User interfaces bridging the gap between user interest and the target task

3. User interfaces needing an explicit mental model for the user

---

[2] CD-I stands for Compact Disc Interactive. A standard for multimedia programs on compact disc as defined by Philips and Sony.

Nielsen's Benchmarks for Hypertext User Interfaces (UIFs)

The relevance of this second research line becomes clear if we examine Nielsen's (1989b) work on evaluating hypertext usability. He distinguished the level of interaction (engine), the level of contents, and the level of structure.

Nielson's benchmark approach (measuring appreciation, easiness, and effectiveness while working with an interactive system), however, mainly stayed at the level of interaction, and not so much at the cognitive level, at which the adequacy of the metaphor and the representation of knowledge play a role. The importance of Nielsen's work lies in the approach of breaking down the determinants of interaction benchmarks into individual differences and different tasks that users have when they use hypertext systems. He compared 92 benchmark measurements of various usability issues related to hypertext that have been published in the hypertext literature in an attempt to find which ones have shown the largest effects.

The most influential factor deciding whether users just look at hypertext systems or actually use it is the age of the user: Young users (ages 20 years or younger) prove to be more willing to actually use hypertext, (Baird, 1988).

The second most influential factor was the general level of motivation and activity of the user. The dependent variable was the number of created new nodes. Users with generally high motivation produced more new nodes in the system (Conklin, 1987). Furthermore, Conklin's research reported on the importance of the task definition for the way the user actually approaches hypertext. This is an important finding for effective implementations of hypertext in the field of education. Nielsen pled for iterative interface refinement as a technique for usability engineering. In fact, this research line concerns the ergonomics of the hypertext task environment.

User Interfaces Bridging the Gap Between User Interest and the Target Task

The relevance of the way an information systems presents itself to the user was recognized several years ago. Still we perceive a fast evolutionary shift in approach.

The psychology of human-computer interaction (Card, Moran, & Newell, 1983), for example, advocates high-level concerns and attitudes about user interface (UIF) design laid down in 10 principles. The first is: "Early in the system design process, consider the psychology of the user and the design of the user interface" (p. 418).

The factual elaborations, however, of how to define user characteristics and the way to relate them to the elements in the UIF designing are observable only at the physical level through pointing devices and the layout of the screen. In the last paragraph the authors overtly condemn the restrictions of their Goals, Operators, Methods (GOMS[3]) such as in the Keystroke-Level-Model: "Can the GOMS analysis be extended to more 'creative', less routine tasks?" (p. 420). The answer they give is: "No, the GOMS analysis is not applicable to less routine tasks such as problem solving."

---

[3] The models hypothesize that the user's cognitive structure consists of four components: a set of Goals, a set of Operators, a set of Methods for achieving the goals, and a set of Selection rules for choosing among competing methods for a goal.

Forrester and Reason (1989) rejected the conception of a UIF design as a representational window through which the human user manipulates and is informed about a software system. They consider it inadequate because it disconnects the user from the system, giving each a spurious autonomy. They suggest a more suitable concept of the UIF design:

> An interface is a dynamic relationship between a User, an Interest, (e.g., problem specification, task solution, browsing) and an ensemble of Representations (via screen, notepad, user's memory, and so on) and Tools (e.g., software manipulation, pencil, user tactics and techniques). For clarity, we call this an intraface. (p. 8).

The UIF approach of Forrester and Reason typically reflects the definition of user interfaces in the third period defined earlier: Intraface suggests that the communication attributes like screen layout, chosen manipulation tools, and metaphoric approach really try to match the user's perception of the task. A helpful addition to Forrester and Reason's approach is the distinction of structural layers in man-computer-interaction as has been described by Hanne and Graeble (1987). They postulate another three levels above the actual (physical) interaction and the syntax to be regarded. Their approach contrasts with Moran's (1981) four-level approach and transcends the level of Command Language Grammar (CLG). They mention:

- The level of semantics expressing a functional representation of thinking in the user and the level of tool representation in the system

- The level of pragmatics expressing the task the user sets for him- or herself and the representation of the application domain in the system

- An overall organizational structure embracing the user and the system and supporting positive feedback for the user if he or she succeeds in reaching the goals.

The last two layers are especially important in UIF design. The intraface pays attention to the subtle congruence between the local (and temporal) interest of the user and the attributes in the system to be used. The multilayered UIF model stresses the sociopsychological elements of the task situation. In fact, it gives attention to the ecology of the user situation, claiming that an organism and its environment are already coupled, as if they resonate and give support or vice versa.

The underlying notion of space in hypertext, expressing the extended connections and consequence of being away from one's starting point, unifies the feelings of the users and the implicit metaphor in many of the hypertext UIFs. Forrester and Reason gave three reasons why the design rationales of current UIFs tend to stay at the levels of the first two phases:

- There is too much stress on the information-processing metaphor.

- The dominant conceptual frameworks for human computer interaction (HCI) theory fail to engage with the experience of using computers in general and computer-assisted learning (CAL) in particular.

• No adequate account has been developed for the user's (changing) adaptations to conceptions of the system in use as an integral and consequential component of the user's experience and the analyst designer's HCI model.

User Interfaces Need an Explicit Mental Model for the User

There has been a great deal of interest in how users develop and employ mental models of the software tools with which they work. (Gentner & Stevens, 1983). The common wisdom holds that good device models aid users, especially in approaching novel tasks. Metaphor-based interfaces acquire their popularity from the belief that they promote effective mental models. Once there is an understanding that a remote disk can contain files and that a file can contain streams of information, a user can accomplish new tasks by analogy from the first understanding. However, three problems may show up:

1. Not all computer tasks have obvious analogies (e.g., archiving in the sense of data compression cannot be understood by imagining air compression or the transport of powdered milk).

2. Metaphors that were initially adequate become inefficient or may even cause misunderstanding and irritation as the user becomes more skilled and needs shortcuts (e.g., preserving the desktop analogy motivates the user to think in spatial consequences).

   In using only one analogy, the teacher will soon discover that he or she must adjust the metaphor, adding new (and often bizarre) features to it or, alternatively, combining various metaphors that are not normally associated. (Halasz & Moran, 1982).

3. Lindsay & Norman (1977) added a third warning: If metaphors are too rich in composition, they can distract too much attention and may obstruct the learning process. "They should be broken down into manageable substructures when presented to the student."

One may still try to argue that there is little empirical support for the usefulness of metaphors in developing effective conceptual models of information systems compared to that for other types of device models.

Young (1980) stressed the value of coherence models that emphasize logical relationships among system elements and make important system relationships explicit. This notion is quite compatible with Bartlett's plea for a meaningful organization of learning material (Bartlett, 1932a).

The coherence model relies on the general observation about human memory that it is hard to remember accurately a set of incoherent facts about the same topic. Instead, what remains after a time is a structuring of the facts round a schema. Individual facts may be distorted either to fit with the schema or to contrast with it, or else may be forgotten.

The experiments of Bransford and Johnson (1972) and Billingsley (1982) gave evidence that understanding a system is facilitated by the appropriateness of knowledge organization, and that it will finally improve the user's performance.

Norman (1983) gave another three levels of the human mental representation for one preparing or using a system:

- The conceptual model as it has been defined by the designer and should be interpreted by the user

- The factual (mental) model being built by the user as he or she gets unpredicted reactions from the system (Inconsistencies between conceptual and factual models can survive for long periods and will give a fictitious feeling about how to coordinate the tools in the system.)

- The scientist's conceptualization of the user's model

Van der Veer and Felt (1988) reported some of their experiences in embedding explicit conceptual models in the teaching of a virtual program such as the Disk Operating System (DOS).

The first conclusion they presented was that Moran's (1981) distinction in four levels of a command language grammar (CLG) is useful for constructing a teacher's conceptual model. The second was that an explicit conceptual model can act as a touchstone to detect inelegant features of the system to be taught.

Most of the examples illustrating the power of explicit metaphors for eliciting mental models in the user are graphically oriented. Boecker, Fischer, and Nieper (1986), for example, concentrate on the role of visualization in software design. Their program *FooScape* generates a graphical representation of the static structure of a computer program. The networks consist of nodes and arrows and enable the user to check for lexical nesting of function definitions. The dynamic aspects: (i.e., what is the program doing?) can be shown by highlighting the nodes (flipping from white to black whenever a function is active).

The explicit metaphor of visualizing states and transitions by means of network diagrams becomes an important one in programming tools, document browsers, and tools for knowledge elicitation.

RESEARCH LINE 3: WHAT USER INTERFACES ARE APPROPRIATE FOR NAVIGATION AND COLLABORATION IN HYPERTEXT?

The third research line goes into more detail and addresses the two lower levels of Nielsen's work: content and structure. This line touches the essential principles of hypertext and the match (or mismatch) with the mental process in the user. Although the problem seems to be quite abstract and hard to solve, we meet many research projects covering the central issue of metaphors for hypertext.

The work of McAleese (1988, 1989) gave strong examples on the relevance of typed hypertext links and the need to differentiate the style of interaction between the user and the system as the situation changes from one learning phase to another.

The basic issue in this line of research is how to upgrade hypertext to a level of externalized knowledge rather than manage interlinked fragments of information. McAleese argued for a freedom of grain size of the information units. Units are represented by a node, that ranges in size from single concept label up to a considerable amount of text.

Hammwoehner (1989) and Hammwoehner and Thiel (1987) were more precise about the desirable granularity of hypertext nodes as they proposed to parse hypertext paragraphs on the basis of text-linguistic regularities. Hypertext units were regarded, not as a more or less arbitrary network of interconnected text units, but as an enhanced notion of text as a more precise (isomorphic) representation of the knowledge to be transferred between the author and the reader. Still, Hammwoehner took the elements of a natural text as the de facto resource for knowledge-based text decomposition.

One of the most predominant problems of consulting large hypertext resources is the risk of disorientation. The study of Nielsen and Lyngbaek (1989) showed that about 56% of the readers of HyperCard documents agree with the statement, "I was often confused about where I was." Nielsen (1989b) described hypertext jumps as

> being orthogonal to the left-right page turning and are visualized as an in-out dimension using an animated iris which opens for anchored jumps and closes for return jumps. The opening iris gives users the impression of diving deeper into the when they take an hypertext jump, and the closing iris for return jumps gives the inverse feeling of pulling back again Nielsen (p. 12).

Nielsen proposed to make use of overview diagrams as navigational aids, providing a course-grained sense of location in the global information space. Additional mechanisms such as backtrack facilities, a history listing, time-stamping, landmarks such as bread-crumb facilities, footprints, and so forth are necessary. HyperCard's HyperTalk (computational hypertext as Nielsen calls it) enables rapid prototyping, for designing and prototyping missing elements such as user history, dynamic overview, and different versions of time-stamping (Nielsen 1989).

Navigation in its pure sense deals with the problem of how to reach a specific point or a set of points in an efficient way. This can be done by prescriptive advice (e.g., "If you want to make a tour while visiting these three concepts, then first go to in this direction.").

Navigation can also be assisted by representing the configuration in space-like maps, schemes, and so forth. Such a representation can help the user to find a comfortable route, and beyond that, contribute to a mental representation so that the user finally builds up a mental representation.

Nielsen was mainly concerned about the question, "How can I go backward quickly and safely?" McAleese (1988) raised the question, "Where can I go next?" This mission has three components:

- Knowing the place (or its name) that meets your interest

- Knowing how to reach it

- Remembering where you have been

The second and third problem could again be defined as navigation problems. The first is often compared with a voyage of discovery and is quite a distinguishing feature of hypertext. On the way to the target information (which essentially could be performed as a straight query task), many associations can rise based on the new elements popping up, and may tempt the user to go in another direction first. Roaming, digressions, and serendipity have not only been recognized as negative elements in browsing, but are also positive characteristics.

McAleese (1989) distinguished between two basic types of browsing tools. The first is the same as that described in chapter 1 and has hot spots to be typed in or clicked on by the mouse, whereas the second provides the user with a graphic outline or a diagram with the pattern of relationships between the nodes of information.

Using studies into the database approach, McAleese gave the relationship between types of browsing and the preference for browsing Tools 1 or 2:

- Scanning: Covering a large area without depth

    Tool 1: medium preference

    Tool 2: medium preference

- Browsing: Following a path until a goal is achieved

    Tool 1: high preference

    Tool 2: low preference

- Searching: Striving to find an explicit goal

    Tool 1: medium preference

    Tool 2: low preference

- Exploring: Finding out the extent of the information given

    Tool 1: low preference

    Tool 2: medium preference

- Wandering: Purposeless and unstructured globetrotting

    Tool 1: low preference

    Tool 2: high preference

The need for Tool 2 is most obvious in the case of global orientations and in case the user is quite open to the potential of the information to be found. The preceding schema also provides us with evidence that presently we must trade off between browsing (narrowing down) and wandering (broadening one's horizon) as two distinct types of information seeking. Scanning, in McAleese's view, can be performed by means of both types of tools, provided that the user is able to resist the temptation to zoom in one of the concepts on the way.

The central problems in network display are

- Focusing

- Zooming

- Pruning

- Positioning the nodes

The first three problems can be integrated into the so-called fish eye view (Furnas, 1986). Its actual use for wandering in a far-reaching hypertext base such as a complete encyclopedia has not yet been explored and has been described in Kommers, Ferreira & Jonker (1989).

HyperCard as referred to before will play the crucial role in chapter 6 and beyond. It has a default hypertext user interface (Tool 1) and also the tools to upgrade itself. Most of the hypertext systems we meet in the research are "plain," in the sense that they cannot be modified by the user. They can only be filled with information and assist in the phase of browsing.

Applying the cognitive mapping and fish-eye techniques has further been described in Kommers (1989). However, it needs dedicated software or in-depth prototyping that goes beyond the technical facilities and flexibility of HyperTalk programming language.

Hypertext Support for Writing and Authoring Collaboration

Hypertext has become popular because of its ability to relate separate elements of text without prescribing the reading sequence. Retrieving information means tracing a line of associations or (if the line is absent) creating it yourself. As long as the document is in use by just you, or a small group of readers (as is most of the electronic mail correspondence of today), there is no problem. However, if several authors are modifying a hypertext document, there are many solutions to the traditional multi-authoring task (as in the updating problem), but still there are a lot of problems to be solved. The experience of authors and readers with hypertext clearly demonstrates that one must do more than just connect documents.

Hypertext offers support for the authoring of complex documents and the processing of ideas, especially in a group or collaborative environment. Duffy and Knuth (1989) stressed that authoring is a critical component in any hypertext application, in the sense that learners require the capability to annotate information frames for themselves and need to be able to collaborate with other students and the teacher over specific units of information.

Duffy and Knuth (1989) warned against the entropy (losing the original meaning after several reinterpretations and annotations) of information that will occur if students simply make annotations without comparing their relevance to other possible annotations they could make: "Authoring should support the learner in extending the ideas in the database and creating his own personalized information" (pp. 199-222).

Duffy and Knuth also mentioned the role of hypertext in the collaboration between student and teacher, and also between students. The teacher should stimulate the students to confront different points of view, and the teacher should be able to discuss and explain communality in different opinions among students. Management of argument development becomes the main task for the hypertext system (Akscyn et al., 1988).

Jonathan Swift said that argument is the worst sort of conversation. Streitz (1987); Streitz, Hannemann, and Thuering (1989); and Streitz (1989) offered a more detailed analysis of the rhetorical space in describing hypertext authoring tools such as TEXTNET (Trigg & Weiser, 1986), NoteCards (Halasz, Moran, & Trigg, 1987), Neptune (Delisle & Schwartz, 1986), and to a lesser extent Guide (Brown, 1987), HyperCard (Williams, 1987), and HyperTIES (Marchionini & Schneiderman, 1988). Streitz (1989b) signaled that most of those systems lack graphical representation of the node-link structure of the hypertext networks.

This deficit results in a number of crucial problems connected with support for navigation (disorientation problem) and for personal information structuring. (pp. 407-438).

Structured Elicitation and Processing of Ideas for Authoring (SEPIA) is an idea processing tool for creating and revising hyper documents. SEPIA intends to solve the two main problems in creating hyperdocuments: cognitive overhead (Conklin & Begeman, 1988) and the problem that most authoring tools for hypertext are rather passive storage and retrieval systems. According to Streitz, an active authoring tool should be able to monitor and guide authors in their problem solving activity and be cognitively compatible by providing different representations adapted to the stage of authoring. This goal is achieved by providing a variety of activity spaces, each residing in dedicated windows open to manipulation by the author. These are

- *Content space*: What to say, in which order, how many details?

- *Rhetorical space*: How to say it; how to use analogies and metaphors?

- *Planning space*: How to create a well-designed balance between the relevance of texts its size?

- *Argumentation space*: How to sketch the line of thought and how to make the reasoning convincing to the reader?

These spaces have been derived from invariant features of the activities to be supported. The editors in all spaces can manipulate nodes and links. Links can have a content that is dependent on the type of link. Streitz (1989a) gave an example: "Activating and opening the so-link in the argumentation space results in displaying the warrant and backing structure of this link."

Streitz's SEPIA system is an excellent example of how interactive tools can specify a more detailed level of theories about authoring and learning. The SEPIA design makes Hayes and Flowers' (1980) widely cited problem-solving model, Kopperschmidt's (1985) idea of hierarchical organization of argumentation, and Van Dijk and Kintsch's (1983) concept of macro and su- perstructures more tangible.

Landow (1989) raised the need for a new rhetoric with the recognition that authors of hypertext and hypermedia material confront three related problems:

- What must they do to orient readers and help them read efficiently and with pleasure?

- How can they inform the reader of a document where the links in that document lead?

- How can they assist readers who have just entered a new document to feel at home there?

Landow supposed that hypertext requires stylistic and rhetorical devices just as does paper-based text. As one might expect, hypertext does not simply match the organizing principles that make page-bound discourse coherent and a pleasure to read.

One task an author must perceive is that of informing the reader what to find at the end of a hypertext trail. In the Intermedia project Landow was involved in choosing the right WEB-view. A web is an overview of the connections between the hypertext elements. It allows readers to benefit from their most recent experiences, simultaneously offering a record of the document at which one has looked and showing the reader's current position.

Instead of traditional rhetoric for speaking or writing on paper, Landow (1989) advised authors of hypertext to anticipate the orientation of the reader. The advice is: "Don't tell the reader how to read the document, but tell him or her what can be expected after choosing a certain direction." (pp. 39-60).

Marchionini and Schneiderman (1988), among many other researchers, mentioned the communication function of hypertext:

> Students could "collaborate" with the system by downloading segments and by annotating and editing them to produce their papers and reports. Students could create their own paths through the hyperdocument, save and annotate them as interpretation of the content, and share these traversals and notes with teachers and fellow students. the potential of computers to facilitate group work is an active area of research. (p. xx)

It is not clear how the term collaboration has intruded into this field. Collaboration has the connotation of working together with the enemy. Cooperation gives a better indication of what most of the authors mean by multi-authoring.

As already illustrated in more detail in chapter 2, Doise (1978) and Doise and Mugny (1984) gave a basic theory for stimulation of the cognitive development when children interact (and have conflict) with each other. Social development defined as being aware of perspectives taken and one's role in the solution of a collective problem seems to be a prelude to the ability to solve intellectual problems for stimulation of the cognitive development when children interact (and have conflict) among themselves.

Hypertext as an interaction device between peers could be helpful in the elicitation of mental conflicts, such as we can often see in self-help groups.

The way current hypertext is exploited for cooperative writing is not defined well enough to promote cooperation in the sense of cognitive exchange. The fresh idea as formulated by Marchionini (Marchionini & Schneiderman, 1988), still is in a primitive stage, especially when compared to dedicated cooperative learning techniques such as Jigsaw (Aronson, 1978), Teams-Games-Tournaments (TGT) and Student Teams and Academic Divisions (STAD) (De Vries & Slavin, 1978), and Small Group Teaching (Sharan & Hertz-Lazarowitz, 1980). The composition of heterogeneous groups may improve the quality of the interactions (Nijhof & Kommers, 1984). However, the cooperation process needs to be coached before cognitive merits evolve. This is especially the case if we consider the narrow bandwidth of written communication compared with social interaction.

Cooperation between students in the use of hypertext has also been studied by Mayes, Kibby, and Watson (1988). They accepted the necessity of social interaction between pupils as a complementary procedure for explicit learning. The method they adopted is called constructive interactions and is primarily intended to observe, transcribe, and analyze pupil's reasoning while the pupil performing the hypertext task.

Rhetoric as a compositional awareness (on an individual level) has been defined in the context of hypertext by Landow (1988) and Streitz (1987). The preference of Marchionini for using hypertext in collaboration is still open with regard to the strategy of the medium.

The experiences and traditions in the field of cooperative learning can offer abundant ideas about how to organize group work by means of hypertext tools. The development of hypertext tools should not be explored without taking notions from the theory on human collaboration.

A clear example of collaboration by means of telematics has been demonstrated by Sligte (1989). Two Canadian schools and one Dutch school devised an electronic field trip using a classroom teleport. The theme of communication was community archaeology. Groups of pupils in the ages 14 to 17 years investigated their own environments and shared their results via computers and satellite. Conversations emanated from the exchanged information and led to a broader understanding of the subject matter. It also bridged intercultural and contextual gaps. The user interface was not equipped with hypertext. The results showed the need to be aware of telematics as a means of collaboration by exchange of electronic text.

Prudent steps to integrate cooperative elements in hypertext environments have been reported by Trigg and Suchman (1989). They proposed that hypertext be equipped with detectors for overlapping information. This contrasts with outline processors in which only one organization at a time can be entertained.

> Such multiple organizations may be especially useful if authors are in the process of progressively reorganizing their work, or if they elect to maintain two or more outlines of a developing paper in parallel. (Trigg and Suchman, 1989, pp. 45-61)

Trigg and Suchman proposed that discussions be facilitated among co-authors at a level removed from the subject matter of their work. Indeed, many of the current hypertext mapping tools enable users to become aware of a meta level stimulating a match between the topic of request and a superordinate level of opinions and perspectives. In fact, this coincides with social techniques as reflection and meta discussions to learn from social interaction (see also the work of Klabbers [1988] in which he introduced the actor-metaphor and the principle of double-loop learning).

Human Factors in the Life Cycle of Hypertext Systems

The software crisis was first signaled in the late 1960s shortly before the term software engineering was invented. Usability engineering goes beyond robustness and user friendliness. It is a reaction to the awareness that human factors probably are the major cost of introducing complex systems. The user interface itself may be important for the final interaction that can be elicited in the application program; however, it does not guarantee the adequacy of the chosen entities to solve the task by the user. Yet the actual relevance of the usability problem has to be recognized by application developers. Usability engineering is the effort to improve human-computer interaction by anticipating all aspects of the task to be performed by the user.

The first step to be taken by the usability engineer is to become aware of the many aspects involved as the user tries to optimize his or her achievement. In terms of hypertext applications, usability is not only covered by the comfort of pointing and browsing actions, but especially concerns the facilities to explicate, modify, and navigate an enormous network of semantic associations. These activities cannot be detected simply by measuring satisfaction or reaction times, but need a more detailed definition of quality criteria such as the match between mental and external representation and versatility for differences in cognitive styles. Hypertext as an add-on to authoring environments may play a crucial role in demanding the utmost from the human imagination, because it attempts to stimulate imagination and creativity in the user.

The first step taken in the design of the two hypertext applications in our project was task analysis, an examination of how the user thinks about the task and the mental data manipulation he or she currently uses (see Card et al., 1983). As system designers succeeded in improving the interaction quality of computer programs, users immediately became more assertive and expected systems to be easy to learn and easy to use. Soon we saw new systems coming out, not because of their usefulness, but because of their easiness. Clear examples are the numerous computer games as well as spreadsheets and data bases promoted by teachers because of their comfort and simplicity.

One way to improve usability is to refer to a set of standard parameters (Nielsen, 1989b):

- Ease of learning: The user can quickly get some work done with the system.

- Efficiency of use: Once the learner has learned the system, a high level of productivity is possible.

- Ease of remembering: The casual user is able to remember what has been learned about using the system, even if it has not been used for some time.

- Few errors: Users do not make many errors during the use of the system, or if they do, they can easily recover from them. Also, no catastrophic errors can occur.

- Pleasure in using: Users are subjectively satisfied by using the system; they like it.

In addition to usability and user satisfaction as Nielsen mentioned, Hilchey and Huriych (1985) mentioned user acceptance as a key variable in the life cycle of interactive systems. She studied the usability of the retrieved information from on-line reference services at Northern Illinois University. Her concern started from the idea that educational use of hypertext needs other criteria than those that pertain to hypertext for public information systems or entertainment. If learning comes in, the quality of knowledge effects should be taken into account during the evaluation of hypertext systems.

RESEARCH LINE 4: WHICH IS THE RIGHT GRANULARITY TO REPRESENT KNOWLEDGE BEYOND THE LEVEL OF ASSOCIATIVE LINKS?

As a practical problem, hypertext authors question how long they should make paragraphs of text and how many relations they should assign from a paragraph. The literature is not clear in answering this question. For this reason, teachers and experimenters need to observe learners as they browse, in order to choose an optimal number of hotshots per paragraph for a certain target group.

An even more fascinating question from the epistemological side is how many types of relations should be allowed while specifying hypertext relations.

The KANT[4] project (Storrs, 1989) focused on the consequence of the chosen grain size. First of all the researchers found that analysts (in the role of an author) tend to create and use a relatively small number of link types. Second, analysts seem to believe that a defined set of links could be a useful addition to a hypertext system, even though they tend to invent quite different sets for themselves.

> The card-based hypertext systems, generally use a whole card as the unit for linking to, while they allow single words or smaller units to link from. Such choices seem to lead to different perceptions of the system being used. (pp. 148-156)

The KANT project showed that hypertext (with free-formatted nodes and un-typed links) is essentially open to be gradually upgraded to more explicit types of relations, and will finally enable the user to express him- or herself on the level of knowledge engineering with facts and rules that can be evaluated by an inference engine.

The many versions of hypertext appearing in the last three years happily stimulated the discussion about the nature of hypertext itself. Most of the re-

---

[4] The Alvey DHSS Large Demonstrator Project Knowledge Analysis Tool: KANT as designed by Graham Storrs. KANT is a knowledge analysis tool that has been developed as part of an Alvey collaborative project. The application has been for the Department of Health and Social Security in the UK. KANT supports procedures for knowledge analysis to facilitate the translation of paper source into hypertext.

searchers acknowledged the idea that the importance is in the links between the information nodes.

The author of information is a neglected actor in regard to the usability of hypertext, especially as one blurs the distinction between authoring and reading. Authoring in hypertext has often been belittled with descriptions like that of Nelson (1981):

- A hypertext system allows authors to link ideas together.

Or a description even more cryptic:

- Creating the Xanalogical structure of the docuverse

Most user interfaces make it easy to perform this task; however, it requires a tough discipline for it to occur in a consistent way: The propagation of links should mirror the relevance of the concepts and the semantics of the relations between them. In other words, important concepts should be elaborated more completely than subsidiary or peripheral concepts (see also McKnight et al., 1989a).

Taxonomy has been an influential method for organizing text on paper. Hypertext can emulate levels of description such as headers, paragraphs, subparagraphs, and so on. As soon as a word in a subparagraph points backward to a header, the taxonomy is destroyed. In fact, it proves that the links between the text entities did not simply express "consists of." It forces us to think about the type of relationships we use in references such as links in hypertext.

The research reports dealing with the granularity of hypertext links focus on the levels of explicit rather than implicit structures in text. Implicit structures in text are much like the network of concepts in the mind of the author, and presumably in the mind of the reader afterwards.

Jonassen (1982, p. 10) highlights the importance of explicit structures in text in order to prompt the reader to main positions in the hyperspace. Hypertext takes the consequence of the need for explicitness and even expresses references in terms of presentation sequences. After all, the reader may use a reference as a jump from one paragraph to another.

There are two reasons for making hypertext relations more clear in their meaning and the configuration in which they are placed:

1. Both authors and readers are familiar with thinking and seeking in hierarchies:

   - Going *down* means "Be more *detailed*"

   - Going *up* means "Be more *general*"

   Simply supplying a hypertext linking tool will inherently amplify the notion of taxonomies: Divide and conquer.

2. Traveling through the network of nodes and links raises the problem of orientation. Hierarchy, as a model for navigating, conflicts with cycles in the network. Heterarchy rather than hierarchy is needed to match the user's model to cyclicity in hypertext.

Heterarchy is inherent in the recursiveness of concept entailments and subsequently asks for a more differentiated notion of hypertext links. In fact, hypertext designers should be more explicit about the semantic implication for the reader traversing a link.

McKnight et al., (1989b) illustrated that the difficulty of defining optimal granularity is highly dependent on context sensitivity in the domain of information. Factual information can more easily be decontextualized, whereas discourse representations might be destroyed if the reader jumps in at the middle of an episode. The arguments for choosing the optimal granularity in discourse are much more problematic. To be frank, at this moment we are still at the level of esthetics and pragmatics rather than the level of theory.

For example, the detective novel is clearly a literary form, that heavily relies on the linear format: A philosophical argument frequently builds from earlier arguments in such a way that it would not be appropriate to jump into the middle without having encountered the earlier material:

> Mathematical theorems may require the building of parallel strands before the final proof, but the strands are logically prior to the proof, and therefore some degree of linearity is inevitable (McKnight, Richardson, & Dillon, 1989b, pp. 277-290).

The fact that we can decontextualize textual passages is not sufficient for embedding them in a larger hypertext system. Readers need strong semantic lines, even in the case of multi-sequential browsing. Causal links and temporal links are clearly bound to a specific presentation order.

Differentiation into several types of links is one possibility for overcoming the danger of fuzziness and semantic ambiguity. Schematic text organization outlining these types of relationships could express Kintsch (1974) and Van Dijk's (1977) gist or macrostructure, legitimizing the reason why certain ideas are more central or important in a passage than others. In other words, the validity of hypertext relations should be based on the cognitive process of the reader rather than the criteria of completeness and semantic correctness.

McAleese (1989) proposed that the granularity of hypertext primarily be determined by the actual preference of the designer rather than the implicit structure of the tool. He uses SemNet as a knowledge acquisition system for constructive and reconstructive learning.

The system McAleese discusses transmits the negotiations between the teacher and the student. The granularity in SemNet equals the level of propositions. Concepts appear in ovals or rounded boxes. Every view (McAleese called it a "frame") contains one central concept, various related concepts, and the types of relationships between them. Examples of types of relationships are:

- type_of

- is_an_example_of

- contained_by

- is_a_part_of

- has_part

- component_of

The facilities for representing nodes and arcs at the level of propositions lead the student to become aware of much more detail than is usually the case in general graphical hypertext browsers. Four remarks can be made:

1. Many more nuances could be added to the two-legged relationships as proposed by McAleese: preconditions, probabilities, personal relevance, and so on. This observation leads to the question of whether SemNet's representations provoke detailed knowledge elements sufficiently. Duffy and Knuth (1989) warned about the inertia of school knowledge and the difficult time students have transferring from school-based learning, because schooling often presents the concepts and principles in an oversimplified framework.

2. It is quite uncertain whether understanding at the level of propositions contributes to problematic or critical elements in the study behavior of students. The examples in SemNet particularly show parts of deterministic and especially causal chains. Denotations of concepts are displayed in networks linking the attention to micro elements in the knowledge to be transmitted.

3. The question arises whether the tendency toward fine-grained representations is a fortunate one after all. In cases of understanding deterministic processes such as those in physics, chemistry, or biology, it may be fine. Many subject areas in school education, however, need the opposite orientation (e.g., being acquainted with the overall view, being aware of the interconnection between points of view).

4. The links distinguished in SemNet reflect only the semantics differences between the concepts in the knowledge domain. It would certainly be necessary to add types of links that express the type of action the user performed in elaborating on a certain concept (e.g., "Annotate," "Example_of," "Argument(s)_pro," "Arguments_contra," "Presupposes").

CONCLUSION

Experiments in education show a general sympathy for the flexibility of authoring and reading in hypertext. Some of them indicate the need for additional facilities such as cooperative authoring, annotating, book-marking.

The need for navigational assistance and trails to find one's way back is somewhat greater as the students are younger; (Leggett et al., 1989). The same tendency was mentioned in respect to learner control: Learners can cope with more freedom as they are older and more capable in the domain of knowledge. Hypertext as a learning tool may evoke a new learning repertoire from younger students; (Kozma, 1987).

These review data indicate that the problems and benefits of hypertext vary among different types of users and possibly also among different types of user settings. Hypertext UIFs, in particular, need usability engineering in order to optimize the relationships between types of users, task demands, and the implicit way of navigation assistance. The design of educational hypertext systems, in particular, calls for anticipation of the cognitive process in the learner and of the increasing capability of the student to deal with complexity.

The implications of different grain sizes and the introduction of various types of relationships in hypertext need further research. The first step in attacking these questions is to observe and categorize browsing sessions while users are (as students) actually exploring information in a hypertext system.

REFERENCES

Akscyn, R. M., McCracken, D. L., & Yoder, E. A. (1988). KMS: A distributed hypermedia system for managing knowledge in organizations. *Communications of the ACM, 31*, 820-835.

Anderson, R. C. (1977). The notion of schemata and the educational enterprise. In R. C. Anderson, R. J. Spiro, & W. E. Montague, (Eds.), *Schooling and the acquisition of knowledge* (pp. 415-432). Hillsdale NJ: Lawrence Erlbaum Associates.

Anderson-Inman, L. (1989). Electronic studying: Information organizers to help students to study "better" not "harder":part II. *The Computing Teacher, 16*(9) 21-23, 25-29, 53.

Aronson, E. (1978) *The Jigsaw classroom.* Beverly Hills CA: Sage.

Asimov, I. (1974). *Words of science and the history behind them*, London: Harrap.

Ausubel, D. P. (1963). *The psychology of meaningful verbal learning: An introduction to school learning.* New York: Holt, Rinehart & Winston.

Ausubel, D. P. (1966). *Educational psychology: A cognitive view.* New York: Holt, Rinehart & Winston.

Baird, Patricia. (1988). HyperCard Opens an Electronic Window on Glasgow. *Electronic Library, 6*(5), 344-53.

Baker, L., & Brown, A. L. (1984). Metacognitive skills and reading. In P. Pearson (Ed.) *Handbook of Reading Research* (pp. 445-456). New York: Longman.

Bartlett, F. C. (1932b). *Remembering: A study in experimental and social psychology.* New York: Cambridge University Press.

Becker, D. A., & Dwyer, M. M. (1994). Using hypermedia to provide learner control. *Journal of Educational Multimedia and Hypermedia, 3*(2), 155-172.

Bernstein, M. (1988). The bookmark and the compass: Orientation tools for hypertext users. *SIG OIS Bulletin, 9,*(4), 34-45.

Billingsley, P. A., (1982, October). Navigation through hierarchical menu structures: Does it help to have a map? *Proceedings of the 26th Annual Meeting of the Human Factors Society*, 103-107.

Boecker, H. D., Fischer, G., & Nieper, H. (1986). The enhancement of understanding through visual representations. Human factors in computing systems-II, *Proceedings of CHI-"86 in Boston.* Amsterdam: North-Holland Press.

Bransford, J. D., & Johnson, M. K. (1973). Considerations of some problems of comprehension. In W. G. Chase, (Ed.), *Visual information processing* (pp. 325-355). New York: Academic Press.

Brown, P. (1987). Turning ideas into products: the GUIDE system. *Proceedings of the Hypertext 87 Workshop* (pp. 33-40). Chapel Hill NC.

Bruner, J. S. (1970). The act of discovery. In C. H. Monson, Jr. (Ed.), *Education for what?* (pp. 233-384). Boston: Houghton Mifflin.

Bruner, J. S. (1974). *The relevance of education.* Harmondsworth, Middlesex: Penguin Education Publishers.

Bruner, J. S. (1960). *The process of education*, New York: Random House.

Burton, R. R. (1982). Diagnosing bugs in a simple procedural skill. In D. Sleeman & J. S. Brown (Eds.), *Intelligent tutoring systems* (pp. 157-183). London: Academic Press.

Bush V. (1945). As we may think. *Atlantic Monthly, 176*, 101-108.

Card. S. K., Moran, T. P., & Newell, A. (1983). *The psychology of human-computer interaction.* Hillsdale NJ: Lawrence Erlbaum Associates.

Carrier, C. A., & Williams, M. D. (1988, summer). A test of one learner-control strategy with students of differing levels of task persistence. *American Educational Journal, 25*(2), 285-306.

Catano, J. V. (1979). Poetry and computers: Experimenting with communal text. *Computers and Humanities, 13,* 269-275.

Chung, J., & Reigeluth, C. M. (1992). Instructional prescriptions for learner control. *Educational Technology, 32*(10), 14-20.

Clancey, W. J. (1987). Qualitative Student Models. *Annual Review of Computer Science, 1,* 5-38.

Collins, A., & Stevens, A. L. (1982). A cognitive theory of inquiry teaching. In C. Reigeluth (Ed.). *Instructional design, theories and models.* Hillsdale NJ: Lawrence Erlbaum Associates.

Conklin J. (1987). Hypertext: An introduction and survey. *IEEE Computer, 20* (9), 17-41.

Conklin J., & Begeman, M. L. (October 1988). GIBIS: A hypertext tool for exploratory policy discussion. *ACM Transactions: Office Information Systems 6*(4) 303-331.

Cumming, G., & Self, J. (1989). Collaborative Intelligent Educational Systems. In D. Bierman, J. Breuker & J. Sandberg (Eds.). *Artificial Intelligence and Education*, pp 73-80, Amsterdam: IOS.

Delisle, N. A., & Schwartz, M. D. (1986). Neptune: A hypertext system for CAD applications. In G. Zaniolo (Ed.). *Proceedings of the International Conference on Management of Data - SIGMOD '86*, (pp. 132-143), Washington DC New York: Association of Computing Machinery.

DeVries, S., & Slavin R. E. (1978). Teams Games Tournaments (TGT): Review of ten classroom experiments. *Journal of Research and Development in Education, 12,* 1.

Dijk, van, T., & Kintsch, W. (1983). *Strategies for discourse comprehension.* New York: Academic Press.

Dijk, van, T., (1977). *Text and context: Explorations in the semantics and pragmatics of discourse.* London: Longman Group Ltd.

Doise, W. (1978). *Groups and individuals, Explanations in social psychology.* Cambridge (Eng): Cambridge University Press.

Doise, W., & Mugny, G. (1984). *The social development of the intellect.* Oxford: Pergamon Press.

Duffy, T. M., & Knuth, R. A. (1989). *HYPERMEDIA and Instruction: Where is the match?* Paper presented at the NATO Advanced Research Workshop, Rottenburg, 3-7 July 1989.

Engelbart, D. C. (1963). A conceptual framework for the augmentation of man's intellect. In B. Howerton & G. Weeks (Eds.). *Vistas in information handling.* Washington DC: Spartan Books.

Forrester, M., & Reason, D. (1989). *The application of an "Intraface Model" to the design of hypertext systems.* Internal report University of Kent, Southampton, Great Britain.

Frederiksen, C. H. (1975). Representation of logical and semantic structure of knowledge acquired from discourse. *Cognitive Psychology, 7,* 371-458.

Frederiksen, C. H. (1977a). *Inference and the structure of children's discourse.* Paper presented at the biennial meeting of the Society for Research in Child Development, New Orleans LA.

Frederiksen, C. H. (1977b). Semantic processing units in understanding text. In R. O. Freedle (Ed.), *Discourse production and comprehension* (pp. 45-68). Norwood NJ: Ablex.

Furnas, G. W. (1986). Generalized fisheye views. *Proceedings of ACM CHI '86 Conference on Human Factors in Computing Systems,* (pp. 16-23). New York: Association of Computing Machinery.

Gal'perin, P. J., & Leontev, A. W. (1972). *Probleme der Lernthreorie.* Berlin: Volk und Wissen.

Gentner, D., & Stevens, A. L. (Eds.). (1983). *Mental models.* Hillsdale NJ: Erlbaum.

Glass, A., & Holyoak, K. (1986). *Cognition.* New York: Random House.

Goetz, E. P., & Armbruster, P. B. (1980). Psychological correlates of text structure. In R. J. Spiro, B. C. Bruce, & W. F. Brewer, (Eds.). *Theoretical issues in reading comprehension.* Hillsdale NJ: Lawrence Erlbaum Associates.

Halasz, F., & Moran, T. (1982). Analogy considered harmful. *Proceedings of the Conference Human Factors in Computer Systems,* Gaitersburg. New York: Association of Computing Machinery.

Halasz, F., Moran, T. P., & Trigg, R. H. (1987). NoteCards in a nutshell. *Proceedings of the ACM CHI+GI'87 conference on human factors in Computing Systems and Graphics Interface* (pp. 45-51), Toronto, Canada. New York: Association of Computing Machinery.

Hammwoehner, R. (1991). *Macro-operations for hypertext construction.* In D . H. Jonassen and H. Mandl (Eds.). *Designing hypermedia for learning* (NATO ASI Series F : *Computer and Systems Sciences*, Vol. 67). ISBN: 0387529586. Berlin: Springer Verlag.

Hammwoehner, R., & Thiel, U. (1987). *Hypertext '87 papers* (pp. 155-174). Chapel Hill: University of North Carolina.

Hanne, K. H., & Graeble, A. (1987). Design and implementation of direct manipulative and deitic user interfaces to knowledge-based systems. In H. J. Bullinger, B. Shackel, & K. Kornwachs (Eds.). *Proceedings of human-computer interaction: Interact '87.* Amsterdam: North-Holland Press.

Hayes, J. R., & Flower, L. S. (1980). Identifying the organization of writing processes. In L.W. Gregg, & E.R. Steinberg (Eds.). *Cognitive processes in writing* (pp. 3-30). Hillsdale NJ: Lawrence Erlbaum Associates.

Hedberg, J. G. (1990). Converging technologies. *Selected papers from the EdTch '90 Conference of the Australian Society for Educational Technology.* Adelaide, Australia: Australian Society of Educational Technology.

Hilchey, S. E., & Huriych, J.. M. (1985). User satisfaction or user acceptance? Statistical evaluation of an online reference service. *Research Quarterly, 24*(4) (452-459).

Huntley, J. S. (1989). *Using the learning tool in developing an expert system in medical education: Utility and impact.* Symposium at the annual meeting of American Educational Research Association, San Francisco CA.

Hypertext '91. (1991). *Proceedings of the third ACM conference on Hypertext at San Antonio,* Texas. ISBN 0-89791-462-9. New York: Association of Computing Machinery.

Jacobs, G. (1992). Hypermedia and discovery-based learning: A historical perspective. *British Journal of Educational Technology, 23*(2), 113-121.

Jonassen, D. H. (1982). *The technology of text, principles for structuring, designing and displaying text.* Englewood Cliffs NJ: Educational Technology Publications.

Kay, A. (1969). *The reactive engine.* Doctoral dissertation, University of Utah.

Kersten, A., Nienhuis, A., Sligte, H. W., Timmer, J., & De Zeeuw, G. (1987). Voorstudie implementatie proefstations. In T.A.M. Kerkhof (Ed.). *Proefstations cluster V, PSOI series no. 25.* The Hague: Netherlands Ministry of Education and Science.

Kibby M. R., & Mayes J. T. (1989). Towards intelligent hypertext. In R. McAleese (Ed.), *Hypertext, theory into practice* (pp. 164-172). Oxford, England: Blackwell.

Kibby, M. R., & Kommers, P. A. M. (1988). *Research proposal for the DELTA-SAFE project on hypermedia authoring,* Internal Report. Brussels: DELTA.

Kintsch, W. (1974). *The representation of meaning in memory.* Hillsdale NJ: Lawrence Erlbaum Associates.

Kinzie, M. B. (September, 1988). Learner control and achievement in science computer-assisted instruction. *Journal of Educational Psychology,* 8(3) 299-303.

Klabbers, (1988). Methodologische aspecten van het ontwerpen van Leeromgevingen. In J. Klep & P. Kommers (Eds.), *Symposiumverslag didactische systeemanalyse.* Enschede: SLO-edition.

Kommers, P. A. M., Ferreira, A., & Jonker, E. (1989). Hypertext as a tool for advanced learning situations. In P. M. Fischer, H. Mandl, & K. Meynersen (Eds.). *Interaktives lernen mit neuen Medien, Ein Forum von Benutzern und Entwicklern.* Tuebingen: Deutsches Institut fuer Fernstudien.

Kommers, P. A. M. (1989). Conceptual mapping for knowledge exchange by hypertext. In D. H. Jonassen, H. Mandl (Eds.) *Designing hypermedia for learning* - NATO Advanced Research Workshop, Rottenburg, 3-7 July 1989. Berlin: Springer Verlag.

Kommers, P. A. M., Jonassen, D. H., & Mayes, T. (1992). *Mindtools: Cognitive technologies for modelling knowledge.* Berlin:Springer Verlag.

Kopperschmidt, J. (1985). An analysis of argumentation. In T. A. van Dijk (Ed.). *Handbook of discourse analysis: Vol. 2. Dimensions of discourse* (pp. 159-168). London: Academic Press.

Kozma, R. B. (1987). The implications of cognitive psychology for computer-based learning tools. *Educational Technology,* 27(11) 20-25.

Lacey, C. A., & Merseth, K. K. (1993). Hypermedia and computer networks: Three curricular innovations for teacher education. *Journal of Curriculum Studies, 25*(6), 543-551.

Landow, G. P. (1988). Relationally encoded links and the rhetoric of hypertext. In J. B. Smith, F. Halasz, N. Yankelovich, M. Schwartz, & F. Weiss (Eds.), *Hypertext '87*, (pp. 331-338). Chapel Hill: University of North Carolina.

Landow, G. P. (1989). *The rhetoric of hypermedia: A guide for authors*. Paper presented at the NATO Advanced Research Workshop, Rottenburg, 3-7 July 1989.

Leggett, J. J., Schnase, J. L., & Kacmar, C. (1989). *Practical experiences with hypertext for learning*. Paper presented at the NATO Advanced Research Workshop, Rottenburg, 3-7 July 1989.

Lessem, R. (1991). *Total quality learning: Building a learning organisation*. Oxford, England: Blackwell.

Levesque, H. J., & Brachman, R. J. (1987). A fundamental tradeoff in knowledge representation and reasoning. In R. J. Brachman & H. J. Levesque (Eds.), *Readings and knowledge representation*. Los Altos CA: Morgan Kaufmann.

Li, D. (1984). *A prolog database system*. New York: Research Studies Press Ltd., Wiley & Sons.

Lindsay, P. H., & Norman, D. A. (1977). *Human information processing*. New York: Academic Press.

Marchionini, G., & Schneiderman, B. (1988). Finding facts versus browsing knowledge in hypertext systems. *IEEE Computer, 21*(1) 70-81.

Mayes J. T., Kibby, M. R., & Watson, H. (1988). StrathTutor: The development and evaluation of a learning-by-browsing system on the Macintosh. *Computers and Education, 12*, 221-229.

McAleese, R. (1988, April 5-9). *From concept maps to computer-based learning: The experience of NoteCards*. Paper presented at the Annual Meeting of the American Educational Research Association, New Orleans LA.

McAleese, R. (1989). *Concepts as hypertext nodes: The ability to learn through navigation through hypertext nets*. Paper presented at the NATO Advanced Research Workshop, Rottenburg, 3-7 July 1989.

McKnight, C., Richardson, J., & Dillon, A. (1989a). The authoring of hypertext documents. In R. McAleese (Ed.), *The proceedings of Hypertext '87*. (pp 138-147). Oxford, England: Blackwell.

McKnight, C., Richardson, J., & Dillon, A. (1989b). *Journal articles as learning resource: What can hypertext offer?* Paper presented at the NATO Advanced Research Workshop, Rottenburg, 3-7 July 1989.

McNamara, D., & Pettitt, D. (1991). Can research inform classroom practice? The particular case of buggy algorithms and subtraction errors. *Teaching and Teacher Education, 7*(4), 395-403.

Megarry, J. (1988). Hypertext and compact discs: The challenge of multi-media learning. *British Journal of Educational Technology, 19*(3), 172-183.

Merrill, M. D. (1980). Learner control in computer-based learning. *Computing in Education, 4*, 77-95.

Merrill, M. D., Richards, R. E., Schmidt, R. V., & Wood, N. D. (1977). *The instructional strategy diagnostic profile training manual*. San Diego: Courseware, Inc.

Moran, T. P. (1981). The command language grammar: A representation for the user interface of interactive computer systems. *International Journal of Man-Machine Studies, 15*, 3-50.

Myers, L. D., & Anderson, J. C. (1994). *Is there too much hyper about HyperCard?* Master's Thesis, University of Virginia.

Nelson, T. H. (1965). A file structure for the complex, the changing, and the indeterminate. *Proceedings of the ACM national conference* (pp. 84-100). New York: Association for Computer Machinery.

Nelson, T. H. (1967). Getting it out of our system. In G. Schechter (Ed.) *Information retrieval: A critical review.* Washington DC: Thompson Books.

Nelson, T. H. (1973). A conceptual framework for man-machine everything. *Proceedings of the national computer conference*, M21-M26.

Nelson, T. H. (1974). *Computer lib and dream machines.* South Bend IN: Publishing House 'The distributors'.

Nelson, T. H. (1980). Replacing the printed word: A complete literary system. *MCC Technical report number STP-356-86, rev. 2.* Available upon request from: Software Technology Program, MCC,. P.O. Box 200195, Austin, Texas.

Nelson, T. H. (1981). *Literary machines, Project Xanadu.* San Antonio TX: Nelson's.

Nelson, T. H. (1987). *Literary machines,* (Edition 87.1). San Antonio TX: Nelson's.

Nelson, T. H. (1988, January). Managing immense storage, Project Xanadu provides a model for the possible future of mass storage. *Byte, 13(1)*, 225-238.

Nielsen, J., & Lyngbaek, U. (1989). Two field studies of HYPERMEDIA usability. In R. McAleese (Ed.). *Proceedings of hypertext II Conference.* York, UK

Nielsen, J. (1989a). Prototyping user interfaces using an object-oriented hypertext programming system. *Proceedings of NordDATA"89 joint Scandinavian computer conference*, Copenhagen, Denmark.

Nielsen, J. (1989b) *Hypertext: Context-in-the-large and individualized interaction.* Working paper JN-1989-4, Technical University of Denmark, Department of Computer Science.

Nijhof, W. J., & Kommers, P. A. M. (1984). Cognitive controversy during cooperation in heterogeneous groups. In R. Slavin, S. Sharan, S. Kagan, R. Lazarowitz, C. Webb & R. Schmuck (Eds.). *Congress proceedings: Cooperating to learn, Learning to Cooperate*, (pp. 125-145). New York: Plenum.

Norman, D. A. (1983). Some observations on mental models. In A. L. Stevens & D. Gentner (Eds.). *Mental models.* Hillsdale NJ: Erlbaum.

Norman, D. A. (1973). Memory, knowledge, and the answering of questions. In R. Solso (Ed.). *Contemporary issues in cognitive psychology: The Loyola symposium.* Washington DC: Winston.

Paine, N. (1989). Helping people learn: A challenge for the future. In R. Tucker (Ed.), *Proceedings of Interactivity '88 The Hague, Holland, interactive media, the human issues*, (pp.45-55). London: Kogan Page Ltd.

Papert, S. (1984). Computer as mudpie. *Classroom Computer Learning, 4(6)*, 36-38, 40.

Pask, G. (1976). Conversational techniques in the study and practice of education. *British Journal of Educational Psychology, 46*, (12-25). Also published in Hartley, J. & Davies, I.K. (Ed.) (1987). *Contributions to an educational technology, Volume 2.* London: Kogan Page Ltd.

Pask, G. (1984). Review of conversation theory and a protologic (or protolanguage). *ERIC/ECTJ Annual Review Paper, 32*(1), (3-40).

Pask, G. (1975). *Conversation, cognition and learning: A cybernetic theory and methodology.* Amsterdam: Elsevier.

Reigeluth, C. M. (1979). In search of a better way to organize instruction: The elaboration theory. *Journal of Instructional Development, 2*(3), 8-15.

Reigeluth, C. M., & Stein, F. (1983). The elaboration theory of instruction. In C. Reigeluth (Ed.), *Instructional design, theories and models* (pp. 335-382). Hillsdale NJ: Lawrence Erlbaum Associates.

Rohwer, M. (1984). An invitation to an educational psychology of studying. *Educational Psygologist, 19,* 1-14.

Ross, S., & Morrison, G. (1989). In search of a happy medium in instructional technology research: Issues concerning external validity, media replications, and learner control. *Educational Technology Research and Development, 37*(1), 19-33.

Scandura, J. M. (1980). Theoretical foundations of instruction.: A systems alternative to cognitive psychology. *Journal of Structural Learning, 6,* 247-394.

Schneiderman, B., & Morariu, J. (1986). The interactive encyclopedia system (TIES). Baltimore: University of Maryland.

Schneiderman, B., & Kearsley, G. (1989). *Hypertext hands-on: An introduction to a new way of organizing and accessing information.* Reading MA: Addison-Wesley.

Sharan, S. & R. Hertz-Lazarowitz (1980a). A group-investigation method of cooperative learning in the classroom. In S. Sharan, P. A. Hare, C. Webb, & R. H. Lazarowitz, (Eds.). *Cooperation in education.* Salt Lake City: Brigham Young University Press.

Shin, E. C. (1994). Effects of learner control, advisement, and prior knowledge on young students' learning in a hypertext environment. *Educational Technology, Research and Development, 41*(1), 33-46.

Sligte, H. (1989). Propelling interaction through telematics - electronic fieldtrip. In R. N. Tucker (Ed.). *Proceedings of interactivity 88 The Hague, Holland. Interactive media, the human issues.* (pp. 163-172). London: Kogan Page Ltd.

Small, R. V., & Grabowski, B. L. (1992). An exploratory study of information-seeking behviors and learning with hypermedia information systems. *Journal of Eduational Multimedia and Hypermedia, 1*(4), 445-464.

Spiro, R. J. (1980). Constructive processes in prose comprehension and recall. In R. J. Spiro, B. C. Bruce, & W. F. Brewer (Eds.). *Theoretical issues in reading comprehension.* Hillsdale NJ: Lawrence Erlbaum Associates.

Stanton, N. A., & Baber, C. (1994). The myth of navigating in hypertext: How a "bandwagon" has lost its course. *Journal of Educational Multimedia and Hypermedia, 3,* (3-4).

Storrs, G. (1989). The Alvey DHSS large demonstrator project Knowledge Analysis Tool: KANT. In R. McAleese (Ed.). *The Proceedings of Hypertext 87,* Oxford, England: Blackwell.

Streitz, N. A. (1987). Cognitive compatibility as a central issue in human-computer interaction: Theoretical framework and empirical findings. In G. Salvendy (Ed.) *Cognitive engineering in the design of human-computer interaction and expert systems* (pp. 75-82). Amsterdam: Elsevier.

Streitz, N. A. (1989). A cognitive approach for the design of authoring tools in hypertext environments. Paper presented at the NATO Advanced Research Workshop, Rottenburg, 3-7 July 1989.

Streitz, N. A., Hannemann J., & Thuering M. (1989). From ideas and arguments to hyperdocuments: Travelling through activity spaces. Available as GMD-IPSI Technical report, Darmstadt.

Symons, S., & Pressley, M. (1993). Prior knowledge affects text search success and extraction of information. *Reading Research Quarterly, 28*(3), 250-261.

Tchudi, S. (1988). Invisible thinking and the hypertext. *English Journal, 77,* 22-30.

Tennyson, R. D. (1980). Instructional control strategies and content structure as design variables in concept acquisition using computer-based instruction. *Journal of Educational Psychology, 72,* 525-532.

Tennyson, R. D., & Buttrey, T. (1980). Advisement and management strategies as design variables in computer-assisted instruction. *Educational Communication and Technology Journal, 28,* 169-176.

Tierney, R. (1989). The influence of high computer access on student's thinking: Second year findings. *ACOT: Apple's Classroom of Tomorrow.* Cupertino CA: Apple Corporation.

Trigg, R. H., & Suchman, L. A. (1989). Collaborative Writing in NoteCards. In HYPERTEXT I: Theory into Practice. 45-61. Intellect, Inc.

Trigg, R. H., & Weiser, M. (1986). TEXTNET: A network-based approach to text-handling. *ACM Transactions on Office Systems, 4*(1). (1-23).

Van der Veer, G. C., & Felt, M. A. M. (1988). Development of mental models of an office system: A field study on an introductory course. In G. C. Van der Veer & G. Mulder (Eds.). *Human computer interaction: Psychonomic aspects* (Chapter 15; pp. 250-273). Berlin: Springer-Verlag.

Weinstein, C. E., & Mayer, R. E. (1986). The teaching of learning strategies. In M. C. Wittrock (Ed.). *Handbook on research on teaching, 3rd edition* (pp. 315-327). New York: Macmillan.

Weizenbaum, J. (1976). *Computer power and human reason.* San Francisco: Freeman.

Weyer, S. (1988). As we may learn. In S. Ambron & C. Hooper (Eds.). *Interactive multimedia* (pp. 87-104). Redmond WA: Microsoft Press.

Whalley, P. (1989). *Models of hypertext structure and models of learning.* Paper presented at the NATO Advanced Research Workshop, Rottenburg, 3-7 July 1989.

Williams, G. (1987). HyperCard, In *BYTE, 12,* 109-117.

Winograd, T., & Flores, C. F. (1986). *Understanding computers and cognition: A new foundation for design.,* Norwood N.J: Ablex.

Young, R. E. (1980). *New directions for teaching and learning.* San Francisco: Jossey-Bass Inc.

PART II

Developing Hypermedia and Multimedia Applications

CHAPTER 4

Nodes and Organization

Joanna C. Dunlap
Scott Grabinger

Chapter Objectives This chapter is about nodes, the basic organizational units of information storage in a multimedia system. In this chapter, we

- explain the concept of nodes in the context of hypermedia and multimedia systems, and

- provide a set of guidelines for determining the organizational structure of interactive multimedia systems.

NODE CHARACTERISTICS

Nodes and Links Nodes and links (see chapter 5) are the basic building blocks of multimedia systems. *Nodes* are information units within a multimedia system. *Links* are the way these information units are physically and conceptually connected and interrelated. Designers use the depth and breadth of content coverage to determine the links and nodes needed to meet the learning and information dissemination objectives of the system.

How Nodes Work Multimedia nodes may be accessed, if supported with the appropriate links, in any sequence that meets the information needs and interests of the user. Rather than coming across a continuous linear flow of information, such as that found in books or videotapes, multimedia systems chunk information into nodes and establish connections between the different nodes. This is called *modularizing* the information in a program. Modularization enables users of multimedia systems to determine for themselves which node to access next. It may be that a node consists of an elaboration, an opposing point of view, an example, or an illustration.

In a typical application, users navigate through the program via links because they want to get from one segment of information to another — one node leads to another. For example, one student engaged in a multimedia system on English history may go to a node on the reign of King James I and see a reference to the works of William Shakespeare. This reference may encourage the student to proceed to a node that provides information on the works of William Shakespeare. Another student viewing the same node on King James I may be intrigued by a reference to Mary, Queen of Scots and choose to access that node instead. Therefore, by modularizing the information in a multimedia system, users are able to access information more easily. This kind of flexibility provides students with opportunities to explore a wider variety of information on the topics that they are studying.

Node Construction

Information contained in a node is provided in one of two ways: designer-constructed or user-constructed. Usually, the designer is responsible for entering all the content information into the nodes of the multimedia system. For example, when *Desert Shield* was developed, the designer had to determine what the nodes would be and enter all the information contained within each node. These types of nodes are *designer-constructed* nodes.

In contrast, collaborative multimedia systems provide users with opportunities to construct the bulk of the nodes in the system. For example, when *Instructional Technology in Teacher Education* (ITiTE) was developed, systems were constructed to let users add information. Such systems are called *user-constructed* nodes.

Designer-Constructed Nodes

Designer-constructed nodes are appropriate for systems in which both the objectives and content are determined by the designers. For example, if the objective of a multimedia system is to describe the rules for trading stocks on the stock exchange, then the system must include information that will help students meet those objectives. The federal government determines the content for these stock trading rules. In this case, we do not want learners determining the rules under which they should trade stocks and bonds.

User-constructed Nodes

Multimedia systems can be designed to make users responsible for filling in the blanks. User-constructed nodes are used if the desired goal is to have students determine the questions they want to investigate. Users will gather, analyze, synthesize, and represent the information they have collected in node shells provided by the developer. Shells are empty nodes that students use for specific purposes such as asking questions, entering information, or making comments as seen in the program *InfoAgent. InfoAgent* helps learners to determine what they need to learn, to develop plans for learning, and to represent the content of their learning in a hypertext system.

Even though students are responsible for entering the actual information in the user–constructed nodes, this does not mean less work for the designer. As the designer, you still have to provide an overall structure so that students cover different areas or segments of the desired content, insuring a thorough examination of the information available. For example, if a multimedia system is designed for use in a graduate-level psychology course in which students are required to investigate psychological paradigms of the 20th century, then you may want to provide the following nodes for students to use: theoretical foundations, assumptions, implications, research support, treatment procedures, and personal perspectives. By determining which nodes are required, you provide a structure that helps to insure that students will consider aspects of the content that you consider important for a thorough understanding.

Determining Nodes
Determining the nodes needed for your multimedia system begins with defining and focusing on your content area. To determine what will be included in the application you must

- determine the purpose of your multimedia system,

- decide how much information will be covered, or

- in the case of an problem-based application, you may need to determine the information necessary for the students to solve a problem or to participate in a simulation.

After you determine what should be included in the system for it to meet your objectives, then comes the tricky part of determining how to organize that information into coherent, modularized, easy-to-digest pieces. This is no easy task, considering that many multimedia systems rely on an abundance of information in order to fulfill the information and/or learning needs (teacher-driven objectives) or interests (student-driven objectives). But how do you decide how the information should be chunked?

In the remaining portion of the chapter, we look at three issues that designers need to consider when determining the kinds of nodes needed for a multimedia system: the kind of content organization that makes the most sense, the size of the node, and the presentation format. Each issue is presented with a set of design guidelines for determining and constructing nodes for multimedia systems.

GUIDELINES

Organization of Nodes
Most multimedia systems limit the types of nodes available to users according to the structure of the content. Therefore, you need to determine the organization of the system by analyzing the content and objectives of the multimedia system, looking for the themes, main topics of the content domain, concepts, arguments, perspectives, and so on that break the information down into logical sections within the program. There are two types of organizational structures to consider in creating the multimedia system. The first is a macro-organization issue related to the design of the main components of the multimedia system. The second is a micro-organization issue related to the design of each individual node.

4.1 Use the primary goals of the multimedia application's role within the whole instructional program to determine the macro-organization.

Desert Shield is an information-based system whose main goal is to provide a database of information related to the national and international politics that led to the Persian Gulf War of 1993. An examination of this goal led to the creation of the basic node divisions of Events, Time Line, People, Documents, Maps, Glossary, and Help. The determination of these node divisions was a function of instructional design considerations, primarily task and learner analyses. In this case, the task of locating information for the database led to the main node divisions because the designer decided that those subjects were of primary interest to potential users. The Glossary and Help sections were included because they were considered basic components of this type of multimedia system.

Instructional Technology in Teacher Education (ITiTE) is a collaboration-based hypertext application. The main goal of *ITiTE* is to provide a point of focus for individuals or small groups to use for working through problems in using instructional technology. The designers decided that the main nodes needed were those for adding information in response to a problem and those for an introduction that helps learners get to the right place. A shell such as *ITiTE* usually requires fewer nodes but needs more tools to help users create empty nodes to fill.

Anchored or situated applications such as *Transfusion Simulation* require nodes for interaction, information presentation, and tutorials. Again, in this case, the bulk of the design effort went into creating nodes that presented information relevant to the problem that the learners would need for practice.

4.2 Use the nature of the content to guide the micro-organization of the nodes.

Each node is constructed to represent its content or purpose. We look now in detail at two nodes to see how this works. We explain why each of the major features was added to its particular node.

First, the Events node of *Desert Shield* contains the following components (see Fig. 4.1):

- *Title:* Every node should have a title, and perhaps a subtitle, to help users keep track of where they are within the program. It is not easy to get a physical sense of location using a computer-based system, so we must provide more information about where a node is within the overall context of the system.

- *Date and Time Fields:* The date is used because the chronology of events leading to the Gulf War is of paramount importance. The date field provides two kinds of information to users: It provides basic information about when an event occurs, and it helps users keep track of where they are within the Events section because the basic organizing structure is chronological. The time field provides an additional organizing cue for multiple events that occurred in one day.

Fig. 4.1. *Desert Shield* **Events node.**

	1230
Event: National Security Council 8-3-90	**Date:** August 3, 1990
See Also:	**Time:** AM

Description:

Scowcroft states that the taking of Kuwait is unacceptable in the long run.

A CIA report argued that the invasion posed a threat to the current world order and could be devastating to the world economy. There was also a serious threat to Saudi Arabia.

Scowcroft stated there would be two tracks: first, the US had to be willing to use force; second, Saddam had to be toppled.

Bush ordered the CIA to plan for a covert operation to destabalize the regime. He wanted to strangle the Iraqi economy and support anti-Saddam groups.

Classification:
Meeting

Location:
White House

Main Participants:
Scowcroft, Wolfowitz, Darman, Bush,

Related Documents:

Return to Index of Events

Notes   Quit   Help   Go Back   Contents   Chart   Glossary   Mark

- *People Involved:* People create history, so again, to meet the objective of understanding the politics and diplomacy leading to the war, the people field provides access to principal players.

- *Control Panel:* The control panel along the bottom of the screen provides the basic tools for navigating and finding information within the program. Again, physical cues such as thumbing through pages is not possible, so the main ways for obtaining access to information are included in the control panel.

- *Description Field:* This field contains the description of the event listed in the title field.

- *See Also Field:* This field refers a reader to other directly related events.

- *Classification Field:* This field was created because the designers believed that the kind of event may be important and may also facilitate other kinds of data search patterns. For example, a user may choose to look at only "meetings."

- *Location Field:* The location of the event described is indicated by this field.

- *Related Documents Field:* Any documents included in the database related to this event are found in this field. The designers planned to include the full text of related government and public documents.

The main components of a node from *ITiTE* are as follows (see Fig. 4.2):

Fig. 4.2. Instructional Technology in Teacher Education (ITiTE) node.

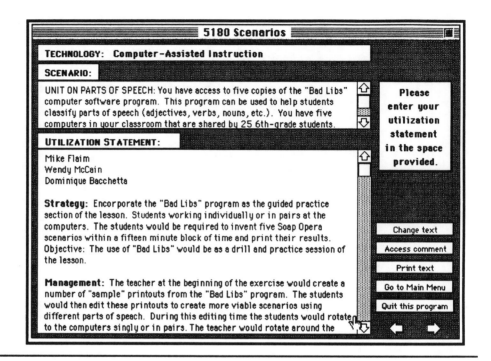

- *Title:* The title field briefly describes the subject of the node: computer-assisted instruction.

- *Scenario:* The scenario field, entered by the designer, presents a task on which a group of three or four students can work. The field contains a brief description of an instructional situation and a series of thought-provoking questions for the group to answer.

- *Utilization Statement:* This field is used for the group's response to the questions presented in the scenario. The students work cooperatively in small groups to discuss answers to the questions.

- *Control Panel:* The control panel is much smaller than in *Desert Shield* because fewer options are necessary. Essentially, the options allow the users to work on this node. Although arrow keys are provided to help students move forward or backward, they are not likely to be used. This program is not a database and does not require users to move about to find information.

The program *Desert Shield* provides multiple links in an information-rich environment, is more complex to design, and needs a number of features. In contrast, the program *ITiTE* is less dependent on content and has a more narrowly defined function, thus fewer components.

Node Size The size of a node raises interesting problems in a computer-based medium. A book gives users direct physical reference cues to its size and to the location of information relative to the rest of the information in the book—visual and touch comparisons are easily made. On a computer, however, the next node always replaces the previous node. The "next" node may be from an earlier or later part of the program. It may or may not be in direct sequence. The physical anchors so important in the print medium (i.e., thickness of the book, position within a chapter, number of pages) disappear and so does our ability to make comparisons and keep track of where we are in the medium. We must also remember that people do not care to read a great deal of text from screens, so information must appear manageable and brief.

4.3 Where possible, modularize information so that each node fits easily on one card, screen, or window.

People need to believe that they are in control of what they are doing and that the task is manageable. If we are reading a book, we can look at page numbers and the thickness of a group of pages to judge the magnitude of a task such as reading a chapter. Even in multimedia applications, users must be able to judge the size of a task.

The amount of information contained in a multimedia system is obviously much more than can fit on one card or screen. Unfortunately, the size of a node can vary from a few words to a document several pages in length, which means that nodes sometimes need to be larger than what can easily fit on the visible portion of a screen. Therefore, it is necessary to break the information down into chunks that can each be more easily handled at one time, preferably so that each chunk fits on a separate screen or window (to observe principles of screen design see chapter 7).

4.4 Label fields within a screen to describe the kinds of information it contains.

Fields must be labeled so that users can see the kinds of information contained in the field. Labels should be directly related to the function of the field or the kind of information contained, such as "Title," "People," or "Date." Labels help users understand the purpose of the screen and of the fields. They help users to find and organize information.

4.5 Avoid scrolling fields, except as lists and indexes.

Scrolling fields make users feel as if they are entering a bottomless pit of information. Use multiple screens organized by meaningful chunks of content rather than scrolling fields. Scrolling fields are more appropriate for lists, tables of contents, and indexes than for narratives.

There are exceptions to this guideline, but each exception should be considered carefully with the user's best interests in mind, not what is easiest to design. For example, the information in *Desert Shield* is chunked so that each node fits on a single card, although the Document section uses scrolling fields.

The "Lang E-Mail 7-30-90" node in the Document section is much larger than what could fit on the card. Therefore, a scrolling field is employed so all the information required for that node can still fit on just one card. A scrolling field is appropriate in this case because the document is included for reference purposes, and the user is likely to understand that it is long.

The *ITiTE* program uses two scrolling fields in its main screen. One presents the scenario, and the other is a repository for the students' response. The information in the scenario is longer than what could fit on one screen and is not easily broken up. In addition, the students need to refer to that information frequently while making their responses, so a scrolling field is used to keep the scenario on the same page the students were using to write their responses. The response field is a scrolling field because it needs to be of an unlimited length to hold the students' information.

Presentation Format

Within each node type, the format of the information can vary significantly, depending on the best way to represent that information. In fact, many different forms may make up one node: text, graphics, animation sequences, videodisc or videotape sequences, or audio sequences.

4.6 Use different backgrounds to distinguish among different node media formats.

In creating an application, a separate background for each node type will need to be created. Each node will probably require different screen design features, such as a different size and number of fields or different navigation options. Keep design principles in mind and maintain a consistent appearance among backgrounds.

We have already seen this to some extent in *Desert Shield*. There are 11 established node types referred to as sections. This means that the users of *Desert Shield* can access nodes that contain information on people, events, documents, places, and so on; therefore, the choice of node type is constrained to those 11. Each of those 11 node types has a separate background because each requires different fields, headings, and labels.

4.7 If multimedia resources are available, use the node form that most appropriately represents the information contained in the node.

For example, *Desert Shield* uses combinations of textual and graphical forms to represent information within different node types. Some nodes use only text. In the People section of *Desert Shield*, some of the nodes represent the information via two forms: text and graphics.

It is because of the format requirements of each node type that we integrate multimedia resources into a multimedia system. For example, imagine that you have to design a system about Italy. You might determine that the types of nodes that should be included in the system are language, geography, art, and literature. You would then have to decide how the information contained in each node type would be best presented. Therefore, you might use video plus audio to present the language so that students would be able to hear how the words are pronounced and see how the mouth is held in order to get certain sounds. For geography it may be appropriate to provide only maps, so graphics would be the best way to present that information. No amount of text can adequately describe a painting, drawing, or sculpture for each person. Therefore, video (videotape or videodisc) would be an appropriate way to present that information. Finally, text-based nodes may be appropriate for literature information.

CONCLUSION

Nodes are the fundamental organizing structure of multimedia systems. The kinds of nodes reflect the main level of organization (macro-organization) of the content. The content itself within each node reflects the microlevel organization of the node. In the next chapter, we discuss how to link those nodes together to provide users with the access necessary to study, organize, and learn the information.

CHAPTER 5

Links

Scott Grabinger
Joanna C. Dunlap

Chapter Objectives Hypermedia and multimedia applications connect nodes of information through links. A link connects one card, window, field, screen, or node to another card, window, field, screen, or node. Links are the essence of multimedia applications. A well-designed set of links reveals information and helps users attain their objectives. A poorly designed set of links misinforms users or inadvertently hides things from them. In this chapter we

- provide you with a definition of links,

- discuss the characteristics that links share,

- describe the types of links you can incorporate into a multimedia environment, and

- present design guidelines to help you understand when and how to use various kinds of links.

CHARACTERISTICS OF LINKS

Link Structures Both users and the program define links. Some programs are highly structured, constraining users to a predetermined path by limiting the options available, such as an online help system for providing information about each entry on a loan application. These highly structured multimedia environments base the link structure on specific, context-sensitive tasks and narrowly defined goals.

Other programs may include large databases with multiple connections from single nodes that provide a means of navigation regardless of contextual relationships. In this case, users define the relationship and meaning of one link to another. They may explore the database aimlessly, browsing from one subject to another. Other users may explore a set of links that are related to their personally defined objectives, with each link providing additional information on that topic. For example, a program may enable a user to jump from information about Washington, DC to information about London, England. For one user this jump may be into two unrelated subject areas. For another, it may be a comparison of two capital cities.

This chapter discusses several kinds of links: contextual links including those that are sequential and relational, and support links including learning and program help (see Fig. 5.1). Before considering link types, we describe characteristics that all links possess: directionality, labeling, size, screen location, visibility, and behavior.

Directionality   Links possess directionality. There are one-way links or two-way links. A one-way link goes to another node but does not provide a way to return to the node of origin. A two-way link goes from one node to another with a provision for returning to the node of origin. A one-way link may be appropriate at the beginning or end of a program when the result of the user's choice is definitive. For example, an option "to return to the beginning of a program" may be a one-way link because it will return users to the original options (e.g., main menu).

However, in most cases, two-way links should be used between nodes. Two-way links provide an anchor (node of origination) and enable comparisons between the first screen (origin) and the next screen (target). *Desert Shield* uses two-way links almost exclusively, whereas the GO BACK button permits users to return to the previous card. One example is the link to the glossary. Users access the glossary by clicking either on the GLOSSARY button or on hot text—words that appear in boldface. After reading the definition, users return to their place of origin by using the GO BACK button.

Labeling   To help users determine the purpose of a link, links include names, icons, or special encoding to identify their type and function (see Fig. 5.2). For example, a link may provide a path to an elaborative node related to a particular concept. If the link has some kind of labeling that identifies that link as elaborative, then the user can make the decision whether to obtain more information or to pursue another route.

Most of the buttons in *Desert Shield* (see Fig. 5.3) use words to indicate their function, although icons (left and right arrows) indicate previous/next node movement. Generally, icons and words are equally effective if users understand the meanings of the icons. Although it takes a bit of time for users to learn the meanings of icons, especially when there are many icons on the screen, users often react quicker to icons once they have learned the meanings. In a series of buttons, pictures may be easier to discriminate from one another than a series of word buttons composed in the same type style. On the other hand, on a crowded screen, icons may take up more space than desirable. Users may also find that a large group of unfamiliar icons are unintelligible. Therefore, standard icons that have universal meanings should be used. In using icons that may not be familiar to users, the meanings should be taught as early in the program as possible. It may be useful to use both words and icons for new icons at the beginning of a program.

Fig. 5.1. Classification of hypertext links.

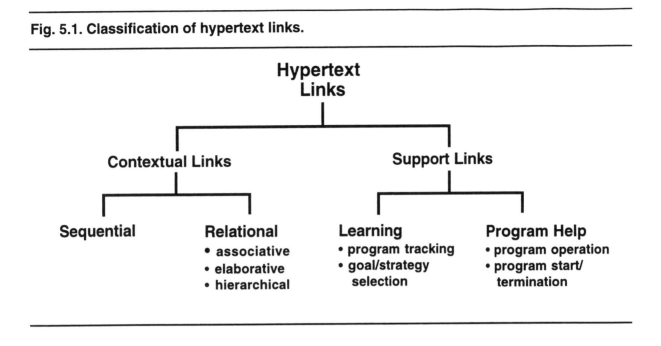

Fig. 5.2. Kinds of labels for links.

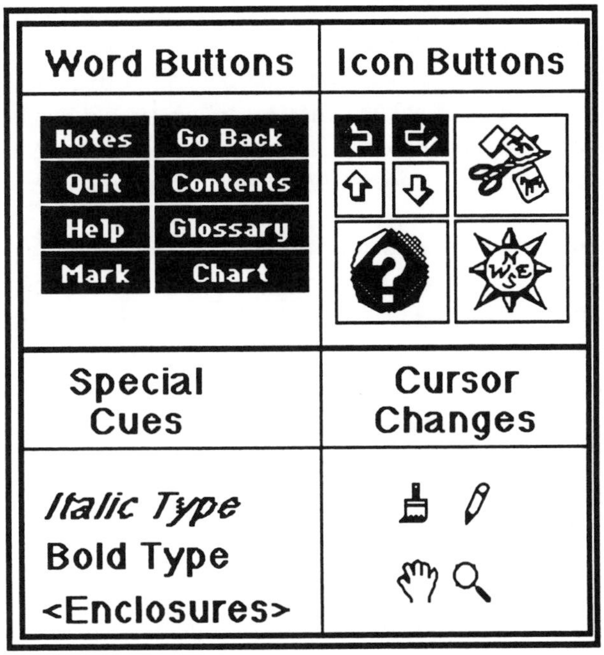

Special cueing is another option for indicating type of link. *Desert Shield* uses words in **bold** type. A word in bold indicates that there is a definition for that word and clicking on the bold word takes users to the glossary entry. Another encoding device is a change in cursor type to indicate the existence of a link to the underlying word. When the cursor is placed over the field "Main Participants" in *Desert Shield*, the cursor changes to a large cross to indicate the presence of links to additional information about people listed in that field.

Size Buttons that initiate links can be any size from a tiny radio button to a transparent button that covers the whole screen. Buttons used throughout the program can be relatively small and organized in one consistent location. Buttons or links that are unique to a node or that offer a unique option must call attention to themselves. One way to do this is to make the button large enough to attract the user's attention (see large button on card in Fig. 5.3).

Screen Location Links that serve a common function throughout an application should be grouped together. Grouping may be achieved by proximity, shading, boxes, and common type style. Links associated with specific words in a text field should be adjacent to (next to or on top of) those words if hot text is not used. For example, in Fig. 5.3 the main user control buttons for the program are located along the bottom of the screen in all of the backgrounds shown, all in the same 10-point Geneva type style and of a similar size.

Visibility Links do not always need to be a separate visible button or object. For example, the field in Fig. 5.3 labeled "Date" has no visible indication of a link. However, a click on the field takes users to the corresponding date node in the "Time Line" section. Hidden links should be described to the user at the beginning of the program or a special encoding technique should be used, such as a cursor change, to remind users of their existence. It is also good practice to remind users of these links' existence periodically through the program.

Interactivity Indicators Visual or audible feedback is a good way to indicate the activation of a link. Some common visual practices include the use of a highlight activation and deactivation or the use of a visual effect to indicate the transition from one node to another. Some of the links in *Desert Shield* alter the highlight from true to false when clicked on to create a quick single-blink effect. Other links between nodes use visual effects, such as a wipe right, wipe left, or dissolve. Most of the links in *Desert Shield* use a combination of both techniques. Audible feedback may take the form of a beep, click, or other sound; however, audible feedback tends to become irritating if used too frequently. The "Date" field in the *Desert Shield* stack uses a chime to indicate a mouse click.

Summary of Characteristics It is important to remember that the characteristics described above are universal regardless of the type of link used. Consideration of the link characteristics in the early stages of multimedia environment design provides the designer with a style guide for reference during development, insuring that links are presented to students consistently throughout the instruction.

Fig. 5.3. Four backgrounds from *Desert Shield*.

Screen 1 (1230):

Event: National Security Council 8-3-90
Date: August 3, 1990
Time: AM

See Also:

Description:
Scowcroft states that the taking of Kuwait is unacceptable in the long run.

A CIA report argued that the invasion posed a threat to the current world order and could be devastating to the world economy. There was also a serious threat to Saudi Arabia.

Scowcroft stated there would be two tracks: first, the US had to be willing to use force; second, Saddam had to be toppled.

Bush ordered the CIA to plan for a covert operation to destabilize the regime. He wanted to strangle the Iraqi economy and support anti-Saddam groups.

Classification:
Meeting
Location:
White House
Main Participants:
Scowcroft, Wolfowitz, Darman, Bush,

Related Documents:

Return to Index of Events

Notes Quit Help Go Back Contents Chart Glossary Mark

Screen 2 (6005):

Card 1 of 1

Glossary Word: CENTCOM
See Also:

CENTral COMmand. The U.S. divided the world in regions of military command. The middle east was in CENTCOM under the command of General H. Norman Schwartzkopf headquartered in Tampa Bay, Florida.

Return to Glossary Index

Notes Quit Help Go Back Contents Chart Glossary Find Mark

Screen 3 (2010):

People — Main Title Card

To find a person: 1) click on the name in the index below; 2) use the "Find Person" or "Find" buttons below; or 3) use Find on the menu bar above. Western individuals are listed by last name first, Middle East individuals are listed by their usual reference, e.g., Saddam Hussein.

Find a Person

People Index:
Abdullah, Saudi Crown Prince
Addington, Dave
Baker, James
Bandar, Prince
Barr, William P.
Bathurst, Admiral Sir Benjamin
Brady, Nicholas
Bush, President George
Cheney, Don
Cohen, William
Crowe, Admiral William J. Jr.
Darman, Richard C.

Return to People Index

Notes Quit Help Go Back Contents Chart Glossary Find Mark

Screen 4 (0222):

Help — Quit Button Description

The QUIT button takes you to a card that provides the QUIT options.

You may quit outright from the Quit card or you may first print out comments entered on the note fields, if the computer is attached to a printer.

Go to Quit Program Card

Quit Help Go Back Contents Chart Glossary

Fig. 5.4. Sequential links.

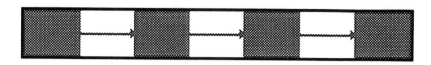

KINDS OF LINKS: CONTEXTUAL LINKS

Contextual links join various parts of a hypertext system to enable users to find the information they need. Contextual links open the system to the user. They provide the doors and windows to help users solve problems, find information, or learn. We have divided contextual links into two groups: sequential and relational links. Although most multimedia environments employ several different types of links, the link types most commonly used are sequential links.

Sequential Links Sequential links create a linear path among a set of related nodes (Fig. 5.4). A set of sequential links is a predetermined path through a program that permits a user essentially two options: next node or previous node. They are most easily represented by the ever-present left and right arrows (see bottom corners of cards in Fig. 5.3).

Some hypertexts provide default routes through the program. Users who do not wish to make their own way through a hypertext may elect to use a path defined by the hypertext designer. This path leads users along a logical path to achieve a specific objective. A linear path is especially useful when a user must view each node in a series to gain complete knowledge in a one-step-at-a-time fashion.

Sequential links reduce the cognitive overhead needed to navigate through a program. They are useful for first-time users or for programs aimed at meeting a narrowly defined objective. Users can usually remember the previous card and know that they are going in one direction related to a single purpose. They are able to maintain a sense of how far they are from the beginning and what is involved in getting to the end. Navigating is like exploring a new city by going to the sidewalk in front of the hotel and walking along the street in a straight line without making any turns — it is easy to remember how to get back to the hotel; you simply turn around and walk back. The tourist can enjoy the sites along the sidewalk without worrying about getting lost or getting distracted by trying to remember street names. Therefore, users of a sequential hypertext path can focus on the content of the nodes along the path without getting lost or distracted by nodes not related to their goal.

However, the primary advantage of sequential links is its main limitation: Sequential links provide only a single path through a hypertext. The tourist who never leaves the sidewalk sees only a limited version of what is available in the city. Hypermedia users also see only a limited version of what is available and may miss information that would help them build richer and more elaborate knowledge structures than when they follow linear paths through the hypertext.

Sequential links are easy to create and produce from a designer's point of view. It is far easier to create a linear set of information with limited access through sequential links than it is to try to plan for links that let users cross different sections, programs, and content areas.

Sequential links form the foundation of most hypertext systems, enabling users to follow a logical linear path through some content. They are usually simple to develop and program

Relational Links Relational links enable users to pursue information tied together by common elements, although not in a sequential manner. There are three main kinds of relational links: associative, elaborative, and hierarchical.

Associative Links. An associative link searches for information related to (or associated with) a specific node, word, or phrase. A set of associations creates a web or network of different kinds of related information (see Fig. 5.5) that can be accessed from multiple points within the program. Compare this to a sequential series in which each node has only two access points, the node before and the node after. These associative relationships are often defined more by the needs of the users than by the content. They permit users to jump across different nodes and program sections to find information pertinent to their needs and interests.

Associative links are significant parts of most multimedia systems because they provide access to information in ways that were not planned by the designer. The goal behind the creation of associative links is to emulate the way humans think. We do not think or process information in a linear manner; instead, we take in information simultaneously from a variety of inputs. The concept of multimedia environments was developed to allow users to follow their own associations. It is these kinds of links, that if well-designed, provide users access to all the information in a multimedia environment.

Associations can be created by using keyword searches or by setting up flexible links. *Desert Shield* uses keyword searches in a number of places. As shown in Figure 5.6, clicking on any name in the "Main Participants" field sets up a search for information related to that name. This type of search is "flexible" because the link is not predetermined but is based on the word or name a user clicks on to instantiate a variable. Similarly, a click on the date in the upper right corner of the screen searches for the date in the "Time Line" section (see Fig. 5.6). The date node provides information about what else happened on that date, but does not elaborate any further on the event. Associative links to other *Desert Shield* sections are available in the menu item SECTIONS on the menu bar.

The primary advantage of associative links is flexibility: the more flexible the links, the more powerful the system. Associative links provide a means of individualization — a means of making information more personally meaningful.

Fig. 5.5. Associative links.

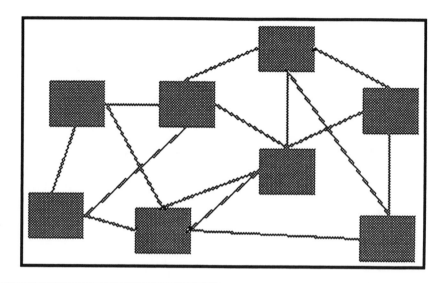

Fig. 5.6. Main participants and date fields in *Desert Shield*.

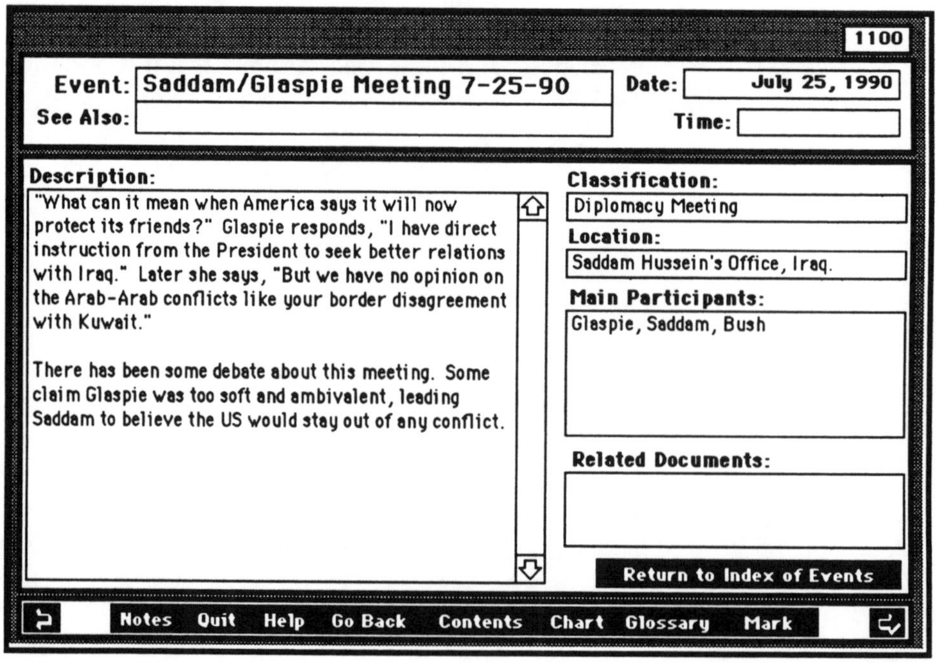

		1100
Event:	Saddam/Glaspie Meeting 7-25-90	Date: July 25, 1990
See Also:		Time:

Description:

"What can it mean when America says it will now protect its friends?" Glaspie responds, "I have direct instruction from the President to seek better relations with Iraq." Later she says, "But we have no opinion on the Arab-Arab conflicts like your border disagreement with Kuwait."

There has been some debate about this meeting. Some claim Glaspie was too soft and ambivalent, leading Saddam to believe the US would stay out of any conflict.

Classification:
Diplomacy Meeting

Location:
Saddam Hussein's Office, Iraq.

Main Participants:
Glaspie, Saddam, Bush

Related Documents:

Return to Index of Events

Notes Quit Help Go Back Contents Chart Glossary Mark

Fig. 5.7. Elaborative links.

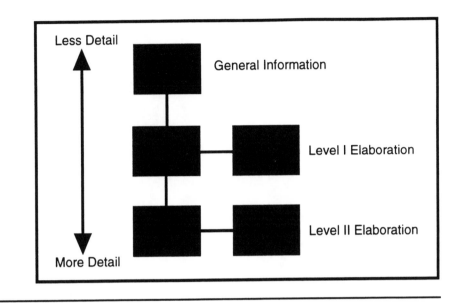

Elaborative Links. Although the relationship between two associated nodes may be defined either by context or by user goal, the relationship between two elaborative nodes is context dependent. An elaborative link is a special kind of sequential link that provides more complex and more detailed information on a specific topic (see Fig. 5.7). A series of elaborative links helps learners to build new knowledge structures and add new features to old structures. An elaborative series differs from a sequential series because users are free to decide whether or not to enter the elaborative series and, once the series is entered, how deep they wish to go.

Desert Shield uses a series of elaborative links when users encounter the "War Powers Act" card in the glossary. This card includes three additional cards that provide progressively more information about the topic (see Fig. 5.8).

Elaborative links are particularly useful for instructional multimedia environments that focus on presenting new information to users. The elaborative structure presents a continuing sequence of more explanation as well as reviews of earlier information. The nature of the elaborative structure lets users access information in more depth when they want additional detail.

Hierarchical Links. A hierarchically linked hypertext is an organizational structure that links information in a progressive manner, illustrating rank or level of importance (see Fig. 5.9). Hierarchical links provide a good overall organizing structure for multimedia environments that deal with several levels of classifications, such as diagnosis within a class of diseases, explanation of genus in biology, or description of an organizational structure. They differ from elaborative links in that the path down through the hierarchy is not usually

Fig. 5.8. Elaboration screens.

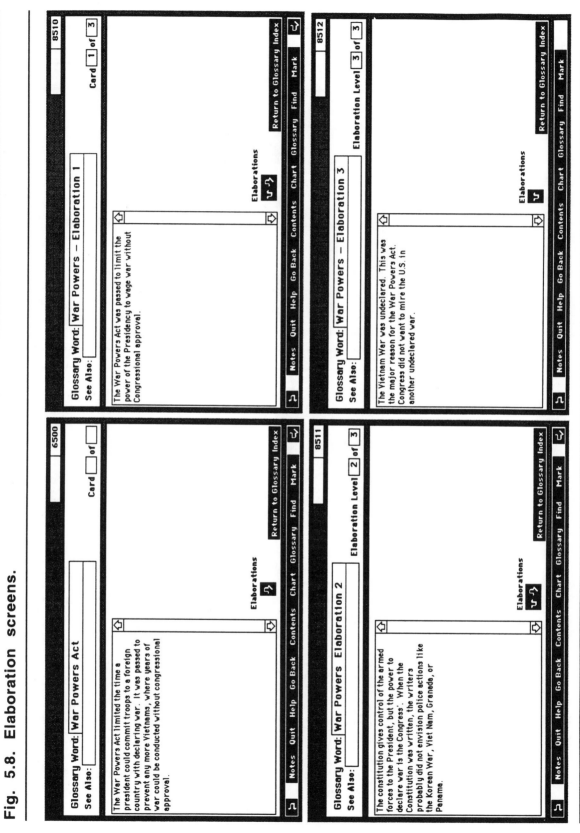

Fig. 5.9. Hierarchical network.

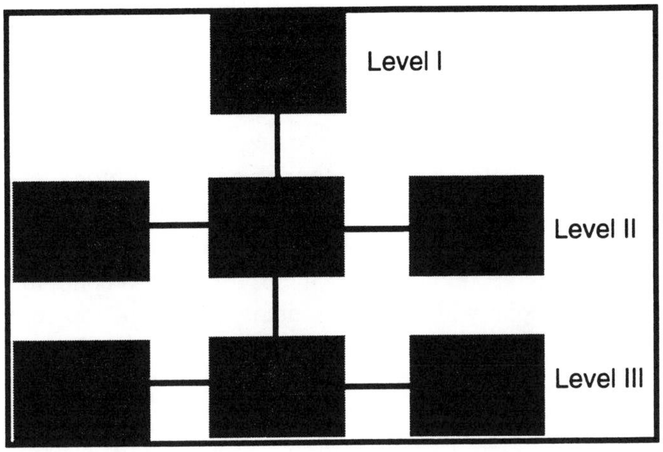

optional: For users to understand the hierarchy, they must continue along the complete path. Therefore, hierarchical links are highly structured, leading users through a logical path with a predetermined end.

Although *Desert Shield* is basically an associative structure of information (the classifications of events, timeline, glossary, people, places, and so on cannot be arranged in a way that makes one topic dependent on a previous topic), it provides an example of a hierarchical path used to describe the administrative structure of the Department of Defense. The path begins with a hierarchical chart that describes the overall structure. Each element on the chart has a related card that is reached by using up/down arrows.

KINDS OF LINKS: SUPPORT LINKS

Support links help to control the overall operation of a multimedia environment by providing users with information regarding how to learn from the hypertext and by providing help facilities related to program operation. Support links are metalinks, connections that provide a structure to help users access and learn from the hypertext. They may provide connections to a help section that explains what the program is and how to use it, connections to tracking information about what the user has seen, connections to a study-help section that provides suggestions on how to study from the program, and connections that lead to starting or concluding the program. Support links fall within two classifications: learning support and program help. They are two-way links permitting a jump from an informational node to the help node and a return to the original informational node.

Learning Support Links

Learning support links join nodes of information that help users organize and structure information. A number of techniques can be built into multimedia environments for the achievement of this objective: program tracking and goal/strategy selection links.

Program Tracking. Program tracking links provide users with direct links from nodes in the program to maps or charts that indicate their position within the hypertext. This provides an overall organizer for users. In more complex programs, it is often necessary to begin with a general map and then to elaborate on the items on the general map with a series of more detailed maps.

Program tracking links can also be used to collect information about nodes accessed by users. Tracking routines, which generally include time stamping facilities, are useful for research purposes, for keeping long-term records of what a user has done with computer-managed instruction functions, and for creating temporary paths that let users retrace prior steps. However, the usefulness of a tracking facility must be balanced by the complexity involved in creating it. Most tracking programs also tend to slow down program operation.

Goal Selection. Trying to use a multimedia system for learning may leave new multimedia users feeling lost and bewildered because the organization, components, and structure of the system are not readily available to users. One cause of this is an undefined sense of purpose or a forgotten goal. There is usually so much information available that users can easily get sidetracked by something else that interests them. One solution to this problem is for the hypertext to ask the users what they hope to learn or why they entered the program. The goal is saved in a field for future reference. *Desert Shield* provides a utility for recording a goal. The User Information card records a goal if the user wishes (see Fig. 5.10).

Strategy Selection. A multimedia system can offer help to users by suggesting learning strategies for them to use. For example, if the user is trying to learn about the solar system, the program may suggest a mnemonic to help him or her memorize the order of the planets from the sun. If the user is trying to learn how to evaluate a prospect for a home mortgage, the program may suggest that the user develop a procedural chart. *Desert Shield* provides users with a strategy deemed appropriate by the designer for helping users learn from the collaborative commenting of hypertext.

For example, to facilitate collaborative commenting as a strategy for learning, each node on most of the sections in *Desert Shield* has a button labeled NOTES (see Fig. 5.11). When users click on the NOTES button, a field appears to permit them to type in their own comments (see Fig. 5.11). When the option key is held down while users click on NOTES, a jump to a node via a two-way link occurs that explains the purpose of the button (see Fig. 5.11). This node also includes information about how to use the collaborative feature that enables them to comment on information within each card.

Hypermedia environments can also provide users with a way to mark paths through the hypertext for future individual navigational purposes or for another user to follow. This is an effective feature for contextually structured hypertexts because it allows the hypertext to continue to be flexible for all users while providing a way for users to construct some structure that may be needed. A path-marking feature also helps users to know what parts of the hypertext they have or have not seen; if the card is part of a marked path, then users know that they have been there before. *Desert Shield* allows users to create new paths or follow previously generated paths (created by themselves or others) by clicking on the MARK button at the bottom of the screen (see Fig. 5.12).

Depending on the selection, the user will be guided through the process of either creating a new path or following an existing path. For example, a user who wants to create a new path will be prompted at every new card accessed as to whether or not the card should be included in the path (see Fig. 5.12).

If the user wants to follow a path, he or she is asked to specify the desired path via the name of the path creator. After entering the path name, the user can begin to follow the indicated path (see Fig. 5.12).

In addition, users are provided with a way of determining if they are following a path; if the MARK button at the bottom of the screen has been replaced by the PATH button, then the user is following a path (see Fig. 5.12). When a path is selected, the left/right arrows are removed to help the user remember to use the PATH button to proceed through the program.

Program Help Links

At this point you may think that we have covered all the links used in a multimedia environment. Sometimes designers get so involved in the development of their multimedia environments that they forget that a novice to the environment may not know how to access information in the hypertext. Links, therefore, can be used to provide novice users with the information necessary for them to comfortably participate in the multimedia environment. The types of links used to provide this kind of support are program help links, including program operation links and program start/termination links.

Program Operation Links

Program operation links are direct, two-way links that take users to information about the operation of the program. An elaborative strategy is probably most useful in explaining the program because some users may need a quick reminder of available options and others may need complete instructions on how to use a specific option. Remember, it is unlikely that new or infrequent users are going to remember the purpose of all buttons and links or where to find hidden links.

Desert Shield has two main paths into information about the program. First, a general screen summarizes the purpose of the program (see Fig. 5.13). Second, there is an expanded help section with one-screen explanations of each button and section (for examples, see Fig. 5.14). The help sections are reached through the main help menu or by an option-click on any of the buttons.

Fig. 5.10. Asking for user goal.

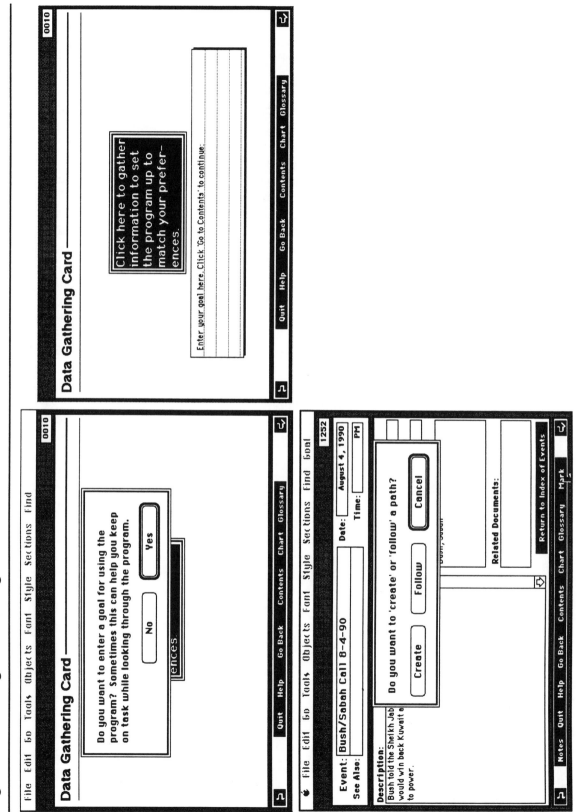

Fig. 5.11. Notes function in *Desert Shield*.

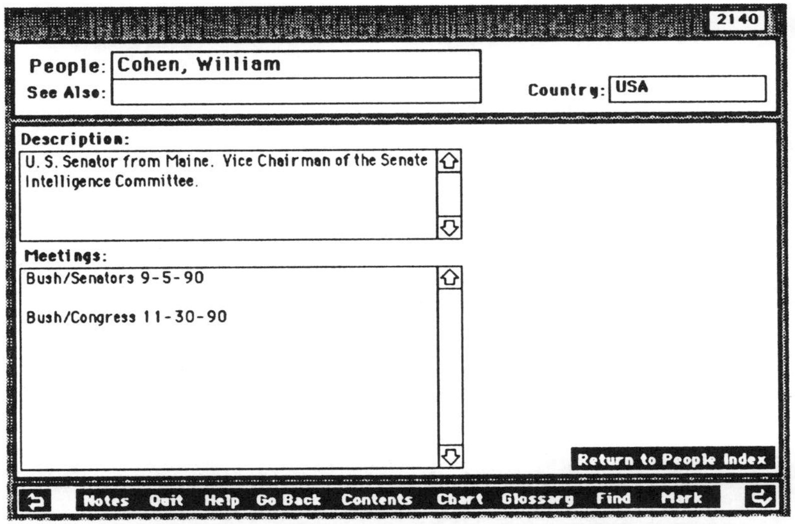

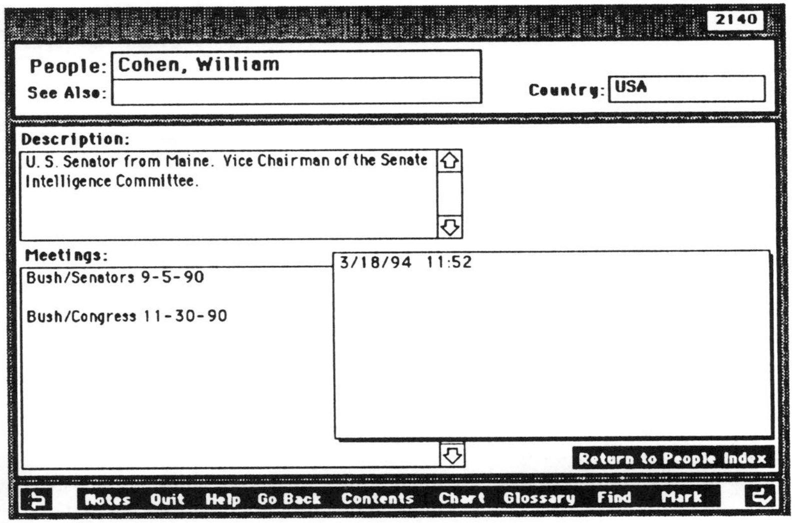

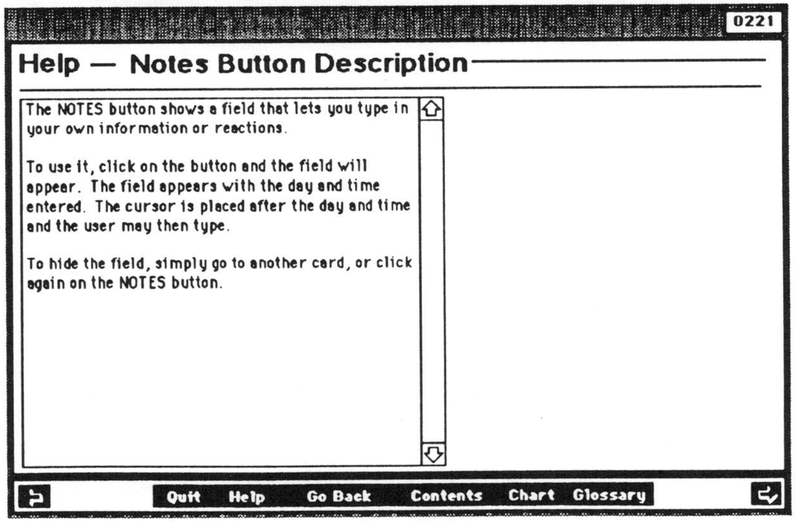

People: Cohen, William   Country: USA
See Also:

2140

Description:
U.S. Senator from Maine. Vice Chairman of the Senate Intelligence Committee.

Meetings:
Bush/Senators 9-5-90

Bush/Congress 11-30-90

Return to People Index

Notes Quit Help Go Back Contents Chart Glossary Find Mark

People: Cohen, William   Country: USA
See Also:

2140

Description:
U.S. Senator from Maine. Vice Chairman of the Senate Intelligence Committee.

3/18/94 11:52

Meetings:
Bush/Senators 9-5-90

Bush/Congress 11-30-90

Return to People Index

Notes Quit Help Go Back Contents Chart Glossary Find Mark

Help — Notes Button Description

0221

The NOTES button shows a field that lets you type in your own information or reactions.

To use it, click on the button and the field will appear. The field appears with the day and time entered. The cursor is placed after the day and time and the user may then type.

To hide the field, simply go to another card, or click again on the NOTES button.

Quit Help Go Back Contents Chart Glossary

Fig. 5.12. Creating paths.

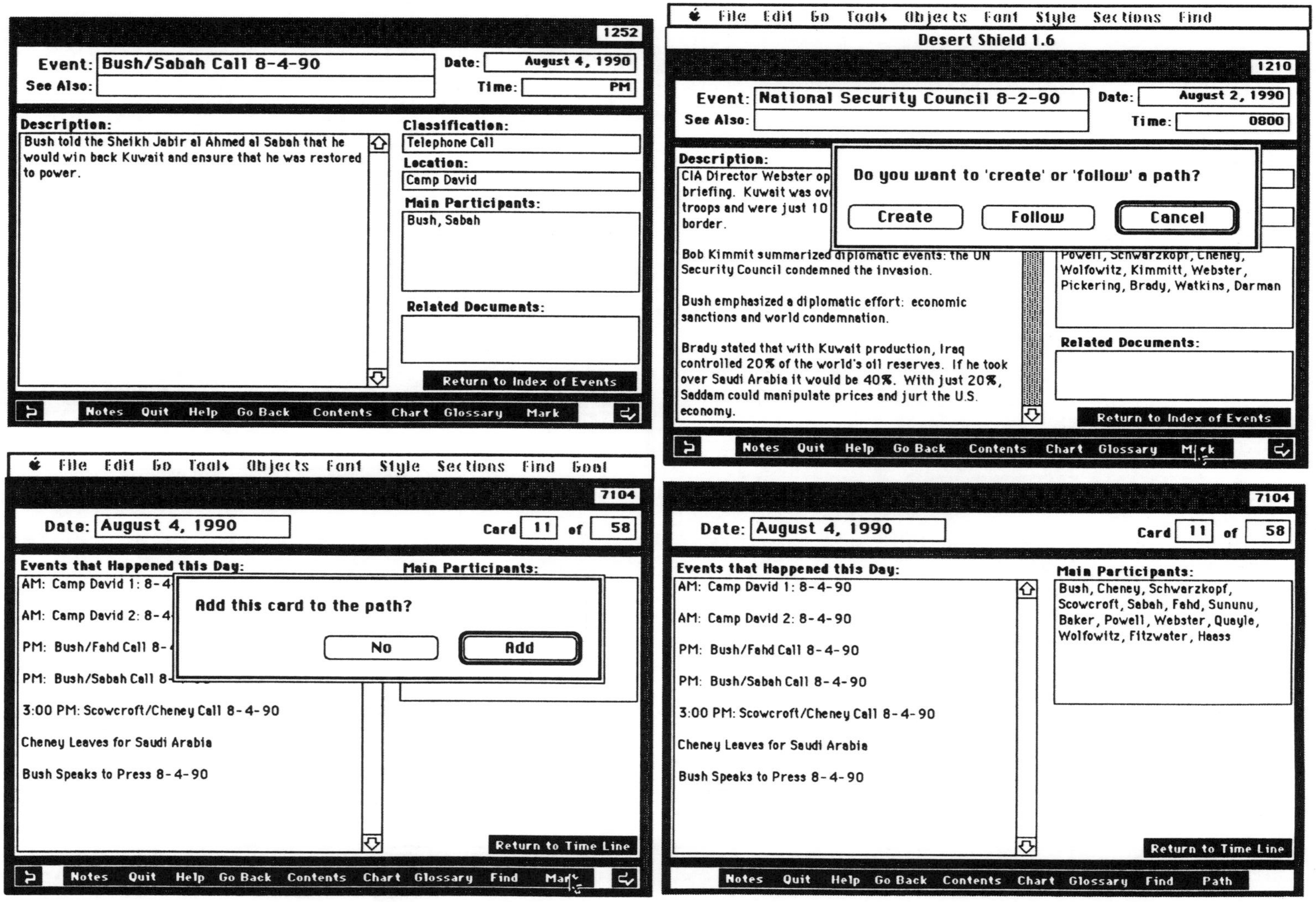

Event: Bush/Sabah Call 8-4-90   **Date:** August 4, 1990   **Time:** ___ PM
1252

See Also:

Description:
Bush told the Sheikh Jabir al Ahmed al Sabah that he would win back Kuwait and ensure that he was restored to power.

Classification:
Telephone Call

Location:
Camp David

Main Participants:
Bush, Sabah

Related Documents:

Return to Index of Events

Notes Quit Help Go Back Contents Chart Glossary Mark

File Edit Go Tools Objects Font Style Sections Find
Desert Shield 1.6

Event: National Security Council 8-2-90   **Date:** August 2, 1990   **Time:** 0800
1210

See Also:

Description:
CIA Director Webster op briefing. Kuwait was ov troops and were just 10 border.

Bob Kimmit summarized diplomatic events: the UN Security Council condemned the invasion.

Bush emphasized a diplomatic effort: economic sanctions and world condemnation.

Brady stated that with Kuwait production, Iraq controlled 20% of the world's oil reserves. If he took over Saudi Arabia it would be 40%. With just 20%, Saddam could manipulate prices and jurt the U.S. economy.

Powell, Schwarzkopf, Cheney, Wolfowitz, Kimmitt, Webster, Pickering, Brady, Watkins, Darman

Do you want to 'create' or 'follow' a path?

Create   Follow   Cancel

Related Documents:

Return to Index of Events

Notes Quit Help Go Back Contents Chart Glossary Mark

File Edit Go Tools Objects Font Style Sections Find Tool

Date: August 4, 1990   Card 11 of 58
7104

Events that Happened this Day:
AM: Camp David 1: 8-4
AM: Camp David 2: 8-4
PM: Bush/Fahd Call 8-
PM: Bush/Sabah Call 8-

3:00 PM: Scowcroft/Cheney Call 8-4-90

Cheney Leaves for Saudi Arabia

Bush Speaks to Press 8-4-90

Add this card to the path?

No   Add

Main Participants:

Return to Time Line

Notes Quit Help Go Back Contents Chart Glossary Find Mark

Date: August 4, 1990   Card 11 of 58
7104

Events that Happened this Day:
AM: Camp David 1: 8-4-90
AM: Camp David 2: 8-4-90
PM: Bush/Fahd Call 8-4-90
PM: Bush/Sabah Call 8-4-90

3:00 PM: Scowcroft/Cheney Call 8-4-90

Cheney Leaves for Saudi Arabia

Bush Speaks to Press 8-4-90

Main Participants:
Bush, Cheney, Schwarzkopf, Scowcroft, Sabah, Fahd, Sununu, Baker, Powell, Webster, Quayle, Wolfowitz, Fitzwater, Haass

Return to Time Line

Notes Quit Help Go Back Contents Chart Glossary Find Path

Fig. 5.13. General program summary screen.

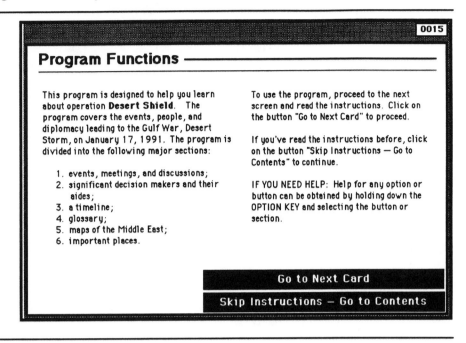

Program Start and Termination Links

There must always be a way to restart in a multimedia environment. A direct link should lead to the main entry point into the program as the CONTENTS button does on *Desert Shield* screens.

Users also need an easy way to quit the program, a way that is always in view. *Desert Shield* uses a QUIT button on the bottom of its screens. Some multimedia environments collect data that need to be closed out through a formal quit routine, which is often part of a termination link.

Support links for learning and program help provide users with information that assists them in meeting their information-gathering, problem-solving, and learning goals and objectives while they are engaged in a hypertext environment. When users are provided with the necessary support mechanisms, hypertext use can be more productive and successful, and therefore more consistent in meeting the users' needs.

With the types of links described, the rest of this chapter focuses on how to effectively use the links just discussed. Each type of link has an associated set of design guidelines to help users design their own links in multimedia systems and applications.

Fig. 5.14. Detailed help screens.

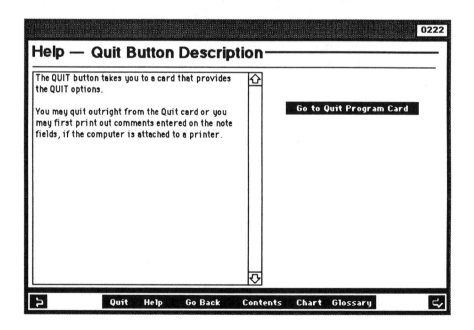

GUIDELINES

5.1   Use left/right arrows when the option of proceeding through a hypertext in a sequential path is necessary.

When it is appropriate to design a sequential path through a hypertext (e.g., presenting chronologies or logical step-by-step processes), providing users with left and right arrow keys informs them that they are proceeding through the information in a sequential fashion. (Note: The use of left/right arrows may be culturally bound. Societies that read from top to bottom may be more comfortable with up/down arrows. This would be a good dissertation topic for some budding graduate student!) *Desert Shield* has made provisions for sequential movement within each section by including left/right arrows.

5.2   When using left/right arrows to proceed through several pages of information related to one idea, remove the left arrow from the first page/screen and the right arrow from the last page/screen.

Sequential links may imply a relationship between one card and another that does not exist. For example, the last card of the "Events" section in *Desert Shield* (Fig. 5.15) has a right arrow on it, yet if it is clicked on, it takes the user to another section, the "People" section. This abrupt change can be disconcerting to the user and create a feeling of being lost. Avoid this problem by eliminating the left arrow on the first card of a sequence and the right arrow on the last card. For example, the bottom two cards in Fig. 5.15 are the same as the top two cards; however, the right arrow is removed from the last card in the "Events" section, and the left arrow is removed from the first card in the "People" section.

5.3   In a multiple page sequence, use the *card x of y* strategy to tell users how many pages are in the sequence and where they are in the sequence.

From a user's perspective, a limitation of sequential links is the lack of knowledge about where he or she is within a sequence. It is disconcerting to start a sequence and not know how many screens it has. This can seem like a bottomless pit to the user. The most effective way of countering this limitation is with the *card x of y* strategy. This strategy uses one or two fields to inform users how many cards there are in the sequence and which card they are currently reading. Note that the screen in Fig. 5.16 shows two fields in the upper right portion of the screen indicating which card the user has and how many are left in the sequence.

Fig. 5.15. Removing left and right arrows.

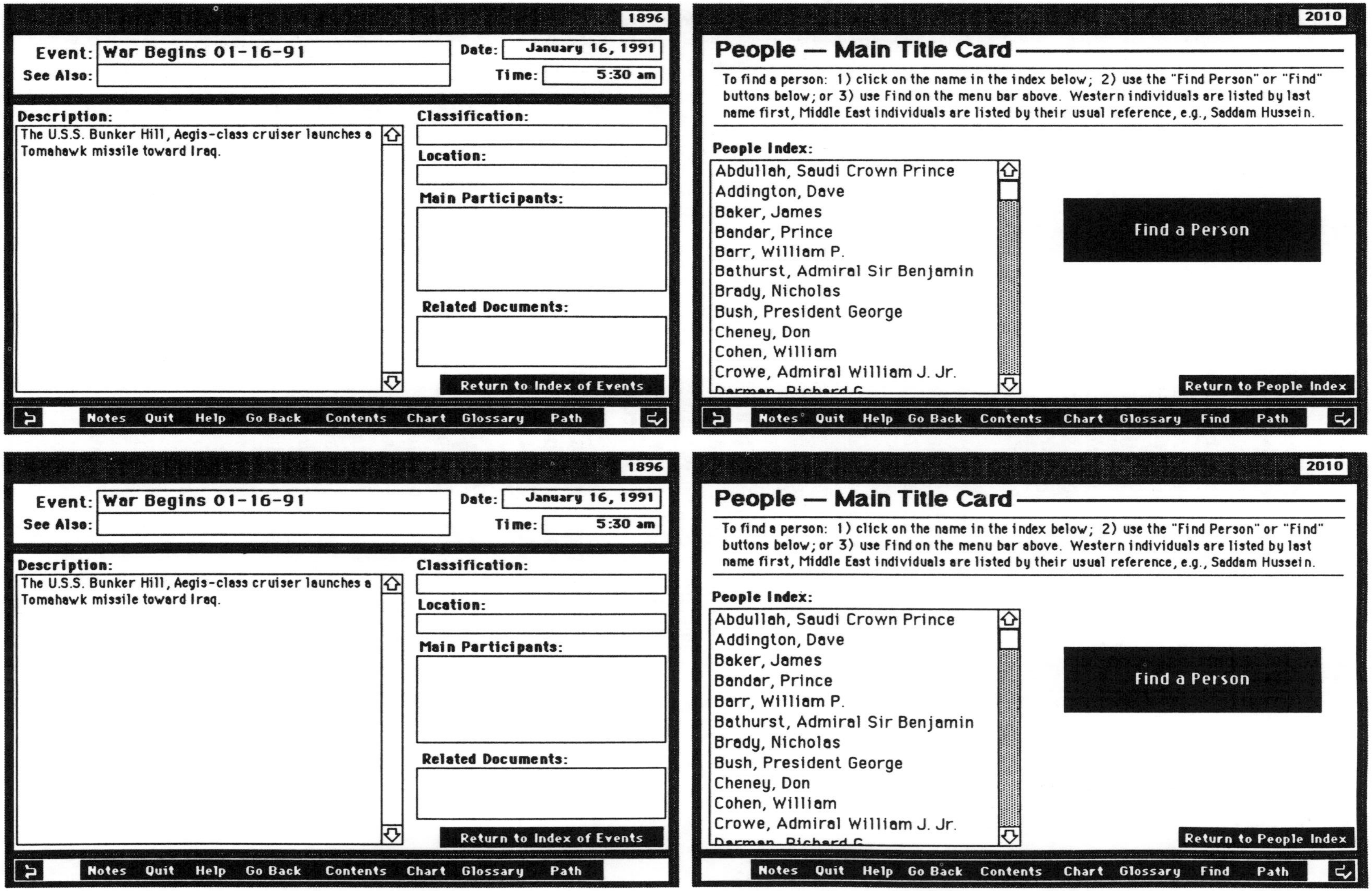

Screen 1 (top-left): 1896

Event: War Begins 01-16-91

See Also:

Date: January 16, 1991   Time: 5:30 am

Classification:

Location:

Main Participants:

Description:
The U.S.S. Bunker Hill, Aegis-class cruiser launches a Tomahawk missile toward Iraq.

Related Documents:

Return to Index of Events

Notes   Quit   Help   Go Back   Contents   Chart   Glossary   Path

Screen 2 (top-right): 2010

People — Main Title Card

To find a person: 1) click on the name in the index below; 2) use the "Find Person" or "Find" buttons below; or 3) use Find on the menu bar above. Western individuals are listed by last name first, Middle East individuals are listed by their usual reference, e.g., Saddam Hussein.

People Index:

Abdullah, Saudi Crown Prince
Addington, Dave
Baker, James
Bandar, Prince
Barr, William P.
Bathurst, Admiral Sir Benjamin
Brady, Nicholas
Bush, President George
Cheney, Don
Cohen, William
Crowe, Admiral William J. Jr.

Find a Person

Return to People Index

Notes° Quit   Help   Go Back   Contents   Chart   Glossary   Find   Path

Screen 3 (bottom-left): 1896

Event: War Begins 01-16-91

See Also:

Date: January 16, 1991   Time: 5:30 am

Classification:

Location:

Main Participants:

Description:
The U.S.S. Bunker Hill, Aegis-class cruiser launches a Tomahawk missile toward Iraq.

Related Documents:

Return to Index of Events

Notes   Quit   Help   Go Back   Contents   Chart   Glossary   Path

Screen 4 (bottom-right): 2010

People — Main Title Card

To find a person: 1) click on the name in the index below; 2) use the "Find Person" or "Find" buttons below; or 3) use Find on the menu bar above. Western individuals are listed by last name first, Middle East individuals are listed by their usual reference, e.g., Saddam Hussein.

People Index:

Abdullah, Saudi Crown Prince
Addington, Dave
Baker, James
Bandar, Prince
Barr, William P.
Bathurst, Admiral Sir Benjamin
Brady, Nicholas
Bush, President George
Cheney, Don
Cohen, William
Crowe, Admiral William J. Jr.

Find a Person

Return to People Index

Notes   Quit   Help   Go Back   Contents   Chart   Glossary   Find   Path

Fig. 5.16. Card x of y strategy.

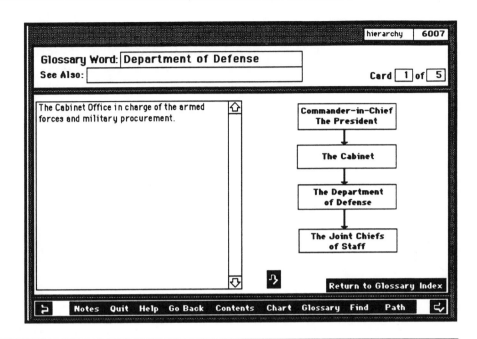

Fig. 5.17. Navigation chart.

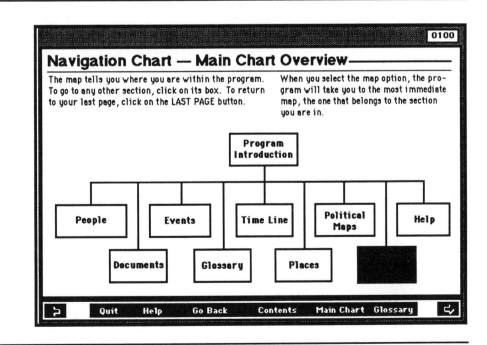

5.4   Use maps, webs, or hierarchical charts to provide users with valuable graphic representations of where they are within a multimedia environment.

Associative links can be very powerful because they enable users to direct their own movement through the information. However, in power there is confusion. The more flexible the hypertext, the easier it is for users to get lost or lose track of their original goals. Therefore, it is important to provide support to help users keep track of where they are in the hypertext. Graphic representations such as maps, webs, or hierarchical charts can remind users of their location so that they will not become lost. *Desert Shield* uses a chart to help orient users (see Fig. 5.17).

5.5   To remind users of where they are within a hypertext, provide extensive verbal/textual support.

Cards should always include headings to indicate what the topic of the card is and to which section it belongs. Extensive use of menu and content lists are also helpful.

5.6   Where there is a sequence representing critical information, build the sequence into the associations so the user does not miss part of the sequence. In other words, use sequential strategies.

It is possible for users to approach a hypertext in the wrong way; that is, they may inadvertently skip some critical information and end up forming incomplete or incorrect knowledge structures. In this case, a more structured approach is needed; therefore, a set of associative links may not be appropriate for a highly structured hypertext. If it is necessary to make sure that users do not miss information within the hypertext (i.e., if there is information you do not want them to skip), then use a sequential strategy to make sure that users see every important card in the sequence.

5.7   Ask users to set a goal upon entry into the hypertext to help them stay on task.

Because associative links allow users to access the information provided in a hypertext based on their own individual needs and interests, it is easy for users to get distracted by the information presented and detour from their original goals. To help users keep track of their reasons for entering the hypertext without taking away any system flexibility, the hypertext program can be designed to ask users to enter a goal before they access the hypertext. Then if they go off on a tangent, they can review their goal and get back on track.

5.8   Use elaborative links to present information in a progressively deeper manner (or in a progressively less detailed manner). Each level within the hypertext should build (elaborate) on the previous level.

It is important to remember that building an elaborative structure requires great care to insure that users can follow the prescribed sequence. In elaboration theory, Reigeluth and Stein (1983) state that no level should be encountered until the user sees the previous level. Although this limitation places a rigid structure on both the designer and user, limiting the flexibility of the hypertext, it may be a necessity to assure accurate assimilation of information.

5.9   Use a field to indicate the depth to which a sequence of elaborations goes (e.g., "level 1 of 5"). If one of the elaborative levels has more than one page or card, then use page/card x of y to indicate the sequence.

In relational links users can encounter a problem that is associated with sequential links: not knowing where they are within the elaborative sequence. Handle this problem with the same *card x of y* strategy described in the sequential links section above, except in this case, use *level x of y*. This indicates to the user how much detail on a specific topic is available. (Combine the "level x of y" strategy with the "page x of y" strategy if each or any level has several nodes that create a sequence about that level.) In addition, remember to remove the up arrow from the first level of the elaborative sequence and the down arrow from the last level.

   Desert Shield also uses up and down arrows to represent more or less depth when providing information about the War Powers Act (see Fig. 5.18). The down arrow indicates that the user can obtain more detailed information about the concept. The up arrow indicates that a more general explanation is available. (The same design guidelines for left/right arrows apply to up/down arrows.)

5.10   Use charts, maps, or webs to help users keep track of where they are in the hypertext.

As with associative links and with hypertexts in general, techniques such as verbal support, maps, charts, and webs can be employed to help users keep track of where they are within a multimedia environment.

5.11   Hierarchies are highly structured. Keep users aware of that structure with verbal and graphic support.

Like sequential paths, hierarchical paths are limited by the structure of the information. The existence of a hierarchy makes it difficult to pursue associations or related information because users cannot just jump out of one hierarchy into another without skipping important information or getting lost; therefore, the design must help users maintain their location and keep informed about where they are within the hierarchy. If a user leaves a hierarchical path early, a warning

Fig. 5.18. War Powers Act screen.

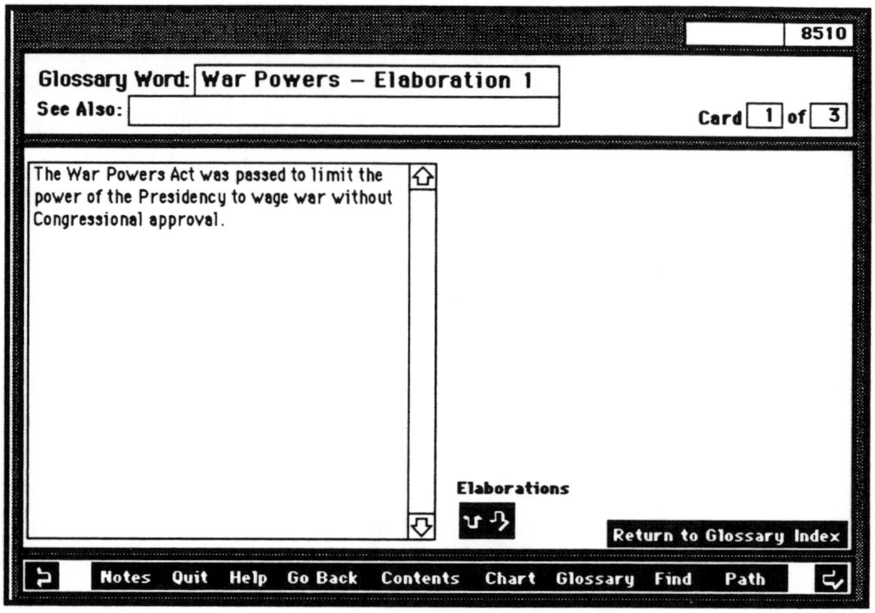

message should alert the user that he or she is leaving before finishing. Furthermore, if users enter a hierarchy somewhere other than at the beginning, a message should inform them that they have missed a portion.

5.12   Use up/down arrows to indicate the path through a hierarchy. Use a field to indicate which level of the hierarchy a user has engaged (e.g., "level 1 of 5").

When up/down arrows are used for continuing through several levels of information related to one idea, the up arrow should be removed from the first level and the down arrow from the last level. A hierarchy can be confusing because it may have both levels and sequences within the levels. Again, much verbal and graphic support is necessary. Hierarchy levels should use the "level x or y" strategy and up/down arrows. Again, when left/right arrows are used for continuing through several pages of information related to one level of the hierarchy, the left arrow should be removed from the first page and the right arrow from the last page.

5.13   Use maps, diagrams, or charts to help users keep track of their positions in the program. In complicated programs, an elaborative approach with general maps and specific maps may be necessary.

Fig. 5.19. Tracking facility screens.

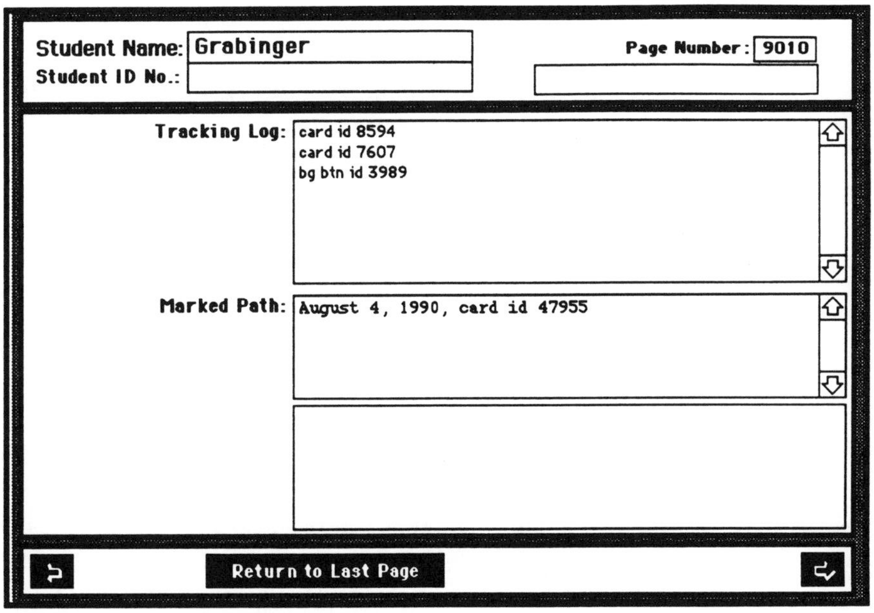

Maps and charts are common tools used to help users keep track of their progress or location in a multimedia environment. *Desert Shield* uses a single chart to indicate which section of the program the user has engaged.

For example, when the user clicks on the CHART button at the bottom of the "Letter to Congress 01-08-91" screen, the Navigation Chart screen is shown with the user's location within the program indicated. Because the "Letter to Congress 01-08-91" screen is part of the Events section of the program, "Events" is highlighted on the Navigation Chart (see Fig. 5.16 for Navigation Chart).

5.14 Use a tracking routine to save information about nodes visited by users only if that information will help users.

A tracking facility for recording events and nodes visited by users is a useful research tool and provides information for users on what they have seen, but it slows down the program. For example, *Desert Shield* includes a tracking facility that, for each user of the program, time stamps each object opened or clicked on in the program, and keeps track of paths that individual users have marked for future navigation through the program and the notes they have made on particular cards within the program (see Fig. 5.19).

5.15 If learning is a prime objective of the hypertext, provide a chance for users to enter a purpose or provide a menu of suggested goals to help users stay focused.

Desert Shield asks the user for a goal early after he or she has entered the program. If the user enters a goal, a new menu option, GOAL, appears on the menu bar for the user to select to recall the original purpose for entering the program. The menu option, GOAL, is a two-way link, so that when the user's goal has been reviewed, the user can return to his or her place of origin in the program by clicking on the GO BACK button at the bottom of the screen.

5.16 Design help systems with an elaborative approach. Keep initial explanations brief and provide options for more in-depth information.

The complexity of multimedia environments often leads developers to create screen after screen of information about how to use the program. By the time users read all of that information, they are too tired to continue using the program with any sense of concentrated purpose. Hypermedia designers must try to keep this information as brief as possible, letting users determine how much depth to study for their own understanding. Brief overviews should be used to explain functions with options for more in-depth information. Users want to get into a program quickly. Therefore, no more than three screens of introductory information should be included. These screens should concentrate on telling users what the program is about, the basic functions of links and buttons, and how to get more elaborate information.

5.17 Always include a way to restart the program (or to return to the beginning).

5.18 Always provide a termination process to inform the learner that the program is closing.

Inadvertent program termination should be avoided by asking users if they are sure they want to quit.

CONCLUSION

Access is everything. The main goal of the designer is to provide the access necessary for users. This chapter provides a way to think about what is needed in a multimedia program. The programming techniques exist to provide users with ways to access almost any node within a program. But, total access may not be the best solution because it takes time to create and may provide more than is necessary. Designers should always let the users' needs and the purpose of the program guide the selection of links.

CHAPTER 6

Human-Computer Interface Design

Rose Marra

Chapter Objectives
The content and information of a multimedia application may be right on target for an intended task, but if the interface between human and computer is not designed well, then the information and instruction may be ineffective or inaccessible. Chapter 7 discusses specific screen design issues (i.e., placement of text, font sizes), and although these issues are certainly a component of the human-computer interface (HCI), this chapter discusses HCI issues at a broader level, dealing with concepts such as intuitiveness and transparency to improve the clarity, usability, and effectiveness of computer systems. Specifically, in this chapter I

- define the field human-computer interface as it applies to multimedia development

- explain the characteristics of intuitive and transparent interfaces and

- present basic principles for effective human-computer interfaces.

The domain, therefore, of HCI design is not clear-cut nor easily defined and ranges into a variety of issues including the physical arrangement and ergonomic configuration of computer systems, user operation of programs, and how the user interacts with the content to solve a task or to learn material (see Fig. 6.1). In the case of an instructional program, the HCI design must not interfere with the instructional design and strategies embedded in the program.

Fig. 6.1. The domain of human-computer interface design.

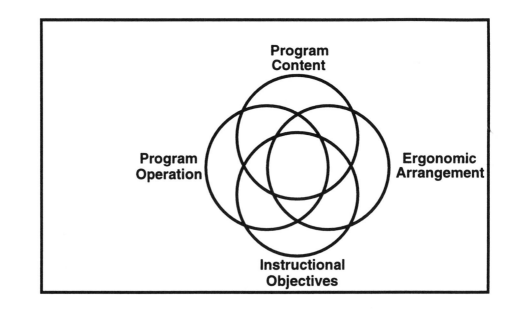

HCI DEFINITION

As it is for many concepts, there are a variety of definitions for human-computer interface design. In broad terms, Carroll (1987) described the notion of human-computer interface as "computers as experienced and manipulated by human users" (p. 23). Reisner (1987) elaborated on this by describing the relationship as two-sided though uneven: We are able to predict specifically what the computer will do as the result of certain input; however, it is the unpredictable human reaction to the computer that we need to study and plan for in our design.

Palme (1983) presented an interesting metaphor that describes why HCI design is such an important consideration in program design. He contrasts the computer and the rules that create its interface with the rules that govern society. There are general rules that govern societal behavior that are valid in numerous different circumstances. For example, loud noises, coughing, and talking are discouraged at movie theaters, concerts, plays, and church services. This is easy for flexible human beings to understand and transfer to different situations. The computer, however, requires a more complete and more rigid set of rules than society does because a computer does not readily understand nuances or similarities in situations. The software must define every possible reaction for the computer. In society things are looser, and there is more interpretation of the rules, which mean the rules are not always followed exactly the same way every time. This difference in flexibility and rigidity is one way of explaining why humans may have trouble dealing with a computer's set of inflexible rules, for although the human user perceives the differences inherent in varied contexts, the computer understands only one reaction or algorithm. This is the reason why the definition of the rules that make up the HCI are so complex.

For purposes of this chapter, then, an HCI is defined as the layer of the software that communicates directly to and interacts with users. A sampling of critical components of an HCI includes

- all messages (error, status, etc.) to users;

- interactions, flow, or navigation between screens or other various parts of the program;

- interrelationships between messages within the program; and

- screen designs.

Note that this list goes beyond the ergonomic factors such as the physical layout of the software and the ways humans access that software (i.e., keyboard, mouse, monitor) through the hardware configuration. An interface is interwoven throughout the entire program. It is in the way that the software reacts to users when they need help, make errors, enter information, or respond to questions. Likewise, the principles and design guidelines that follow must deal with these diverse aspects of a HCI.

BASIC HCI PRINCIPLES

6.1 Conduct an audience analysis to guide the development of the human-computer interface.

Audience Analysis A central HCI design principle is to analyze the characteristics and needs of the audience (Carroll & Rosson, 1987; Bailey, 1985). Although instructional programs include an audience analysis as part of any instructional design, audience analysis for the HCI differs slightly from audience analysis in instructional design (ID). ID learner analysis focuses on the cognitive, affective, and prior learning characteristics of the learners. It looks for characteristics that will facilitate or inhibit learning. Task and performance analyses for HCI emphasize analyses of intended usage patterns and technological attitudes and abilities. The following guidelines address how to get at these HCI issues.

6.2 Analyze the problem that the user intends to solve with the software.

Problem Analysis Although this guideline relates to ID's task analysis, one must go a bit further in this HCI analysis. ID always examines the principle subtasks inherent in completing the main task. One factor to consider in the HCI analysis is whether any of the subtasks can be performed by the interface rather than the user to help the user maintain appropriate cognitive involvement.

For example, if the task is one familiar to users (e.g. writing a check, solving a common mathematical problem, or entering data in a frequently used program), then the HCI can take advantage of commonly known terms and perform mundane steps to enable the users or learners to focus on new steps and new learning. That is, users may know how to write a check without a computer; therefore, in a new computerized version of the task, the HCI would guide the user through the well-known steps using common terminology and emphasizing unfamiliar tasks of the computer version.

However, the opposite may be true. Students may be so engaged in a new, large task (e.g., simulating a science experiment, comparing geographic information) that they fail to see and adequately perform the subtasks. The interface must insure proper attention to detail and cognitive subtasks necessary to complete the larger task.

Another situation arises when a task is known but the program, most likely a teaching program, expects users to accomplish a familiar task by a new method. This might occur, for instance, in a learning environment that is encouraging math students to solve quadratic equations with a different method. Learners may already be familiar with one method, but it is the job of the interface to model a different one and point out the differences to the learners.

This guideline, although having its beginnings in ID's task analysis, asks designers to look more closely not just at the components of the task, but at the way they are expected to be accomplished within the interface.

6.3 Analyze how the prospective users accomplished the objective or task prior to using the computer and software.

This guideline is closely related to the previous one and somewhat difficult to separate from it. Whereas the previous guideline looks at the task objectives, this one focuses more on user performance. Admittedly, there is some overlap, but to implement this guideline and make a thorough analysis, designers need to look at users' prior behavior patterns in performing the task. Sometimes a new program is built to replace an old program. In that case, the following questions are asked:

- Did users perform the task on a computer before? If so, will the new solution be a similar type of program or very different (i.e., going from a DOS environment to a Macintosh)?

- What did users like and dislike about the prior program? Were disliked factors a result of poor implementation?

- Were users forced to use the program against their will, thus creating a bad attitude that no matter how good the program, it would not be appreciated?

If software was not used before, the following questions should be examined:

- What are the users' attitudes toward using computers? For instance, have they had or heard of experiences in which computers have replaced people, or that may cause them to have a negative predisposition to any software introduced?

- Should the program imitate the existing way of accomplishing the task exactly? The wider the difference between the computer method and noncomputer method, the flatter and longer the learning curve.

- How will a computer program improve user performance? Will users save time? Will they save money? Will quality of performance significantly improve?

Once designers have collected this information, it can be used to make decisions about not only the HCI, but also what else might have to be done to achieve success with the product. For instance, if there is a negative attitude regarding computers, the software may have to be accompanied with assurances from some trusted body or individual that this software is not threatening anyone's job, or that a learner's prior bad experience with a "drill and practice" program does not necessarily mean they will not succeed with the current environment.

6.4 Examine the users' experience level with computers and other relative kinds of software packages.

The users' experience with other software packages tells something about what expectations and what metaphor they may bring to the product being designed. If users have experience with command-line systems and programs (e.g., a DOS or UNIX system in which users must know the command to enter to achieve the desired action versus a menu driven system), then a system or program that relies on icons and menus, although supposedly easier to use, may be unfamiliar and difficult to those users. This means that a significant amount of education will need to be done before users will adapt to the new system, and more on-line help may be required.

The interface can also address the sort of metaphor familiar to the users from their prior experience. The interface can facilitate learning and performance if the metaphor model for the interface gives a high-level view of the assumptions and guidelines used to design the program. Users can then relate the metaphor to actions within the interface. For instance, if users are aware that designers built a hypermedia program around a travel metaphor, then they may be able to interpret a pull-down menu bar labeled "Travel Agent" as related to making plans for solving the hypermedia program's main topic or problem.

An interface can also attempt to relate the current interface's functionality to a system with which users are familiar. Therefore, a help message about pull-down menus might define them in terms of a command-driven system. An extension of this concept is to actually create an interface that allows multiple modes for running the system; that is, there might be an option to emulate a command-line system (or whatever system type users understand) rather than use the pull-down menus. If the user community's prior experience is not homogeneous, as is likely to be the case, designers may not be able to accommodate all familiar styles within an interface (just as instructors are not able to adapt to all individual learner characteristics), but may need to model the interface metaphor as described before, so that users may have a better chance of knowing what to expect from the interface.

6.5 Examine user attitudes toward using a computer for the intended task.

Users bring many attitudes to computers. Some may see as a great "tool" that can make them more powerful on their jobs, while others may feel quite threatened. The latter group may have experienced or heard of jobs being lost as the use of computers increased.

Knowing this type of information can affect the final product in a several ways. First, although designers should always strive for the best, in a case such as this, being extremely sensitive to a friendly, easy-to-use interface that clearly shows the benefits to users becomes even more important. Even sensitive interface design, though, may not totally compensate for these preexisting attitudes, so a design team may want to suggest that the product introduction be accompanied with written or verbal materials that attempt to ease users' concerns.

On the other hand, if users bring a positive attitude to the system, then they ought to be able to find the kind of functionality they expect in the product. The interface should make this functionality obvious and simple so it can capitalize on users' enthusiasm.

The rub for designers comes when they try to adapt a system to work well both for users looking for functionality and for those who are more timid with the product. Some suggestions for scaffolding progressive turnover of functionality to users as their expertise increases are discussed later. For example, *Desert Shield* might have chosen to keep a count of how many times a user has accessed the system. At a certain predetermined count, then, new functionality that allows users to edit links could be introduced. Thus, the system could have turned more control over to the user as experience increased.

Section Summary   To summarize how HCI's audience analysis principles should be factored into instructional design:

- Task and front-end analyses should be expanded beyond learner characteristics to include user attitudes and task accomplishment patterns.

- All stages of design and implementation should balance and measure themselves against the needs of users in terms of program operation and program purposes.

- When in doubt or when other principles or heuristics are in conflict, always turn back to users' needs and characteristics and make decisions based on them.

PRODUCTION BIAS

6.6 **Design an interface that encourages exploration and makes learning efficiency a rewarding experience.**

Production bias (Carroll & Rosson, 1987) means that users are interested in completing their target tasks; they use of an interface for getting their jobs done. In other words, they are intent on being productive, not on learning the program. This is not a bad tendency if the path users take to accomplish their tasks is the most efficiently designed path. However, using the computer efficiently or as the program designers intended is often of little consequence to users. Their production bias motivates them to finish the task any way they can-efficient or not. This bias discourages users from taking time to do any system exploration, experimentation, or documentation reading, because anything not directly associated with getting the job done seems to be a deviation from their goal and a waste of time. Users may desire a more efficient way to perform a task and may even suspect that such a method exists, but the desire for task completion will outweigh the desire to find a more efficient alternative.

Although knowing users' degree of production bias is not totally possible, there are a few things to consider that may be helpful in both estimating the bias and determining how to deal with it. Once again these come back to the importance of a thorough audience analysis. A design team may try to determine the users' prior patterns of use with previous pieces of software particularly patterns associated with learning new functionality or willingness to conduct system exploration. In many programs it may be possible to collect evidence for use frequency of *help* facilities or of training and documentation.

If users do not use these help facilities, then the design team should find out why. Is it that they have tried and have been frustrated by not finding what they need, or is it that they just haven't tried? In either case, the implication for the HCI may be to couple the interface with other aspects of the product that encourage exploration and new learning. For example, a button labeled CATALOG may result in a pop-up window that says

---

Enter the name of the new catalog: _____.

For more information about what catalogs are and how they are used, press the HELP button below.

To make it as easy and nonintrusive as possible (which may be ways to get users to try things they have not used before), place the HELP button within the pop-up window.

Production bias also affects the instructional design of the program. For example, students may want to finish the program as quickly as possible to get back to work activities (or recess). Extrinsically motivated students tend to do the minimum to finish an assignment (Keller, 1983). Their level of learning is not the goal, but simply assignment completion. The strategies the student uses to learn the material are basically a matter of student choice, but can be affected by careful instructional design. Moreover, careful HCI design can help make sure that the strategies are implemented. Handling the production bias may be a simple matter of limiting user options. If it is important for users to read and study a particular sequence, the interface and strategy can require a thoughtful response before users continue and can also prevent users from escaping to another part of the program before the section is completed or before the objective is achieved. Similar to interface design, the instructional design of the program tries to develop strategies for the instructional interface to motivate learners to go beyond the minimal target goal. If high-level learning is a goal of the program then the program interface should support this via exploration that encourages methods such as inquiry teaching (Collins & Stevens, 1983).

Desert Shield uses this technique when it provides an elaboration on the topic of the War Powers Act. Figure 6.2 presents the screens that are part of this elaboration. Once in the sequence, users must complete it to prevent partial knowledge.

A second instructional design factor affected by production bias is the opposite of the previous example. Instead of lightly covering material, students try to memorize everything they encounter because they believe that this is their task. For example, programs that implement cognitive flexibility theory such as KANE (Spiro & Jehng, 1990) require the learner to link dynamically back and forth between a number of nodes examining many perspectives on the complex topic (KANE explores the motivations of the character Kane in the movie *Citizen Kane*). The learners may be so unaccustomed to this mode of learning that they assume their task is to be learning (that is, memorizing) everything encountered in the system and not using the interconnections between nodes to construct their own views as the program intended. Their production bias therefore leads them to accomplish the wrong task.

6.7 Given that production bias leads users away from exploring and learning, make efficient task completion obvious within the user interface.

Realizing that users may perform shortcuts or, conversely, accomplish a simple task with an unnecessarily complex routine, HCI designers need to strive to make efficient task accomplishment obvious within the user interface. In other words, the interface should lead users to the most efficient ways to accomplish a task. In *Desert Shield*, for example, information access is the prime purpose. Therefore, the interface design focuses on letting users access information in multiple ways: from the menu bar, from a main table of contents, and within fields on the screens. The designer's goal was to provide direct access (one mouse click) whenever possible.

Another way of providing direct access is to utilize a functional organization of on-line help rather than (or in addition to) a topical organization. For example,

Fig. 6.2. Elaboration screens.

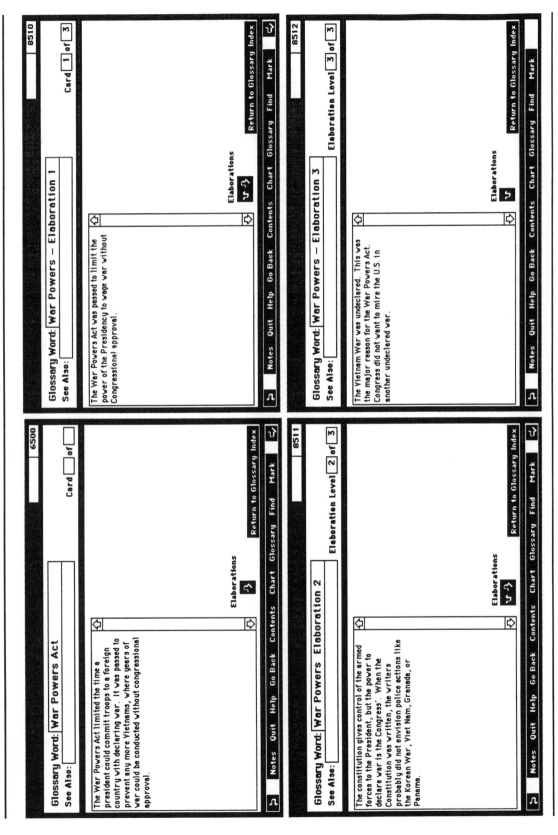

if users need help on step five of a process, the interface should not force them to look at steps one through four. *Desert Shield* uses context sensitive on-line help by letting users access a help topic for a menu or button choice directly by holding the OPTION key down when clicking. Again, this gives direct help without taking the user through a long set of hierarchical screens.

6.8 **Describe task functions, buttons, and menu options using words, phrases, and icons that are familiar and have meaning to the target audience.**

A great deal of good interface design is in the language used for describing objects and tasks. For example, a table of contents or index entry should read "moving text" rather than "steps in cut and paste". "Moving text" is the task users try to accomplish; "cut and paste" are names for the operations defined by the system developers. The names may be descriptive, but they are not as descriptive as terms that may be familiar to users.

The notion of simple and direct naming should also apply to the design of icons. Graphics-based interfaces such as Windows and Macintosh foster the development of icons instead of words to label buttons and functions. Although a lot of thought goes into these icons, they are often a mystery to common users. All words, phrases, and icons need to be tested in a formative evaluation process. (More information about icons is found in chapter 9.)

Section Summary The production bias says that users are interested in task completion. This interest is so strong that they may not take the time to discover the most efficient way to accomplish their task. Although there is probably no way to eliminate this bias, instruction or an HCI can try a several strategies. Functionality that you want users to utilize (most likely functionality that leads to efficient task completion and that might be "help") needs to be clearly and easily available. Users should not have to look far. Additionally, designers should try to find out how much the production bias is in effect by looking at how users have learned new concepts and methods in the past.

ASSIMILATION BIAS

6.9 **Correct any misconceptions or inappropriate knowledge brought to a new way of accomplishing a task from prior experience and learning.**

Assimilation bias (Carroll & Rosson, 1987) states that users' previous knowledge base may obscure new learning. It is similar to the production bias described previously in that users end up sticking with the familiar way to get the job done rather than exploring or looking for more efficient methods. In assimilation bias, users are led to an inefficient way of task completion because of preconceptions from prior learning. Users are comfortable with their previous ways of accomplishing a task and resist a change to another method. They are reluctant to assimilate the new methodology into their working or study habits.

Assimilation bias is evident in HCI design when the computer program operation may be so new and different that users seek a familiar sequence and methodology to accomplish their tasks. User-familiar items can be defined by prior knowledge of and experience with other systems or they can be those learned from a coworker who, even though a novice also, may be perceived to be an expert by comparison. In this way, system misinformation and incomplete information spreads among users. From this incomplete information, users may also formulate theories and rules about the rest of the system that may be incorrect.

6.10 Write informative error messages to tell a user why something went wrong, not just that something went wrong.

Error Messages Inappropriate prior knowledge and its consequences must be discovered and remedied. Much of this must be dealt with in the original planning and formative evaluation of the interface, because the HCI tends to remain static once implemented. In an interface, a misconception generally takes the form of an incorrect system view. In most systems, the only opportunity there is to correct such views is when an error occurs. Therefore, interface designers must not only consider designing clear error messages, but also suggesting ways to correct not only the error at hand, but the underlying misconception as well. For example, Fig. 6.3 shows two responses to an input error. The first announces to the user that the input entered was not correct. The second announces that the input entered was not correct because it expected numbers rather than letters. It seems to be a small item, but error messages are notoriously uninformative.

6.11 Within the interface, correct low-level user errors as soon as possible.

In the context of interface design, some lower-order errors probably should be corrected immediately-things such as pressing a tab key when the interface prompts users to press a return to continue. There is no benefit in allowing such an error to go uncorrected because users will become frustrated with the inflexibility of the program. Correcting low-level errors as soon as possible improves accuracy and facilitates error handling (Bailey, 1985). This prevents users from proceeding and reinforcing an improper view of how the system operates. This, in effect, mitigates the assimilation bias, by stopping incorrect actions early, and in the process encouraging or teaching correct ones.

6.12 Design the interface so that users cannot "hurt" anything, nor have the perception that they have hurt something.

This guideline can mitigate the effects of the assimilation bias. If users believe that they "hurt" something, they may become shy with the system and reluctant to try new things, thus exacerbating both production and assimilation biases.

Fig. 6.3. Types of error messages.

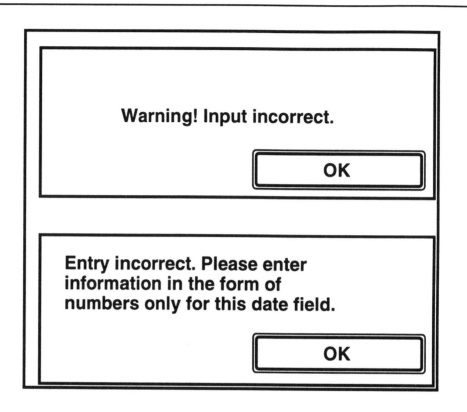

This guideline is probably most critical as applied to the novice user who approaches the computer with some trepidation. A significant factor in implementing this guideline is a thorough system evaluation.

A second way to encourage users to learn different routines is to build "undo" and "go back" functions into the system. Unfortunately, these commands may be difficult and expensive to implement because they require the system to save snapshots before and after every given command. Less expensive attempts at user safety include warning messages when the user is about to do something with sweeping consequences, such as removing the contents of an entire directory/folder or not saving the results of a two-hour computer aided instruction session.

Section Summary The assimilation bias states that a user's prior knowledge may obscure new learning. The functional ramifications are similar to those of the production bias in that users may not use the interface's full functionality but rather stick to tasks they know. Designers can use the following strategies to counter-balance the effects of the assimilation bias:

- Use error messages to correct/modify incorrect system views.

- Correct errors as soon as possible so that incorrect system models are not cognitively strengthened inadvertently.

- Make the interface impervious to harm so if learners do explore, they will not have the perception that they have damaged anything; this friendly exploratory environment may lead to further exploration and the discovery of new interface functionality.

INTUITIVENESS

6.13 Design an interface that is intuitive, logical, transparent, and direct to users.

Intuitive Interface To be intuitive in the context of HCI design, the interface must adapt to the reality of how users think rather than expect users to adjust their thinking schemata and strategies to an arbitrarily designed interface. If an interface is intuitive, it falls easily within the expectations and experience of the users. Therefore the users will not have to make such a leap to place their cognitive processes about the problem they seek to solve within the confines of the system. The way they normally approach the target task should be readily represented within the system's interface.

Transparent Interface Concepts related to intuitiveness include transparency and directness. Designing a *transparent* system means that program operation does not interfere with users performing program tasks. Transparency in an interface helps to create a system that is easy and nonintimidating to use. A transparent interface takes little cognitive overhead and puts few, if any, demands on users. Icons (pictorial representations of interface functionality) are a potential example of interface transparency. A small picture of a computer printer on a button is thought to be transparent for most users because it involves an easy leap to understand the function the button activates.

An interface that is *direct* helps users to believe that they are engaged in accomplishing their goal. In contrast, an indirect system serves as an obstacle to accomplishing goals (Hutchins, Hollan, & Norman, 1985). For example, a word processor that is direct helps users to believe that they are writing a story and not that they are using a word processor to write a story. A CAI program that is direct helps students to believe that they are learning valuable information rather than operating a computer program about information.

Another way of describing the principle of intuitiveness is via metaphor matching. Users come to an interface with a metaphor about how the program functions. A metaphor creates a set of expectations among users about how difficult a task will be and how they will perform that task. For example, when Apple Computer introduced the Macintosh, they also introduced a new metaphor for computer operation-the desktop. Users have been encouraged to view the computer as a desktop with a series of folders to organize their work. If the interface operates consistently with the users' metaphor, then the interface feels intuitive or natural. If not, users must adjust their metaphor or expectation in order to use the system most effectively. Then the interface is not intuitive, transparent, or direct.

For example, frequent users of command-line-driven systems (a command-line-driven system takes most of its user input via commands that the computer understands typed in via a keyboard), such as UNIX and DOS may expect computer interactions to consist of typing a command at a prompt and then getting a response. When command-line users are first exposed to a system using the desktop metaphor (e.g., Windows or Macintosh), they find that their expectations are not met. Such users have to adjust their expectations in order to use the desktop system without having to translate the commands they would normally have typed into the equivalent desktop inputs. What was actually intended to be a very easy interface to adapt to, turns out, at least to a subset of users, to be quite a leap.

Windows As effective as a metaphor is in tapping into something familiar and easy to grasp for the users, it can be overused and actually decrease transparency. Jonassen (1989) cites an example of using multiple windows in an interface. Programs and files in windows placed on the screen can be an intuitive interface device because they extend the concept of the single view of an application or task to multiple views. This may be intuitive to a point, but when too many windows are available on the screen, they have the opposite effect. Users can effectively juggle only a few windows at once, just as a person can keep only a few items in short-term memory. Therefore, once the number of windows gets beyond a threshold, depending on each user and the context in which they are using the interface, they become a hindrance because the user must concentrate on the windows rather than the tasks they contain.

The interface should also help make the instruction intuitive. Instructional design theories such as cognitive apprenticeship (Collins, 1991) also have goals of intuitiveness and directness. These instructional methods strive to immerse learners in a real-world learning experience to make the learning effort intuitive while they are focusing on a realistic task.

6.14 Keep the interface simple and basic with a limited number of options.

Avoid designing an interface that is too feature-rich or too busy. There is a basic set of functionality that users need in a software package for it to provide an enhanced way of accomplishing the desired task. Although it is true that multiple ways to achieve a task may help an interface work for novices and experts, too many options may confuse users (especially the novices) and actually detract from the interface's usability. From a cognitive processing point of view, users must chunk away all the options in short-term memory, and if there are too many of them, the users' own processing is bogged down causing confusion and reduced interface transparency (Andre & Phye, 1986).

For example, the development of software for phone switches (which these days are complex computers) results in the conclusion that most users do not want or need the feature richness provided in these systems. The multitude of ways to answer calls and place them on hold, and many of the features provided for accomplishing those functions, often go unnoticed and unused. Users evidently find one way or possibly two intuitive ways that accomplish the task, such as answering the call, and do not search any further for others unless their needs change, thus outweighing the effort of looking for and learning a new feature. Users, in this case, actually provide their own simplicity in an interface that offers too many options.

6.15 Balance the locus of control between the interface and users.

Locus of Control Designers should build an interface that encourages users to interact with the system in substantive ways that reflect the actual nature of the task. For example, some of the older, line-oriented word processing programs had such severe limitations on how to represent information that users had to format text in their minds rather than on the screen to meet the text editor's demands. The antithesis of these editors are today's WYSIWYG (what you see is what you get) editors with which users have almost total control over the final appearance of the text. Although in the first case, users may eventually memorize all of the editor's interface rules, these rules are not substantive parts of the actual task. In the second case, the interface design has adapted to the users to give them more control over the job. This frees users to concentrate more on the content of their text than on how to use the tool.

Section Summary Ironically, there is no intuitive way for a designer to necessarily create an intuitive or transparent interface. However, designers need to consider their audience and design interface attributes that fit as easily as possible into the users' cognitive structures. Keeping the interface relatively simple and balancing control between the interface and users are ways designers may use to promote interface intuitiveness.

Intuitiveness, directness, and transparency are important elements of a successful interface. To design these characteristics into the interface, designers must understand the characteristics of the intended users and the targeted use of the system. This level of understanding includes the expectations and metaphors that users bring to the program, as well as how best to engage the learners actively in the completion of their tasks. In sum then, the interface must allow users to concentrate on their target task instead of the interface itself. If an interface can accomplish this, it has achieved an important level of intuitiveness, directness, and transparency.

COMPUTER AS TOOL

6.16 The interface should help the tool adapt to users.

The idea of "computer as tool" emphasizes that an interface should clearly support the computer program working for users rather than the other way around. Although this seems like an obvious suggestion, users are quite often in the position of having to do things the way the computer wants it to be done, rather than being able to impose their processes on the system. As other guideline explanations indicate, users may then have to adjust their processes because interfaces have little capability in adjusting to individual users. But the interface should strive to ease necessary user adjustments by making those expectations clear.

The primary purpose of human-computer interface design is that the interface should lend itself to allowing users to be directly engaged in their task without having to expend effort focusing on the tool they are using to accomplish that task. This simple idea, however, may get lost in designers' fascination with the technology that allows these interfaces to exist. When this idea is lost, users are forced to wade through an interface that may not directly aid them in accomplishing their target task, and which is no longer transparent (Hutchins, Hollan, & Norman, 1985). For this reason and also to keep the interface design focused on the users' needs, the design process should include many opportunities for user feedback so that the users or their representatives can verify that the design is going to meet their needs.

The view that technology should adapt to users has not always been the case. Older computing systems, which were often much less powerful than those readily available today, required users to have specific knowledge about the computer and software internal design. Not much effort was made in computer design to create what we now refer to as a friendly interface. In addition to the newness of the entire HCI field, another factor, the state of technology, contributed to the more cryptic interfaces. Computer processing power was too precious to spend on extras such as a nice interface. Because computers were not as ubiquitous as they are today, and because computer users were highly trained, technically literate individuals did not need a user-friendly interface to accomplish tasks. The UNIX operating system is a good example of that type of software. It was specifically designed for the research and development community of AT&T Bell Laboratories and today still retains a more primitive, if not extremely powerful and flexible, user interface. Today's diverse set of users demands a more sophisticated interface that a nontechnical user can easily master.

This guideline is complex because users approach the interface with varying degrees of expertise. In other words, how does a single interface effectively adapt to novices, experts, and every user in between? This is one of the more difficult HCI heuristics to implement, but it is also one of the most important. The following associated principles illustrate several tactics that HCI designers may employ to adapt the software to users with different levels of expertise.

6.17 Design an interface that can grow with users as their level of expertise increases.

Palme (1983) suggested the idea of an interface for growth. Such an interface may be characterized by menus and help facilities in the interface's early release. Then in subsequent interface releases, as the user community may be assumed to have more expertise, designers can add more sophisticated functionality such as command parameters, a command-line interface (such as the Macintosh's keyboard sequences), and even the ability for users to write their own script programs within the interface.

In an instructional situation, the software may use a progressive turnover strategy. This is a concept similar to that of mastery learning in which users must demonstrate their competence in one area before being allowed to progress to the next. In a HyperCard stack, users may be restricted from writing or modifying scripts until they know enough to set their scripting level high enough; persons simply browsing a stack will not have this ability.

The level of expertise could be determined through a count of how many times the individual has used the software. (Of course this makes an assumption that the more users have used the system, the more expertise they have acquired.) Another way to determine expertise is through a series of self-evaluation questions, such as, "Do you consider yourself not at all familiar, familiar, or very familiar with this system?" Depending on a user's response, the interface would vary. This tactic should also include examples of what each level means so that users can more accurately choose, and it should *always* allow users to change the expertise level in case they are not comfortable with their current choice.

A simple example is how the Macintosh allows various operations to occur, either via a novice-oriented pull-down menu and mouse selection or via a sequence of keyboard strokes. Novices are satisfied because they do not have to go look up the operation in a document, but can use the keywords on the screen and the mouse to find and execute the function. Experts are satisfied because they have the flexibility to execute the known function without having to move their hands from the keyboard to the mouse.

In *Desert Shield*, this interface-flexibility based upon a user's experience level might be implemented by having a front-end tacked onto the existing environment that walks novices through an already-created path in the stack. This would serve to introduce novices to the available functionality in a gradual way, as well as reinforce how various portions of the environment (i.e., place, person) may be used. *Desert Shield* could accommodate novices via the progressive turnover strategy as well. Initial sessions with the environment might be limited to using only the persons and places portions of the stack. Internal counts could be kept of a novice's use of various *Desert Shield* functions, and when a certain predetermined threshold is reached, more functionality could be turned over to the user.

6.18 The interface should keep the user informed to keep the interface and underlying software from seeming mysterious and out of the user's control.

Keeping users informed (Bailey, 1985) gives them a sense that the computer is still at their service rather than off performing some task that no longer involves them. In other words, informing users keeps them involved with the interface. This feedback can take several forms:

- Status messages are used to show progress of a task being performed. For example, when copying a file from the hard drive to a diskette using the Macintosh, a message box is displayed that tells users "Items remaining to be copied: 1". This is accompanied with a thermometer-like rectangle that is progressively filled up with colored shading so the user knows that the copy is actually being made. When the rectangle is filled up, the copy is complete and the box is removed.

- Warning messages let users know the consequences of the action to be performed. Once again, the Macintosh provides a good warning message example. When users place files in the trash and then request that the trash be emptied (so the files are actually removed from the hard disk), a warning message/question is presented. Once warned, users can either continue with the removal or cancel it.

> The Trash contains 2 items which use 113K of disk space. Are you sure you want to permanently remove these items?

- Correctness feedback indicates whether an action or response is correct. Instructional programs handle this in varying ways including the static, "You are correct. Press any key to continue," or the phrases indicating that the user is correct: "You got it," or "That's right; press RETURN to move on."

    Learning environments that promote complex problem-solving skills may require much more complete correctness feedback. For example, in an environment designed to teach medical students transfusion medicine, students must analyze a particular medical case involving transfusion medicine. Correctness feedback for these cases involves much more than a simple "correct" or "wrong, try again." Correctness feedback here includes information on the case diagnosis and treatment choice. Correctness feedback must therefore vary with the nature of the task being taught.

- Navigational feedback shows users where they are in a program. This is particularly important in potentially complex programs such as those proposed in cognitive flexibility theory (Spiro & Jehng, 1990) in which the structure of the program is not necessarily hierarchical. *Desert Shield* provides users with a navigational chart, which, as the name implies, is a chart or map that highlights the portion of the program that the user has engaged. This helps prevent learners from getting lost in the stack.

Like other guidelines, implementing this one requires balance. Too much feedback interferes and reduces interface transparency. Using software full of user-status messages can be a maddening experience, especially if users are quite experienced and have seen these same-messages many times.

Too little feedback might result in a different type of frustration. Take, for example, the situation in which the user requests a certain function from the computer, and then, at least it seems to the user, nothing observable happens. A user may ask the system to save a document, and it appears that the system is just sitting there doing nothing. Because many users are not familiar with computer operations, they may mistake the apparent inactivity for an error and become

Fig. 6.4 Feedback for a lengthy operation.

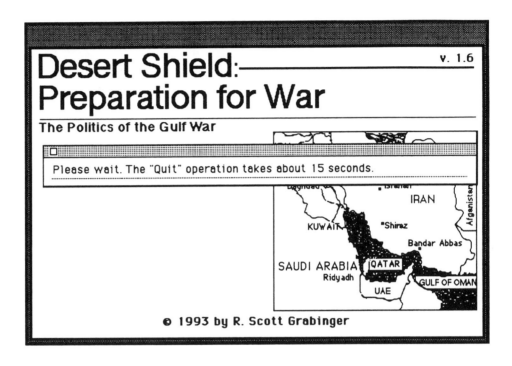

impatient or fearful that they have done something wrong. This may result in repeating the previous user action and, depending on the robustness of the HCI software, may ultimately result in a real error. A similar situation may occur in a HyperCard stack such as *Desert Shield* during a search or find operation. In a large stack, the system may actually be working away at the requested task, but unless it gives users some clear indication of its progress, they may feel frustrated at the apparent inactivity. Some interfaces accomplish such status messages via a thermometer-like graphic that fills up showing the approximate percentage completed as the task is performed. *Desert Shield* provides feedback whenever a long operation occurs (see Fig. 6.4).

Section Summary Interfaces all too often lose sight of the guideline that the tool should do as much as possible to adapt to users rather than have users needing to adapt to the tool. Whereas in earlier computing systems, limitations in technology often did not allow designers to achieve this goal, this is not the case today. When designers overlook this goal today, it may be because they are so enamored with what the technology allows them to do that, they overlook the need to keep user needs as the top priority.

Designing interfaces to support adapting to users' needs is one of the most important and most difficult guidelines to implement. Users' needs and abilities vary, especially with levels of expertise. This section describes two subguidelines to help in designing adaptive interfaces. The first guideline, based on Palme (1983), suggests techniques for building an interface that grows with users as their expertise grows. Strategies such as counting the number of times users have accessed the program are suggested. The other guideline discusses user feedback messages that keep users in control of their use of the interface rather than leave them with the feeling that the interface is operating on them.

CONCLUSION

This chapter discusses the principles and guidelines for HCI design with emphasis on these principles for hypermedia and multimedia design. Principles discussed include

- doing a thorough audience analysis to determine both users' abilities and prior experience with computers and interfaces as well as attitudes;

- accommodating the users' production bias by encouraging exploration within the interface;

- accommodating users' natural assimilation bias with an interface that corrects inappropriate prior knowledge that may limit users' abilities within the interface;

- designing an interface to be intuitive, logical and clear to users;

- and building an interface that supports adapting and growing with the users rather than the other way around.

There is no doubt that these concepts are difficult to grasp and even more difficult for designers to implement. However the importance of a well-designed HCI cannot be over stated. The HCI is the primary means by which users interact with a learning environment, and if they find it difficult to use, their learning may be compromised. Conversely, any design effort that results in an HCI that allows users to focus on the learning task at hand and enhances their abilities in that arena, although it may not be overtly acknowledged by users, will pay off with users having a more satisfactory experience with the learning environment.

REFERENCES

Andre, T., & Phye, G. D. (1986). Cognition, learning and education. In T. Andre & G. D. Phye (Eds.). *Cognitive classroom learning: Understanding, thinking, and problem solving* (pp. 1-19). New York: Academic Press.

Bailey, R. (1985). *Human performance engineering: A guide for systems design* (pp. 293-299). New York: Prentice-Hall.

Carroll, J. M. (1987). Preface. In J. Carroll (Ed.), *Interfacing human thought*. Cambridge MA: MIT Press.

Carroll, J. M., & Rosson, M. B. (1987). Paradox of the active user. In J. Carroll (Ed.). *Interfacing human thought* (pp. 80-111). Cambridge MA: MIT Press.

Collins, A. (1991). Cognitive apprenticeship and instructional technology. In L. Idol & B. F. Jones (Eds.). *Educational values and cognitive instruction: Implications for reform* (pp. 121-138). Hillsdale NJ: Lawrence Erlbaum Associates.

Collins, A., & Stevens, A. (1983). A cognitive theory of inquiry teaching. In C. M. Reigeluth (Ed.). *Instructional-design theories and models: An overview of their current status*. Hillsdale NJ: Lawrence Erlbaum Associates.

Hutchins, E. L., Hollan, J. D., & Norman, D. A. (1985). Direct manipulation interfaces. *Human-computer interaction*. Hillsdale NJ: Lawrence Erlbaum Associates.

Jonassen, D. H. (1989). Functions, applications, and design guidelines for multiple window environments. *Computers in Human Behavior, 5*, 185-194.

Keller, J. M. (1983). Motivation design of instruction. In C. M. Reigeluth (Ed.). *Instructional-design theories and models: An overview of their current status*. Hillsdale NJ: Lawrence Erlbaum Associates.

Palme, J. (1983). A human-computer interface encouraging user growth. In M. E. Sime & M. J. Coombs (Eds.). *A designing for human-computer communication* (pp. 139-156). New York: Academic Press.

Reisner, P. (1987). Discussion: HCI, what is it and what research is needed. In J. Carroll (Ed.), *Interfacing human thought*. (pp. 337-352). Cambridge MA: MIT Press.

Spiro, R. J., & Jehng, J. (1990). Cognitive flexibility and hypertext: Theory and technology for the non-linear and multidimensional traversal of complex subject matter. In D. Nix & R. J. Spiro (Eds.). *Cognition, education and multimedia: Exploring ideas in high technology* (pp. 163-205). Hillsdale NJ: Lawrence Erlbaum Associates.

CHAPTER 7

Screen Design

Scott Grabinger

Chapter Objectives Interactive multimedia applications tend to rely heavily on the written word to present information. Even programs using a large number of sophisticated graphics and animation combine those graphic forms with written words. All of this information is presented by combining text elements including type, illustrations, and graphic devices (e.g., lines, shading, boxes) in an empty space to present information (see Fig. 7.1 for a larger list of text elements). The combination and arrangement of text elements in meaningful ways are problems of message design and layout. Designers work to lay out information in ways that reflect the content as well as the shapes and quantities of letters, numbers, and graphic images. In this chapter, we

- define the fundamental concept of legibility and

- discuss guiding concepts of aesthetic qualities, macrolevel organization, and microlevel organization.

Text Elements The arrangement of text elements is an increasingly complex matter. Each element portrayed in Figure 7.1 each have an almost infinite number of values. For example, typestyle could include Helvetica, Chicago, Times, New Century Schoolbook, Monaco, Arial, Avant Garde, and so on. The element of background color could easily take over 16,000,000 values on most of today's color computer systems. Therefore, finding the "correct" combination could be an impossible task if there were only one correct combination. But, like most things, there are a number of ways to create a screen or set of screens of information that are effective for users. The trick is to learn some basic guidelines that can help a designer put the elements together in a way that maintains the meaning of the content and encourages the reader to process the information.

Fig. 7.1. Screen design elements.

typesize	typestyle	leading
background color	leading	color
foreground color	typeweight	kerning
contrast	wordspacing	boxes
letter color	kerning	lines
graphic resolution	shading	bold type
inverse type	flashing	progressive disclosure
animation	buttons	fields
uppercase	lowercase	shades of gray
	special effects	

LEGIBILITY

Effective instructional text, whether presented on paper or via computer screens, is more than a collection of alphanumeric characters and graphic devices. The objective of effective instructional text is to communicate information and ideas to a specific audience. Hartley (1978, p. 13) presented the following definition of instructional text:

> Instructional text normally contains a wide variety of components — such as listed information, programmatically developed statements, numbered items, diagrammatic presentations, explanatory notes and pictorial features of many kinds.

> Furthermore, such materials are not intended for continuous reading. In an instructional setting the reader's focus of attention is constantly ranging from a place on the page to somewhere else. From this point of view instructional materials are tools for use in a highly interactive and relatively unpredictable sequence of events.

Thus, an instructional program requires more design consideration regarding the display of text on a page than does a work of fiction such as a novel or short story. Novels maintain reader involvement with literary devices such as plot, story, characterization, theme, and dialogue. In instructional texts, reader involvement through literary devices is not always possible nor desirable. Though fiction gets by quite well with page after page of one word beside another, instructional programs use more than words. Multimedia programs are for learning and require different techniques to maintain reader involvement and encourage cognitive processing of content.

Techniques used to facilitate learner involvement with instructional programs presented via computer screens fall within the domain of legibility. *Legibility* is the influence of the *total format* of the page or screen.

Fig. 7.2. Visibility examples.

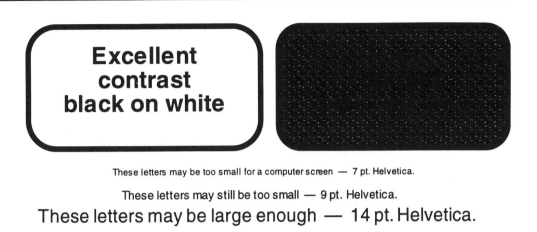

These letters may be too small for a computer screen — 7 pt. Helvetica.

These letters may still be too small — 9 pt. Helvetica.

These letters may be large enough — 14 pt. Helvetica.

Legible text possesses two primary design qualities that designers must work to enhance: visibility and recognizability (Reynolds, 1979). The designer must work, to some extent, with these three qualities to facilitate retention of information by encouraging deeper reader involvement.

Visibility   *Visibility* refers to the perceptual detectability and discriminability of the printed character. Visibility includes characteristics related to the clarity of the image, crispness of type, and contrast between foreground and background. A visible display presents symbols clearly and accurately. Visibility variables interact with the eyesight of the reader, as well as with conditions external to the reader such as lighting. For example, a screen with poor contrast between letters and background fails the visibility test of legibility because without adequate contrast the shapes of the letters would not be discriminable from the background (see Fig. 7.2). Another important factor in visibility is the size of the text. Letters that are too small may not be perceived for what they are (see Fig. 7.2). Visibility is a prerequisite for recognizability, because without adequate visibility the reader fails to recognize the meaning of individual symbols on the display. (See Fig. 7.3 for other variables that affect visibility.)

Research in the visibility area of legibility for both printed text and text displayed on screens has determined many typographic factors, including type sizes and contrast factors that contribute to optimal visibility. Work reported by Tinker (1963, 1965) and later updated by Rehe (1979) covers the area of visibility quite thoroughly for printed text. Research pertaining to the legibility of monitors is less than 20 years old with the bulk occurring in the last decade. Most of the effort has focused on the visibility of different typestyles, sizes, and contrast values (Cakir, 1980; Mills & Weldon, 1987; Snyder & Taylor, 1979; Wright & Friend, 1992). For computer screens, Mills and Weldon (1987)

Fig. 7.3. Legibility and Text Element Variables

Visibility	**Recognizability**
ambient lighting	typestyle
typesize	leading
background color	typeweight
contrast	word spacing
letter color	kerning
monitor resolution	symbol meaning
typestyle	

---

reported that reading rates are faster for smaller type sizes, but that searching tasks are better performed with larger letters. Galitz (1993) reported that lines on computer screens should contain no more than 40 to 60 characters, and he recommended using two columns of text between 30 and 35 characters wide. Lenze (1991) compared serif and sans serif type fonts in continuous text presented to subjects via a microcomputer. He found no apparent difference in reading speed or comprehension; however, his subjects preferred sans serif type. These findings for both paper and screens are usually widely practiced, because a publisher who does not produce visible materials will not remain a publisher for long.

Recognizability *Recognizability* refers to the ability of a display to convey the meaning of letters, words, and objects. A recognizable screen display presents meaningful symbols so that the meaning of each symbol can be identified and understood. Recognizability interacts with both text elements and reader characteristics — the background or prior knowledge of the reader. For example, a first-grader may be able to recognize each of the letters on this page, but would have difficulty recognizing the meanings of all the word symbols even though they are quite visible. Additionally, a screen display in Russian may be quite visible, but it would not be recognizable to most North Americans because they would not be able to perceive the meaning of each symbol nor the words made up by the symbols. Format variables that effect recognizability (see Fig. 7.3) include typestyle, word spacing, leading (amount of space between lines), and kerning (amount of space between letters). (See Fig. 7.4 for examples of recognizability problems.)

The works of Rehe (1979) and Tinker (1965) sets forth many widely accepted standards for variables listed under the recognizability factor of legibility. Although these same standards are assumed to be applicable to screen displays, the generalizability of paper standards to screen displays has not been verified.

Fig. 7.4. Recognizability examples.

Wordspacing
Thesewordsdonothaveanyspacebetweenthemmakingthemhardtorecognize.

Letterspacing
Some of t h e s e le t t ers are too far apart, making it
hard to read.

Linespacing
Line spacing can effect recognizability

too. Too much space can break the mental

connection between lines.

Focus   Whereas legibility includes both the appearance of the display and the
comprehensibility of the writing, the focus of this chapter is on the arrangement of
text elements to create meaningful displays. We look at the overall guiding
concepts of aesthetic qualities, macrolevel organization, and microlevel
organization. Each concept will present a set of guidelines for constructing screen
displays in multimedia applications.

AESTHETIC QUALITY GUIDELINES

**7.1   Use accepted aesthetic publication guidelines. Strive for balance,
harmony, and simplicity.**

Balance, harmony, and simplicity are general constructs often given to designers
as the basic elements of design. All three constructs can probably be summed up
in the word "moderation." Screens that display balance, harmony, and simplicity
are not jammed with information, have elements distributed throughout the screen,
and maintain a consistency in styles and locations from one screen to another. The
following related guidelines operationalize these ideas.

Fig. 7.5. Internal margins and white space.

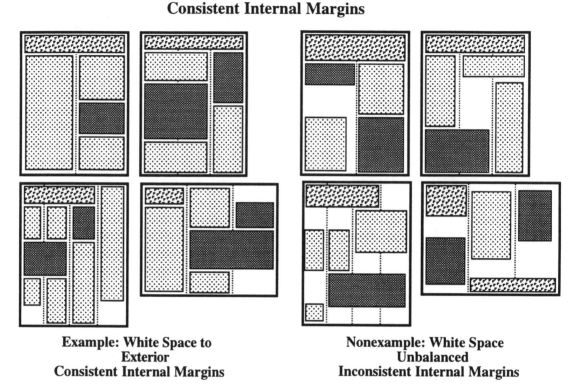

**White Space and
Consistent Internal Margins**

Example: White Space to
Exterior
Consistent Internal Margins

Nonexample: White Space
Unbalanced
Inconsistent Internal Margins

7.2   Maintain consistent internal margins and distribute the bulk of the white (empty) space around the exterior margins of the screen to help create a sense of balance,.

The notion of balance is a complicated concept in which both the weight of objects and the use of space are used to create that sense of balance. *White space* is space that contains no information; it is empty space on the screen. The first step in creating balance is to group the text elements together on the screen and to distribute the white space around the exterior margins. Consistent internal margins should be maintained among the elements on the screen. Note that in Figure 7.5 the drawing labeled "Example" the largest amount of white space is around the exterior margins. The text elements themselves are separated by smaller internal margins of white space, although the size of the margin between each element is the same. The drawing labeled "Inconsistent" has varying sizes of internal margins. The white space distributed around the exterior is also inconsistent in size. This combination creates a disorganized, unbalanced appearance.

Fig. 7.6. Harmony.

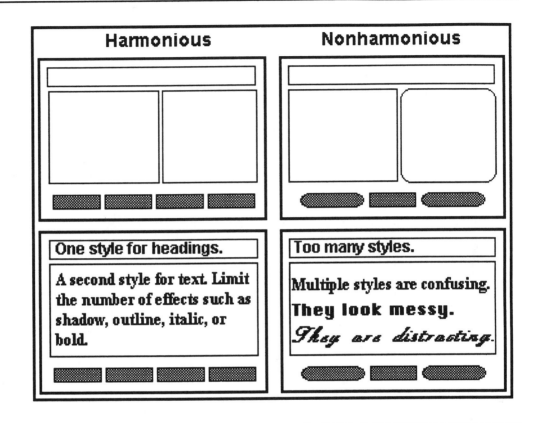

7.3 To help create a sense of balance, distribute light and dark areas and objects evenly around the screen.

Light and dark, black and white, or the visual weight of screen objects must be distributed evenly. It really is not an either/or situation. There are many colors and many shades of gray that can help balance a screen. Note that in Figure 7.5 the drawing labeled "Example" has dark areas at both the top and bottom of the screen to maintain a sense of balance. However, the drawing labeled "Nonexample" has all of the black area at the top of the screen creating a top-heavy and unbalanced appearance. Black does not have to be balanced with black. Sometimes the size of an object or a shading of gray may also balance the screen.

7.4 Use consistent design styles in objects and appropriate typestyles to create a sense of harmony.

Consistent design features refers to the overall style of the elements used. For example, in Figure 7.6 the drawing labeled "Harmonious" uses the rectangle as a basic design feature. The fields and buttons all use the rectangle style as a basic shape. Boxes around items also use the rectangle. However, in the drawing labeled

"Nonharmonious," the screen is composed of a mix of rectangle and rounded rectangle objects. The mix of these two different styles decreases the sense of harmony and the sense of organization.

The same sense of harmony can be created by using consistent type faces. In the "harmony" example in Figure 7.6, only two type faces are used in the fields on the screen: one for headings and one for the body of the text. The "Nonharmonious" example shows what happens when too many styles and too many sizes of type are used on one screen. A group of buttons can be harmonized by using the same button style, font, and size for all buttons in a cluster. The *Desert Shield* backgrounds create a sense of harmony by using the same button style for all of the control buttons along the bottom of the screen.

7.5 Keep screens simple. Avoid too many buttons, text fields, or graphic objects.

Designers often begin with a simple concept, but wind up adding "just one more button" or "one more field" to add that extra option or that last bit of information. Finally, by the time they are finished, the screen is cluttered with too many buttons, too much text, and too many design elements. Try for a minimalist look. Use as few buttons and fields as possible. Put options in the menu bar and avoid creating a button for every possible item. Don't feel obligated to fill in every piece of white space on the screen with text, graphics, or buttons. Standard options in the *Desert Shield* stack are placed in the menu bar at the top of the screen under the titles SECTIONS and FIND to prevent the screen from being too cluttered.

However, this does not mean that the other end of the extreme is desirable either. Plain, simple, and bare are not liked by viewers of either model or real screen samples (Grabinger, 1993). Screens must hold some visual interest. Visual interest refers to screens that use text elements to create an environment that looks worth exploring. A moderate degree of complexity is part of this environment and the following factors that can help to create organized screens and contribute to complex, visually interesting screens: lines, boxes, illustrations, and the placement of white space along the exterior margins of the screen.

7.6 Avoid screens that are solely text without any graphic devices or illustrations.

Viewers seem to think that screens without any illustrations or graphic devices are unorganized and uninteresting, making them harder to study or to read (Grabinger, 1993). Lines, boxes, buttons, diagrams, illustrations, charts, and graphs provide interest, organization, and can create a sense of control.

BASIC TYPOGRAPHY GUIDELINES

After Gutenburg invented the printing press, the primary focus on the science of typography was the creation of visible and perceptible documents. The principal typography factors related to the visibility and perceptibility of a document include type size, typestyle, line length, leading, case, and justification. A great deal of research has been performed with these type variables in the printed page world leading to accepted standards (Rehe, 1979; Tinker 1963). Generally, research into the application of these standards to computer monitors has supported the findings of print researchers, and has generated research findings regarding characteristics unique to the use of screens: contrast, resolution, brightness levels, color, font style, and visual fatigue (Cakir, 1980; Christ, 1975, 1977; Kolers, Duchincky, & Ferguson, 1981; Reynolds, 1980; Riley & Barbato, 1978; Snyder & Taylor, 1979; Tullis, 1981; Vartabedian, 1971). The following guidelines help to operationalize the general findings of these researchers.

7.7   Use only a few simple, familiar, and portable typestyles.

A *typestyle* is a particular shape distinctive to the characters that make up the type or font. Some fonts are intended only for display or use as titles and headings. They often set a tone for the text that follows. For example, **Avant Garde** is a modern typeface useful for display purposes in screens that need to project a feeling of modernism and recency. Other fonts are more appropriate for masses of text. Helvetica, Times, and Bookman are often used for presenting information in text. They are familiar and easy to read for a long time. Figure 7.7 shows some typical font families that are appropriate in each area.

Fonts come in two basic styles: serif or sans serif. Figure 7.7 provides a selection of each. Serif fonts have extenders on the letters to provide a higher sense of style. These fonts often provide more cues to the uniqueness of the letters and are easy to read. Sans serif fonts are simpler with straight strokes and no extenders. They are also fairly common and usually take up less space than serif fonts. Either font is appropriate.

The font family that is used must be portable, that is transferable from one machine to another. Unusual fonts such as Arial, Book Antigua, or Monotype Corsiva are not found on most machines. Therefore, a program created with these fonts may not work properly on a computer that does not have these styles installed. For programs that will go to a wide variety of machines, use only the most common fonts for that machine, or attach the font to the application. For the Macintosh, these include Times, Helvetica, New York, or Geneva, with Geneva being the most portable of the group. *Desert Shield* standardized on the Geneva font because it was the font most likely to be found on any machine that used the program.

Finally, choose, at the most, two typestyles. One font family may be chosen and used for both headings and text, or one family may be chosen for the headings and another for the text for visual interest. However, if you find yourself using three or more styles, analyze the reasons carefully. Too many font styles destroy unity and result in busy screens.

Fig. 7.7. Fonts and font families.

12-Point Text Fonts

Helvetica
Bookman
Times
Palatino
Arial

12-Point Display Fonts

Avant Garde
Desdemona
Mistral
Centaur
Bauhaus 93

Sans Serif Type Faces

Arial
Arial Narrow
Avant Garde
Century Gothic
Chicago
Geneva
Helvetica

Serif Type Faces

Book Antigua
Bookman
Bookman Old Style
Boston
Century Schoolbook
Courier
New Century Schoolbook
New York
Palatino
Times

7.8 Use type sizes appropriate for the audience and the amount of reading to be done. Be consistent in their use.

Type size is a matter of courtesy to the reader of the material. Frequently, a designer decides on a type size on the basis of trying to fit as much material as possible on the screen. Remember that the reader is going to be between 18 and 24 inches from the screen. Any text presented on the screen must be large enough to be read from the furthest distance by the average reader. Figure 7.8 shows some examples of font size for Arial from small to large. The larger sizes are used for headings. The 12-point size is probably most appropriate for text, although 14-point size may be appropriate for younger audiences or people reading from over two feet from the screen. The 10-point size may be satisfactory for mature audiences reading near the screen.

Fig. 7.8. Type sizes.

Arial 8 point
Arial 9 point
Arial 10 point
Arial 12 point
Arial 14 point
Arial 18 point
Arial 24 point
Arial 36 point

Consistency, as usual, is important here also. Readers pick up cues from the size of the text used. Large sizes indicate headings. Smaller sizes indicate bodies of information. If the size changes from one screen to another, the reader may become confused about the importance of the information or the meaning of the size change. The sizes used for headings, subheadings and text should be chosen and maintained throughout the program.

Finally, it should be remembered that not all point sizes are equivalent. Figure 7.9 shows the relative sizes of several 18-point fonts. Do not assume that because you are using a 12-point font that it will be large enough to be read.

7.9   Use both lower- and uppercase text.

Although the use of all UPPERCASE letters may be appropriate for cueing an important word, phrase, or heading, it is easier to read words in lowercase or mixed case. Examine Figure 7.10. Note that both samples are the same text, although one is in traditional mixed text and the other is all in upper case letters. Uppercase letters provide fewer cues about their uniqueness, making it more difficult to recognize individual letters. Now that most computers give the options of italics and bold for emphasis, solid uppercase type should be used sparingly. (Special Note on Italics: Depending on the font being used or the size of the type, italicized text can be difficult to read on a screen. Be sure to test it out before settling on its use.)

Fig. 7.9. Point size comparison.

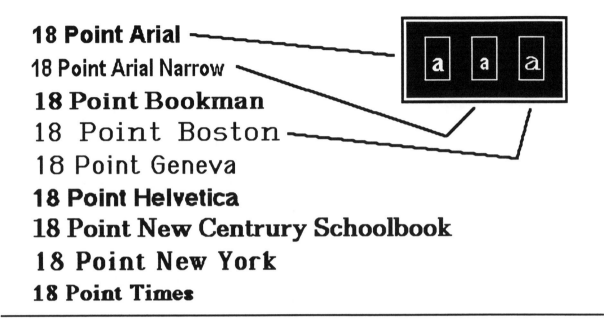

18 Point Arial

18 Point Arial Narrow

18 Point Bookman

18 Point Boston

18 Point Geneva

18 Point Helvetica

18 Point New Centrury Schoolbook

18 Point New York

18 Point Times

Fig. 7.10. Upper and lowercase.

WHILE ALL UPPER CASE LETTERS MAY BE APPROPRIATE FOR CUEING AN IMPORTANT WORD OR PHRASE OR HEADING, IT IS EASIER TO READ WORDS IN LOWER CASE OR MIXED CASE. EXAMINE FIG. 7.10. NOTE THAT BOTH SAMPLES ARE THE SAME TEXT, THOUGH ONE IS IN TRADITIONAL MIXED TEXT AND THE OTHER IN UPPER CASE. UPPER CASE LETTERS PROVIDE FEWER CUES AS TO THEIR UNIQUENESS, MAKING IT MORE DIFFICULT TO RECOGNIZED THE UNIQUENESS OF THE LETTERS. NOW THAT MOST COMPUTERS GIVE YOU THE OPTIONS OF ITALICS AND BOLD FOR EMPHASIS, ALL UPPER CASE SHOULD BE USED SPARINGLY.

While all UPPER CASE letters may be appropriate for cueing an important word or phrase or heading, it is easier to read words in lower case or mixed case. Examine Fig. 7.10. Note that both samples are the same text, though one is in traditional mixed text and the other in upper case. Upper case letters provide fewer cues as to their uniqueness, making it more difficult to recognized the uniqueness of the letters. Now that most computers give you the options of italics and bold for emphasis, all upper case should be used sparingly.

Fig. 7.11. Justification.

In this article, the implications of constructivism for instructional design (ISD) are summarized as five principles that integrate the affective and cognitive domains of learning. Distinguishing characteristics of the two. **Left Justified**	In this article, the implications of constructivism for instructional design (ISD) are summarized as five principles that integrate the affective and cognitive domains of learning. Distinguishing characteristics of the two . **Right Justified**
In this article, the implications of constructivism for instructional design (ISD) are summarized as five principles that integrate the affective and cognitive domains **Center Justified**	In this article, the implications of constructivism for instructional design (ISD) are summarized as five principles that integrate the affective and cognitive domains of learning. **Fully Justified**

7.10 Keep line lengths reasonable.

Readers prefer short lines of about 8 to 10 words or 45 to 60 characters long. Although there is some flexibility in this recommendation, Grabinger (1993) found, in studies looking a viewer preferences, that readers prefer shorter rather than longer lines of text. On a normal screen, this is probably in the neighborhood of the previous recommendation. When lines are too long, it becomes difficult to follow them across the screen; it is easy for readers to lose their position on the screen. Another reason for keeping lines reasonably short is that lines of about 8 to 10 words permit more line breaks based on syntax.

7.11 Generally, use single spacing between lines of text.

The amount of space between lines of text, *leading* (rhymes with *heading*), is closely related with the length of the. Readers prefer shorter lines that are single spaced, perhaps because this produces shorter blocks of text that appear to be manageable chunks of information. However, as lines get longer (more than 60 characters or 10 words), double spacing may be needed. The longer the line, the harder it is for readers to maintain their position on that line. Space between the lines helps the reader to maintain vertical position in the text.

7.12   Left justification is adequate in most circumstances. Use full justification only when proportional spacing is available.

Justification refers to the point on the screen at which a line of text begins (see Fig. 7.11). *Left justification* refers to text that begins at the left margin and flows to the right. The right margin is *ragged*; that is, it is not even like the left margin. The text in this book is left justified. *Right justification* begins at the right margin and flows left leaving an even right margin and a ragged left margin. *Center justification* refers to text that begins at the center of the line and flows equally in both right and left directions leaving ragged margins on both the right and left. *Full justification* refers to a line of text that begins at the left and ends at the right, leaving even margins on both the right and left.

Left justified text is easiest to read. Fully justified text is also common, but is slightly harder to read because of the artificiality of creating line breaks based on the end of a margin rather than on the syntax. Fully justified text relies on hyphenation and thus breaks phrases and words. In text that uses a nonproportional font (see Fig. 7.12), an effort to fully justify often creates rivers of white space running down the screen or page. This sometimes occurs with proportional fonts as well. Generally, people use the fully justified style because of an inherent sense of neatness, thinking the page looks better if both right and left margins are even. Although justified text may look neater, it is more difficult for the viewer to follow and read, so left justification should be used as often as possible.

MACROLEVEL DESIGN GUIDELINES

The macrolevel organization of the screen refers to the general layout. The constructs of organization and visual interest provide some rules of thumb for arranging text elements to create screens from which readers want to read and study. Instead of wondering about each individual text element, computer-based instruction and hypermedia producers can focus on arranging whatever elements they use to create organized, structured, and visually interesting screens.

7.13   Begin macrolevel organization of the screen by dividing the screen into functional areas appropriate to desired tasks and consistent with the knowledge level of the users. Maintain this level of organization with only minor changes throughout the program.

The designer-defined areas of the screen represent the tasks the screen will allow users to perform. Heines (1984) described the standard screen components as orientation information, directions, student responses, error messages, and student options. In hypermedia and multimedia applications, we can add areas for information presentation and illustrations. Not every screen needs a place for each of these tasks; it depends on the program.

Fig. 7.12. Proportional vs. nonproportional fonts.

Bookman is a proportional font.
```
Courier is a nonproportional font.
```

Times is a proportional font.
```
Monaco is a nonproportional font.
```

For example, look at the "Events" screen (top) in Figure 7.13. The control buttons and options are located in two areas. Options particularly relevant to that section in *Desert Shield* are located along the bottom. That functional area is separated from the other parts of the screen by a box and shading to unify the options. The titles are in large print along the upper portion of the screen. The main information area is in the center of the screen and is composed of three fields of information. Each field is separated from the others by a box, yet all are unified by the white background that serves to tie them together.

Now look at the lower screen in Figure 7.13. *Desert Shield's* "Help" screen shows a simpler screen with fewer tasks. However, the same basic style is maintained with a control ribbon on the bottom, the information area in the center, and titles and orientation information in the upper portion of the screen.

7.14 Create a separate area to indicate important status and orientation information: location, page, topic, subtopic, objective, and so on.

Because computer programs show only one page at a time, users must be continually informed as to what they are seeing and where they are within the program. With books and magazines, a user can quickly thumb back and forth through the pages. The mass or width of a book is an indicator of where users are in the book. Unfortunately, it is simply not possible to relate the concept of mass in a computer program. Therefore, a functional area that provides users with status and orientation information such as that shown in Figure 7.13 is needed on all computer screens. For more examples of this, refer to chapter 6.

7.15 Keep any controls (e.g., left and right arrows, section buttons) in a separate area. Throughout the program, consistently use the same area of the screen for the controls.

Options and control buttons should be located in the same functional area throughout the program. Use shading or boxes, or join the buttons together to set the options and control buttons apart from the other elements on the screen and create a sense of unity.

Fig. 7.13. Functional areas.

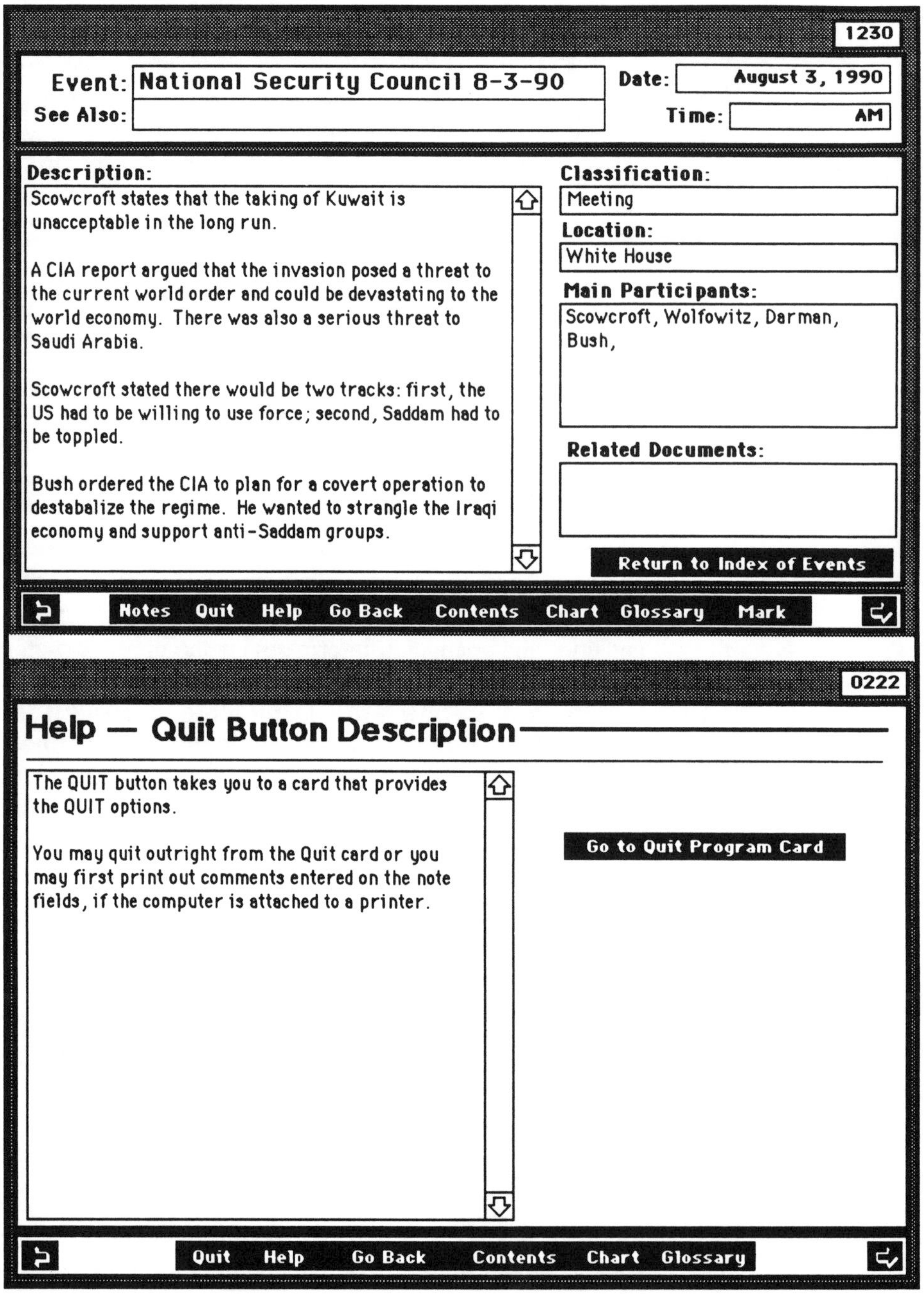

1230

Event: | National Security Council 8-3-90 | Date: | August 3, 1990
See Also: | | Time: | AM

Description:

Scowcroft states that the taking of Kuwait is unacceptable in the long run.

A CIA report argued that the invasion posed a threat to the current world order and could be devastating to the world economy. There was also a serious threat to Saudi Arabia.

Scowcroft stated there would be two tracks: first, the US had to be willing to use force; second, Saddam had to be toppled.

Bush ordered the CIA to plan for a covert operation to destabilize the regime. He wanted to strangle the Iraqi economy and support anti-Saddam groups.

Classification:
Meeting

Location:
White House

Main Participants:
Scowcroft, Wolfowitz, Darman, Bush,

Related Documents:

Return to Index of Events

Notes   Quit   Help   Go Back   Contents   Chart   Glossary   Mark

---

0222

Help — Quit Button Description

The QUIT button takes you to a card that provides the QUIT options.

You may quit outright from the Quit card or you may first print out comments entered on the note fields, if the computer is attached to a printer.

Go to Quit Program Card

Quit   Help   Go Back   Contents   Chart   Glossary

7.16 **Use graphic devices including boxes, shading, color, white space, and textures to organize the functional areas and set them apart from each other on the screen.**

This is where "art" comes in — the artful arrangement of graphic devices to create interesting and organized screens. Begin with simple pencil and paper sketches to rough in the main areas needed for the screen. Then, experiment with lines, boxes, shading, color, textures, and white space to create separate areas that stand apart from each other on the screen.

MICROLEVEL DESIGN GUIDELINES

Microlevel organization of the screen refers to structural techniques to reflect the organization of the content. The constructs of structure and organization provide some rules of thumb for arranging text elements to create screens that help readers to organize the content. Microlevel organization refers to how the content is presented within the overall macrolevel design.

7.17 **Reflect the substance and organization of the subject matter in the design of the display.**

Designers should consider how the screen can reflect the structure of the content to make it meaningful for the user. This is referred to as micro level organization. Generally, users prefer screens that use headings, directive cues, and spaced paragraphs to indicate the structure of the content and to break the content into chunks of information that are easy to read and/or study. For example, headings can be used as organizers and directive cues to point out important terms and phrases; increased spacing can be placed between paragraphs rather than traditional indentation; and comparisons can be shown in side-by-side columnar arrangements (see Fig. 7-14).

7.18 **Keep one idea per screen.**

Use the natural separation of screens to separate ideas into meaningful units. Large ideas may need to be separated into several screens, but make them discrete and separate units. There is no need to crowd screens with several ideas.

7.19 **Use headings as organizers.**

Headings of at least three levels are useful in organizing points for users. Main headings providing orientation can be placed in the area of the screen that serves that task. Subheadings referring directly to the information presentation should be placed within the text. Phrased headings, such as questions, can direct users' attention and facilitate learning.

Fig. 7.14. Directive cues.

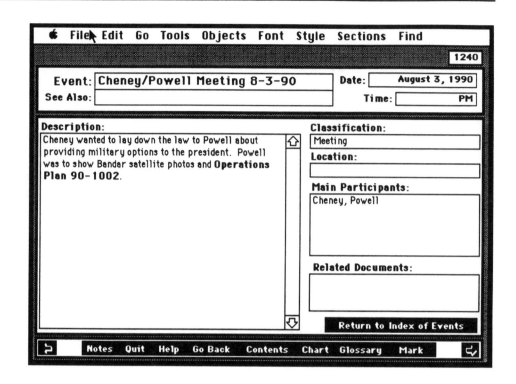

7.20 **Put paragraphs into bite-sized bits of information by single spacing within the paragraph and using increased space rather than indents to separate paragraphs.**

This gives readers manageable chunks of information because the information appears to be in bite-sized pieces. Unlike fiction, computer text needs built-in pauses between each piece of information so that readers have a chance to reflect on what they have just read before continuing to the next unit of information.

7.21 **Use indents to indicate hierarchically related subject material.**

Subsume related material under other material. Traditional outline formats or lists with numbers, letters, and bullets should be placed under the superorganizing concepts.

7.22 Group closely related items within a box or a common background color or shading. Use the same graphic devices, as well as white space, to separate unrelated or contrasting ideas.

Graphic devices provide a visually interesting way to link common ideas or to separate unrelated ideas. If shading is used, make sure it does not reduce the visibility of the text it surrounds. See Figure 7.13 for examples of this technique.

7.23 Use directive cues (i.e., bold, italic, underlining, inverse) to emphasize important terms or ideas.

Used sparingly, directive cues (see Fig. 7.14) such as color, size, bold, italic, flashing, shape, direction, brightness, underlining, uppercase, and inverse can facilitate learning by calling attention to (i.e., making more perceptible) important words or phrases. This technique should probably be limited to one to three items per screen. Flashing should probably never be used. It can be extremely distracting to users.

7.24 Set up comparison-contrast situations in a side-by-side columnar arrangement.

Columnar arrangements are particularly useful for both comparisons and contrasts because it keeps in view all the items being compared.

CONCLUSION

Good interface design requires close attention to student behavior and attitudes as well as system capabilities. The screen is the central point of the interaction between student and program; therefore, much of interface design focuses on the screen. Although an attractive screen requires both artistic talent and a good sense of organization, almost anyone can design appealing, functional screens by applying some common sense. A good place to start is with a design that looks useful to you. Alter it to meet the needs of your program.

REFERENCES

Cakir, A. E. (1980). Human factors and VDT design. In P. A. Kolers, M. E. Wrolstad, & H. Bouma (Eds.). *Processing of visible language, Volume 2.* New York: Plenum.

Christ, R. E. (1975). Review and analysis of color coding research for visual displays. *Human Factors, 17*, 542-570.

Christ, R. E. (1977). Four years of color research for visual displays. *Proceedings of the Human Factors Society 21st Annual Meeting.* San Francisco CA.

Foster, J. J. (1965). Commentary: Psychological research into legibility. *Journal of Typographic Research, 2*, 279-282.

Galitz, W. O. (1993). *User-interface screen design.* Boston: QED Publishing Group.

Grabinger, R. S. (1993). Viewer perceptions: Model and real screens. *Educational Technology Research and Development, 40*(1), 35-73.

Hartley, J. (1978). *Designing instructional text.* New York: Nichols Publishing Company.

Heines, J. M. (1984). *Screen design strategies for computer-aided instruction*. Bedford MA: Digital Press.

Kolers, P. A., Duchincky, R. L., & Ferguson, D. C. (1981). Eye movement measurement or readability of CRT displays. *Human Factors, 23*(5), 517-527.

Kolers, P. A., Wrolstad, M. E., and Bouma, H. (Eds.). (1980). *Processing of visible language, Volume 2*. New York: Plenum.

Lenze, J. S. (1991). Serif vs. sans serif type fonts: A comparison based on reader comprehension. In D. G. Beauchamp, J. C. Baca & R. A. Braden (Eds.). *Investigating visual literacy*, (pp. 93-98). Commerce TX: International Visual Literacy Association.

Mills, C. B., & Weldon, L. J. (1987). Reading text from computer screens. *ACM Computing Surveys, 19*(4), 330-358.

Rehe, R. E. (1979). *Typography: How to make it most legible (3rd ed. revised)*. Carmel IN: Design Research International.

Reynolds, L. (1979). Legibility studies: Their relevance to present day documentation methods. *Journal of Documentation, 35*(4), 307-340.

Reynolds, L. (1980). Teletext and Viewdata — a new challenge for the designer. In J. Hartley (Ed.), *The psychology of written communication* (pp. 207-224). New York: Nichols Publishing Company.

Riley, T. M., & Barbato, G. J. (1978). Dot-matrix alphanumerics viewed under discrete element degradation. *Human Factors, 20*(4), 473-477.

Snyder, H. L., & Taylor, G. B. (1979). The sensitivity of response measures of alphanumeric legibility to variation in dot matrix display parameters. *Human Factors, 21*(4), 457-471.

Tinker, M. A. (1963). *Legibility of print*. Ames IA: The Iowa State University Press

Tinker, M. A. (1965). *Bases for effective reading*. Minneapolis MN: University of Minnesota Press.

Tullis, T. S. (1981). An evaluation of alphanumeric, graphic, and color information displays. *Human Factors, 23*(5), 541-550.

Vartabedian, A. G. (1971). Legibility of symbols on CRT displays. *Applied Ergonomics, 2*(3), 130-132.

Wright, C., & Friend, L. (1992). Ergonomics for on-line searching. *Online, 16*(3), 13-27.

CHAPTER 8

User Support Strategies

Joanna C. Dunlap

Chapter Objectives This chapter is about user support, a part of the human-computer interface process that makes it easy for people to use our applications. In this chapter, we

- explain the concept of user support in the context of multimedia systems and

- provide a set of guidelines for orienting users to a program, facilitating navigation, keeping the user informed, and providing general support.

Need for User Support Hypermedia and multimedia applications are often highly complex owing to the flexibility of environments in which they can be used and the depth and breadth of information they make available to users. This level of complexity can leave users feeling confused and frustrated. Unfortunately, designers of hypermedia and multimedia consistently make a serious error. They forget or ignore what it is like to be a novice user of a program. For example, designers developing applications for Macintosh computers or MS-DOS computers running Microsoft Windows often forget to provide instructional support for users who have never used a mouse and menu-driven program. Because initial support is lacking, users may be unable to access the program's contents. This problem can be quite a disappointment for both the user and the designer. Regardless of how wonderful the multimedia program is, it is useless to users who have neither the tools nor the information to access the program. Therefore, providing this support based on the users' characteristics and determined needs helps to insure that users are able not only to access and use the application appropriately, but also to have the positive experience that results from using the program.

ORIENTING USERS TO THE APPLICATION

The next step after you determine a need for a multimedia application is to decide what the application's content will be, who will be using the application, and how you will present the content to those users. These decisions are different for every project you undertake. But in the majority of cases the users' need for support is the same: They need to understand the program's structure, purpose, and rules so they can more easily learn how to use the program effectively, efficiently, and without overwhelming frustration.

Starting the Program

The first area of support you need to consider is a way to orient users to the application itself. In other words, how can you, as a designer, provide users with the information needed to get them up-to-speed and ready to use the application?

8.1 **To provide users with a good first impression of your application, introduce users to the program by providing a title screen.**

First impressions are important, especially in computer applications. From the moment users open an application, they begin to learn about the program. When designing a multimedia application, think of the first few screens as a formal introduction, information that helps users begin to get to know your program. Opening the program to a meaningless, ambiguous, untitled screen does nothing to reassure users that they are even in the right program.

Title Screens

A formal title screen gives users confidence in your program and assures them that they are using a professionally designed product. When a user opens *Desert Shield*, for example, the first screen they see is the program's title screen (Fig. 8.1). *Desert Shield*'s title screen provides users with the name of the program, the copyright information, and all necessary legal and contributor information (see scrolling field beginning with "READ ME FIRST"). This title screen lets users know they are in the right place if they want to access the *Desert Shield* program.

8.2 **Immediately following the title screen, provide users with information regarding the purpose, structure, and rules for using the application.**

Users want to know as soon as possible whether using the program can fulfill their learning goals and objectives. After that, they want to know how to use the program. Therefore, you need to provide users with screens that contain information regarding the application's purpose, structure, and rules. If they know this information up front, they can confidently use the program because they know what to expect.

Program Functions

Following the title screen in *Desert Shield* are two additional information screens. First, there is a Program Function screen (Fig. 8.2) that describes the purpose of *Desert Shield*, explaining the content and the sections. It also provides

Fig. 8.1. *Desert Shield* **title screen.**

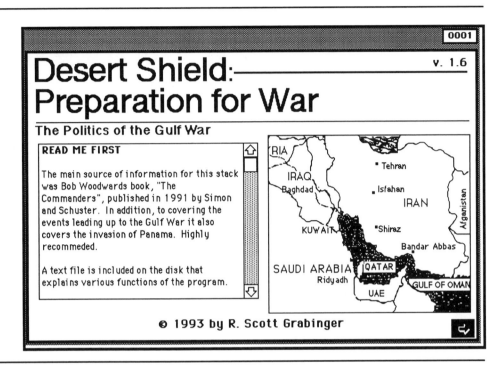

a brief overview about program use and a brief description of the program's special features. Following the Program Function screen, *Desert Shield* has a Program Instruction screen that provides users with more details about using the program's main features (Fig. 8.2).

Two important design heuristics should be noted at this point. First, even though *Desert Shield* uses only two screens to present users with an explanation of the program's purpose, structure, and rules, this information is presented clearly and completely. If you want to avoid boring users and insure that they will probably read the information, keep the orientation screens down to a bare minimum. Write concisely.

The second heuristic involves giving users the ability to bypass orientation screens that present them with information they do not need. Often, users will use a particular application more than once. The first several times, they may want to refresh their memories regarding how to use the program, but after they gain more experience, those screens cease to be useful. *Desert Shield*'s Program Function screen (Fig. 8.2) lets users skip these orientation instructions and jump directly to the Contents screen by clicking on a button at the bottom of the screen.

Fig. 8.2. *Desert Shield* program objectives and operation screens.

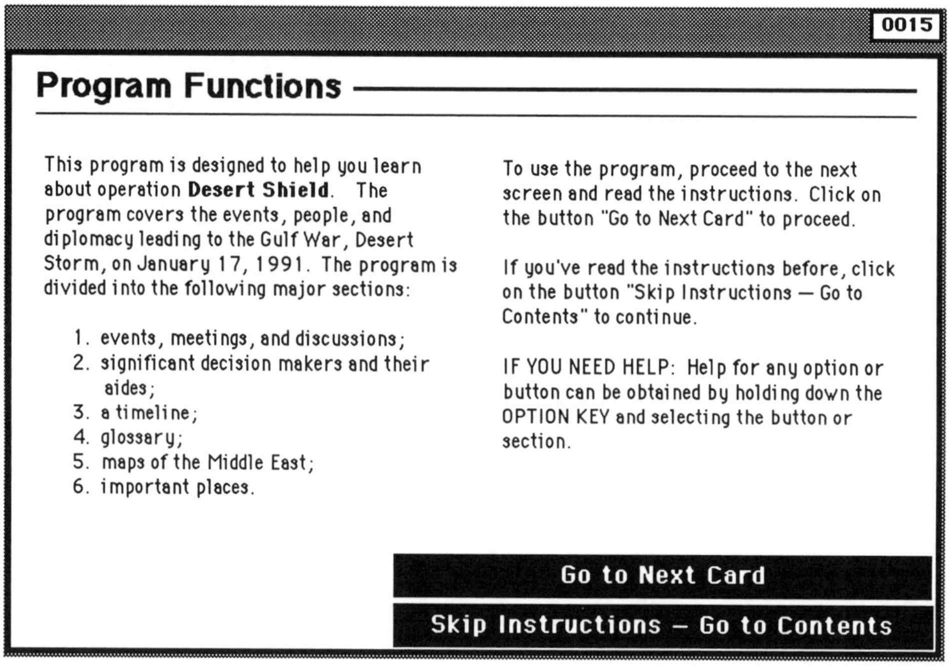

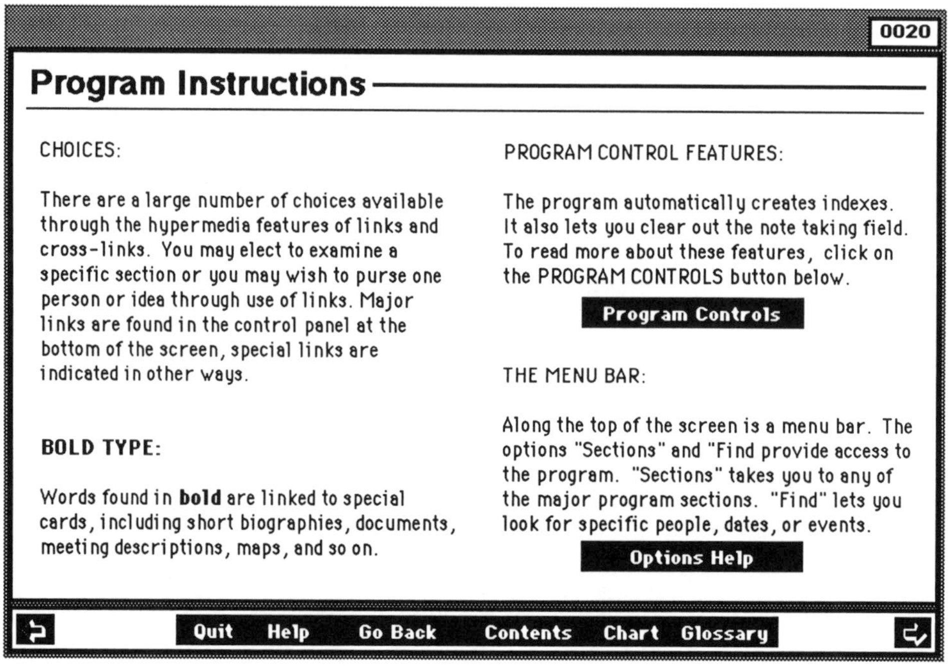

`0015`

Program Functions ────────────────

This program is designed to help you learn about operation **Desert Shield**. The program covers the events, people, and diplomacy leading to the Gulf War, Desert Storm, on January 17, 1991. The program is divided into the following major sections:

1. events, meetings, and discussions;
2. significant decision makers and their aides;
3. a timeline;
4. glossary;
5. maps of the Middle East;
6. important places.

To use the program, proceed to the next screen and read the instructions. Click on the button "Go to Next Card" to proceed.

If you've read the instructions before, click on the button "Skip Instructions — Go to Contents" to continue.

IF YOU NEED HELP: Help for any option or button can be obtained by holding down the OPTION KEY and selecting the button or section.

Go to Next Card

Skip Instructions — Go to Contents

`0020`

Program Instructions ────────────────

CHOICES:

There are a large number of choices available through the hypermedia features of links and cross-links. You may elect to examine a specific section or you may wish to purse one person or idea through use of links. Major links are found in the control panel at the bottom of the screen, special links are indicated in other ways.

BOLD TYPE:

Words found in **bold** are linked to special cards, including short biographies, documents, meeting descriptions, maps, and so on.

PROGRAM CONTROL FEATURES:

The program automatically creates indexes. It also lets you clear out the note taking field. To read more about these features, click on the PROGRAM CONTROLS button below.

Program Controls

THE MENU BAR:

Along the top of the screen is a menu bar. The options "Sections" and "Find" provide access to the program. "Sections" takes you to any of the major program sections. "Find" lets you look for specific people, dates, or events.

Options Help

Quit Help Go Back Contents Chart Glossary

8.3 **If you anticipate users who are unfamiliar with a certain aspect of computer use (e.g., using a mouse or pull-down menus), build prerequisite instructions into the application.**

Depending on the needs of your users, it may be necessary to provide some preliminary instruction about how to use the computer before they reach the meat of the application. For example, you may need to introduce users to using a mouse. This type of prerequisite instruction is not needed by all users. Be sure to provide experienced computer users with a way to skip such instruction.

8.4 **To avoid early boredom, get users involved in the application as quickly as possible.**

Because most people learn best by doing, early interaction is important in getting users familiar with using the program. Even if the interaction is as simple as clicking on a button to get to the next screen or having users choose menu items, it is important to create some level of interaction to keep users motivated and interested and to give them an early feeling of accomplishment (something which is especially important for novice users). Because early interaction is so important, asking users to control the program's movement is better than having the initial screens provide an animated display of the information that users are supposed to just sit back and read.

8.5 **If the application has several sections (two or more), use a table of contents as a reference point for the program.**

Multimedia applications often contain a lot of information. To successfully use an application, users have to know how that information is organized and where it is in the program. A table of contents is an excellent device for orienting or introducing users to the way the content is organized and divided into sections. By referring to a table of contents, users can get the gist of what types of information are available to them. A table of contents also gives users a starting point from which to pursue specific information that will help them to meet their learning goals and objectives. *Desert Shield* uses a table of contents as a reference point for users. It acts like a standard main menu and is the method by which users access the different sections of the program (Fig. 8.3).

FACILITATING NAVIGATION

Navigation tools help users to access information contained in hypermedia and multimedia applications. Depending on the size and functionality of an application, these tools range from simple left and right arrow keys for moving through screens of information organized linearly to a more complex and flexible system of menus, hot text, and buttons that let users move relationally and elaboratively through screens of information (refer to chapter 7 for a more detailed discussion of links and navigation.) The following design guidelines present suggestions for using navigational elements to help users access the information they want and

Fig. 8.3. Table of Contents screen.

```
                                                              0050
  Contents─────────────────────────────────────────
   Choose one of the sections to begin your exploration of DESERT SHIELD.
   Remember, numerous cross-links among sections are available.


     ○ People

     ○ Events

     ○ Political Maps

     ○ Timeline              ○ Help Sections

     ○ Documents             ○ Indexes

     ○ Glossary              ○ Program Charts

     ○ Places                ○ Program Controls


   ↵      Quit   Help    Go Back   Contents   Chart  Glossary    ⤵
```

need (such as the use of menus, program networks and maps, metaphors, textual reminders, screen and section names, and "you are here" and progress indicators).

8.6   Make menus accessible to users regardless of their position in the program. Strive for the "two-click" rule.

Two-Click Rule   The "two-click" rule states that users should make, at most, only two clicks (and preferably one) to go anywhere in the program. Instead of requiring a series of button clicks, use pull-down menus to make navigation more simple by creating menu items for each section of the program. In this way, users can quickly get to the information they need.

In *Desert Shield*, users have three means of access to the different sections. The first is the table of contents. The second is the menu bar. This menu bar has a selection called *Sections* that allows users to select the beginning of a section with one click. The third involves buttons at the bottom of the screen that let users have single click options to the Glossary and Table of Contents.

8.7   For more complex programs involving more than one level of information (e.g., main sections, primary sections, and subsections), provide users with a program network or map that, when accessed,

allows users to click on the area of the map they want to travel to regardless of its level in the section hierarchy.

Program networks or maps are powerful navigation tools because they give users a visual representation of an application's components and the connections between those components. These tools allow users to move to subsections within the main sections of the program. They are especially helpful when the application has a complex structure and connections.

Program Maps Although program maps are like menus and tables of contents in that users can use these navigational aids to access another section of the program, a network or map is a more appropriate navigational tool when the program includes several hierarchical levels of sections, such as a series of main sections, primary sections, and subsections. By using a map to navigate through a complex program, users can get closer to the actual information they want and need than they could if they used a pull-down menu or a table of contents.

For example, if you are developing a hypermedia application about the European Renaissance, the application's structure might require a program map that looks something like Figure 8.4. If you provide users with a pull-down menu, table of contents, or both, then you may be able to include only the first level of sections (e.g., English Renaissance, Italian Renaissance, French Renaissance, etc.) due to the lack of space in a pull-down menu or table of contents for the level of detail included in the program. Therefore, if a user is interested in learning more about the changing role of the monarchy in England during the Renaissance, she or he would have to choose "English Renaissance" from the pull-down menu or Table of Contents and then go through a series of additional, subsequent menu choices or steps to get to the subsection "Role of the Monarchy." Using a program network/map, the user could simply click on "Role of the Monarchy" and instantly go to that subsection of the program with no additional steps.

Desert Shield uses a simpler version of Fig. 8.4, called the "Navigation Chart" (Fig. 8.5). Users can move to another section of *Desert Shield* by clicking on the box that represents the appropriate section. For this feature to be the most useful, program networks/maps must be made available to users regardless what level of the program they are accessing.

8.8 Use metaphors to help convey an application's navigational options to users.

Depending on the content contained in your application, the application's purpose, and the structure of the content, you can use metaphors to convey different things. For example, HyperCard uses stacks of index cards to help users understand the functionality and feel more comfortable in using the program. This metaphor works because people are used to organizing information onto index cards and then sorting those cards into stacks.

Fig. 8.4. European Renaissance map.

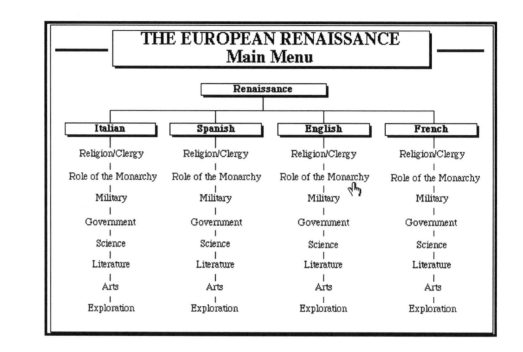

Fig. 8.5. *Desert Shield* program map.

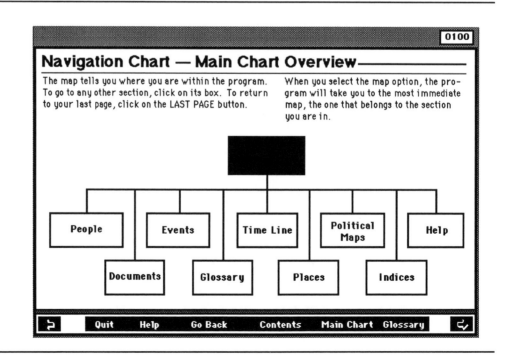

Macromedia Director, which allows users to create animated and interactive sequences, uses a movie metaphor to explain its functionality. If you are designing a program to provide information about Europe's historical sites, you might choose a road map or travel brochure metaphor to present the content. Information on painting throughout the ages might lend itself to a museum floor plan metaphor.

8.9   Prominently display the section and screen names so users know where they are in the application at all times.

Names that identify sections and screens within an application are an effective way to show users their location at any given point. For example, users need to know that they are where they want to be. If users of a geometry program click on a button that is supposed to take them to a screen showing them the formula needed to calculate the area of a hexagon, they want to know that they are on the right screen looking at the correct formula.

Users can also get so involved in what they are learning or get so distracted by an activity or a question from a colleague that they forget where they are and why they are there. Knowing what section and what screen they are on can help to remind users of what they should be doing.

Desert Shield prominently displays the section and screen names at all times. For example, Figure 8.6 reminds users that they are in the "People" section of the program and that the name of the screen is "Powell, General Colin L."

8.10   Progress indicators should be used as navigational aids when one piece of information has to be divided into more than one screen.

When users control their movements within a hypermedia application, they navigate as they see fit, based on their information needs and desires. This can become a problem when one piece of information is divided into more than one screen and the user is unaware of that division. If users are not informed that there is more than one screen for a particular piece of information, they may move to another subject prematurely. You can avoid premature movement by using process indicators to inform users that there is more information on the particular subject they are investigating. Use the *card x of y* strategy discussed in chapter 5.

FEEDBACK TO KEEP USERS INFORMED

Feedback keeps users informed of a number of things and comes in a variety of styles:

- When users click on a button, you could have it flash to let them know that the computer is reacting to the input.

- When users move from one screen to the next, you could insure that a visual effect takes place to indicate that the screen has changed.

Fig. 8.6. *Desert Shield* **People screen.**

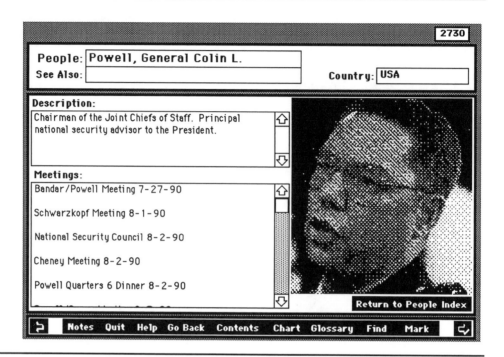

• When users move from one section to another or begin a time-consuming operation, you can have an hourglass or watch appear to indicate that the user must wait until the operation is complete.

• When a user is taking a quiz and gets the answer wrong, you could have a field pop up showing that the chosen answer is incorrect then provide a hint pointing to the correct answer.

• When users accidentally hit the QUIT APPLICATION button, you could have a message come up asking them if they really want to do the indicated action.

These feedback examples show ways in which designers of hypermedia and multimedia applications can help to keep their users informed during application use. This section of the chapter provides some design guidelines for using these examples.

8.11 Use interactivity indicators to keep users informed about their actions within the program.

Interactivity
Indicators Frequently, owing to the size and complexity of a hypermedia application, user-initiated actions, such as clicking on a button to go to a new section or the next screen, can take longer than users anticipate or expect. Unless you inform users when they have initiated an action, they may decide that they have made a mistake and reinitiate the action, or they may click on the button again. These actions can

become a problem when the program follows through on both user actions and moves users to a screen or into a section to which they did not want to travel. The worst-case scenario is one in which users end up lost in the program, missing important information because they lost track of where they wanted to be and how to get there. The solution is to give users feedback when they have initiated an action.

Desert Shield provides this feedback in three ways. First, when users click on a button, the button flashes so users know that their click was understood. Most button clicks in *Desert Shield* do, in fact, initiate movement either to another screen or to another section of the program. Second, when a user action involves traveling, *Desert Shield* uses visual effects to reinforce the fact that the user is moving from one screen or section to another. Finally, *Desert Shield* also provides users with feedback when an action requires more time for completion by replacing the normal cursor with a wristwatch that warns users to wait until the action is complete.

When using visual effects to reinforce movement through an application, be consistent, unobtrusive, and keep the number of different visual effects used to a minimum.

8.12 If the application includes test items, use immediate and individualized feedback to inform users about the status of their answers to praise them for correct answers and to be supportive in cases of incorrect answers.

This guideline shows the power of computers in instructional situations. When students answer a question on a quiz in the classroom, they rarely get immediate or individualized feedback. Feedback usually comes a day or a week later when the quiz is returned to the students. Often this feedback simply consists of the number of right or wrong answers. However, when students are quizzed within a computer application, they can receive instant individualized feedback based on their performance. In other words, users are informed when they have done something well (e.g., "Good job. You have mastered this section!") and when they are not quite right and need some guidance or a hint (e.g., "You are close. What about looking at...") Therefore, when users are asked to do anything within an application that asks or requires them to perform, a feedback feature should be provided that supports them during their performance.

8.13 When users make easily reversible mistakes, provide a forgiveness feature that allows them to undo their last action.

Quitting a Program Inevitably users accidentally select a menu item or click on a button that erases their work, takes them back to a starting point, or quits the application. When users can accidentally do something unwanted, inform them of their action and check to make sure that they really want to complete the action. This forgiveness feature gives users a chance to undo or cancel an unwanted action.

Fig. 8.7. *Desert Shield* quitting action.

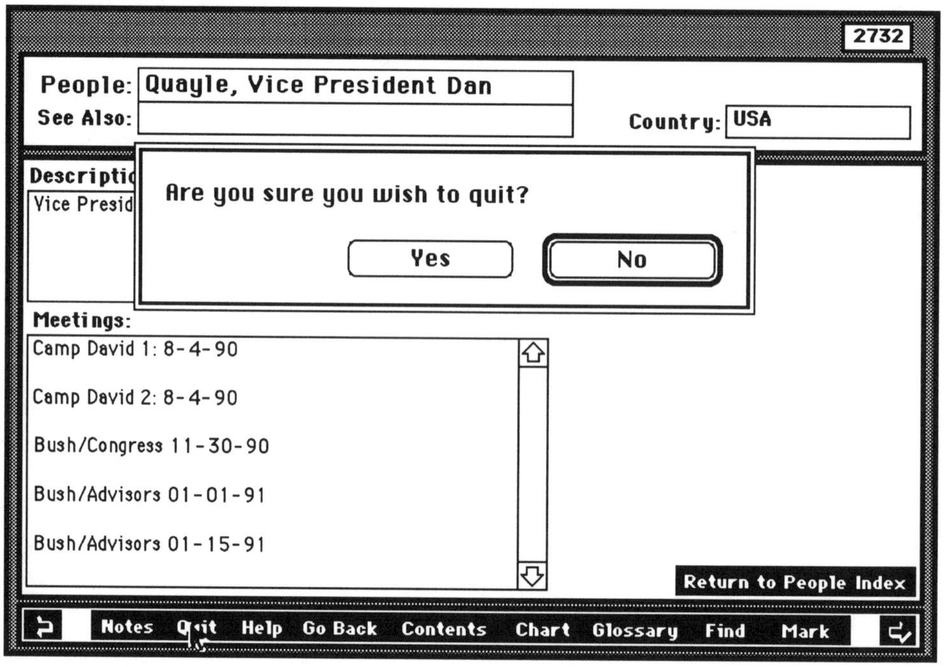

For example, when users click on the QUIT button in *Desert Shield*, they are asked, "Are you sure you wish to quit?" (Fig. 8.7). If a user clicks on the NO button, the action is canceled.

GENERAL USER SUPPORT

The following is a set of design guidelines for user support features that require customization for each hypermedia application. Keep in mind that for some design projects it is not necessarily appropriate to include these features.

8.14   Provide users with a glossary of terms that they can access at any time if the program includes new or unknown terms.

Desert Shield uses a glossary to provide users with definitions for terms that may be unfamiliar to them (Fig. 8.8). They can access the glossary from anywhere in the program via a GLOSSARY button at the bottom of each screen or by clicking on a "hot" word found in the text in **bold** type (Fig. 8.9).

Fig. 8.8. *Desert Shield* **Glossary screens.**

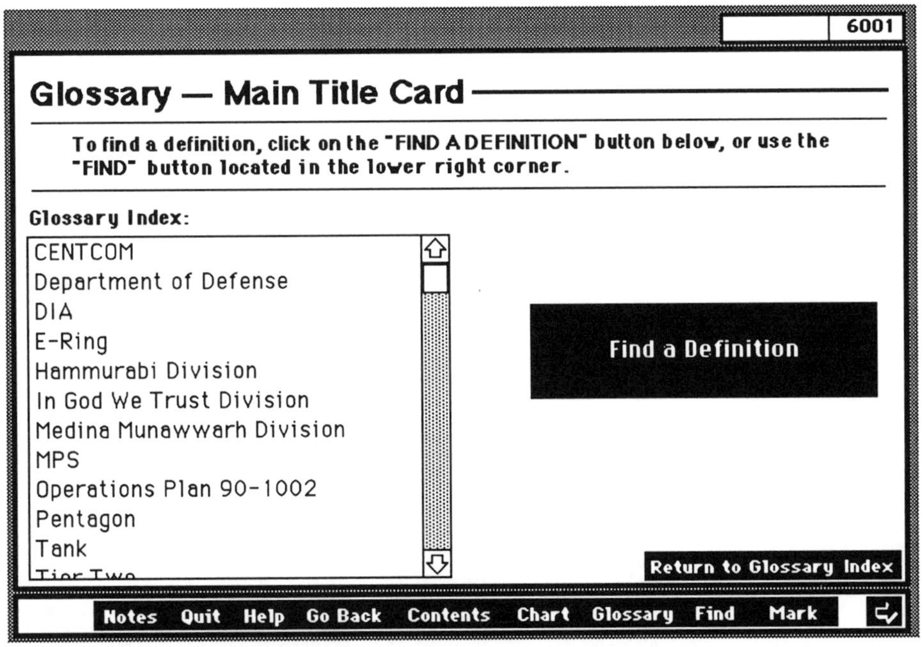

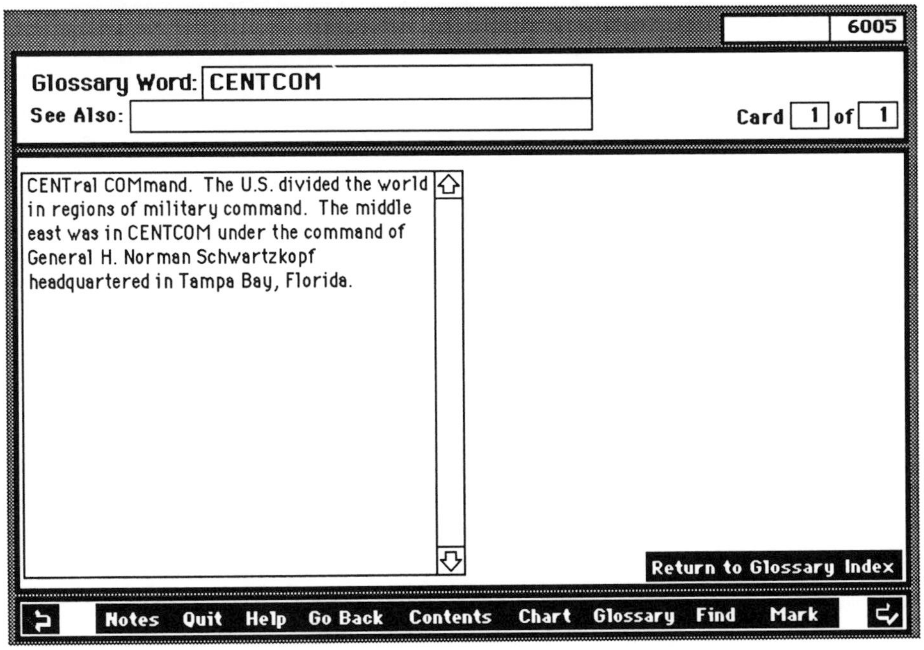

```
                                                                    6001

Glossary — Main Title Card ─────────────────────────

   To find a definition, click on the "FIND A DEFINITION" button below, or use the
   "FIND" button located in the lower right corner.

Glossary Index:
┌──────────────────────────────────┐
│ CENTCOM                          │⬆
│ Department of Defense            │
│ DIA                              │
│ E-Ring                           │
│ Hammurabi Division               │        ┌──────────────────────┐
│ In God We Trust Division         │        │                      │
│ Medina Munawwarh Division        │        │   Find a Definition  │
│ MPS                              │        │                      │
│ Operations Plan 90-1002          │        └──────────────────────┘
│ Pentagon                         │
│ Tank                             │
│ Tier Two                         │⬇                Return to Glossary Index
└──────────────────────────────────┘

       Notes   Quit   Help   Go Back   Contents   Chart   Glossary   Find   Mark
```

```
                                                                    6005

Glossary Word: │CENTCOM                                         │
See Also:      │                                          │    Card  1  of  1

┌──────────────────────────────────────┐
│ CENTral COMmand.  The U.S. divided the world │⬆
│ in regions of military command.  The middle  │
│ east was in CENTCOM under the command of     │
│ General H. Norman Schwartzkopf               │
│ headquartered in Tampa Bay, Florida.         │
│                                              │
│                                              │
│                                              │
│                                              │
│                                              │
│                                              │
│                                              │⬇        Return to Glossary Index
└──────────────────────────────────────┘

        Notes   Quit   Help   Go Back   Contents   Chart   Glossary   Find   Mark
```

Fig. 8.9. *Desert Shield* **hot text screen.**

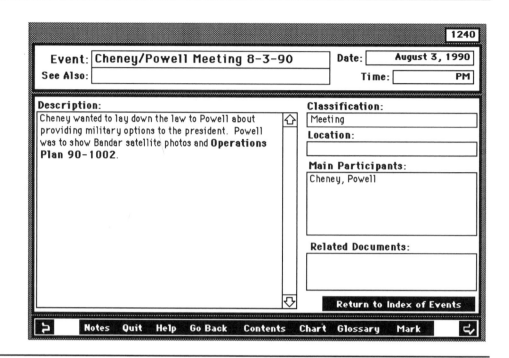

Hot Text When reading the description of the Bandar briefing held on 8-3-90, users may find that they are unfamiliar with Operations Plan 90-902. They can get to the definition by clicking on the GLOSSARY button at the bottom of the screen and going to the Glossary Index or, because the phrase **Operations Plan 90-902** is in bold type in the text, they can click on the actual reference in the text and instantly go to the definition entry in the Glossary (Fig. 8.9).

8.15 If the application includes any real-time or timed features, provide users with the ability to take a time out by including a pause feature.

For some applications, you may need to include an activity that requires users to react to stimuli in real-time fashion (e.g., flight simulations for student pilots). Other applications may require users to complete a series of steps in a certain amount of time (e.g., simulations involving the running of a business, performing scientific processes, and so on). In these situations an element of time is involved. With instructional applications that involve adhering to a set time limit, it is appropriate to allow users to take times out to gather additional information from elsewhere in the program or to review facts that might affect their performance. You can easily provide for these actions by including a pause or wait feature in your application.

For example, suppose you develop an instructional application that includes a performance section in which users must act as surgeons in operating rooms. You have included as part of the exercise a real-time element that requires users to respond to patients' needs in a timely manner. Because this application is designed to help users learn more about surgical procedures in emergency situations, you should let them stop the clock (pause the simulation) and refer to patients' case histories, textbook sections, or a program that describes appropriate procedures for different surgical situations.

8.16 All applications should include detailed help information specific to the application.

Regardless of the type of hypermedia application, users need to be able to refer to detailed explanations of different features of the program. You can provide this information by giving users help screens that they can access from anywhere in the program. The types of help screens included and the number of help screens needed for each application depend on the number of features and the complexity of the program's structure, navigation, and purpose.

Desert Shield provides users with detailed help screens that explain how to use each of the sections, describe the screen design, and remind users how all of the buttons work (Fig. 8.10). The ability to access this kind of detailed explanation for the different features of the application not only helps users understand more clearly how to use the application but also helps them to feel more comfortable and secure about using the program, knowing that they can always get help when they need it. This is the reason why you must consider user support and make this support part of all hypermedia applications.

CONCLUSION

User support is a crucial part of any hypermedia instructional application. Providing users with features that help them learn how to use the application, while at the same time giving them a sense of security in knowing that help is always available, can help to make the experience of using the application more meaningful, useful, fulfilling, and nonthreatening. Regardless of how great the potential learning outcomes may be from using a particular application, if users cannot figure out the purpose of the application, how to navigate through the information, when they have done something correctly or incorrectly, or how and where to get additional help when they need it, then the application will be deemed a failure because users were unable to use it effectively or efficiently. Including simple user support features such as the ones described in this chapter can help to insure that learners use your applications to meet their learning goals and objectives and have a positive experience doing so.

Fig. 8.10. Help screens.

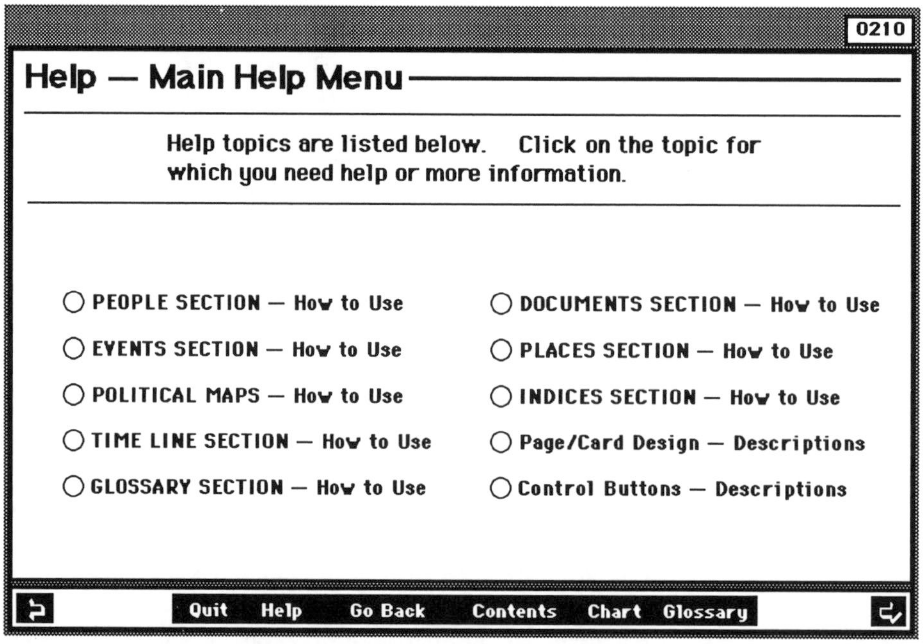

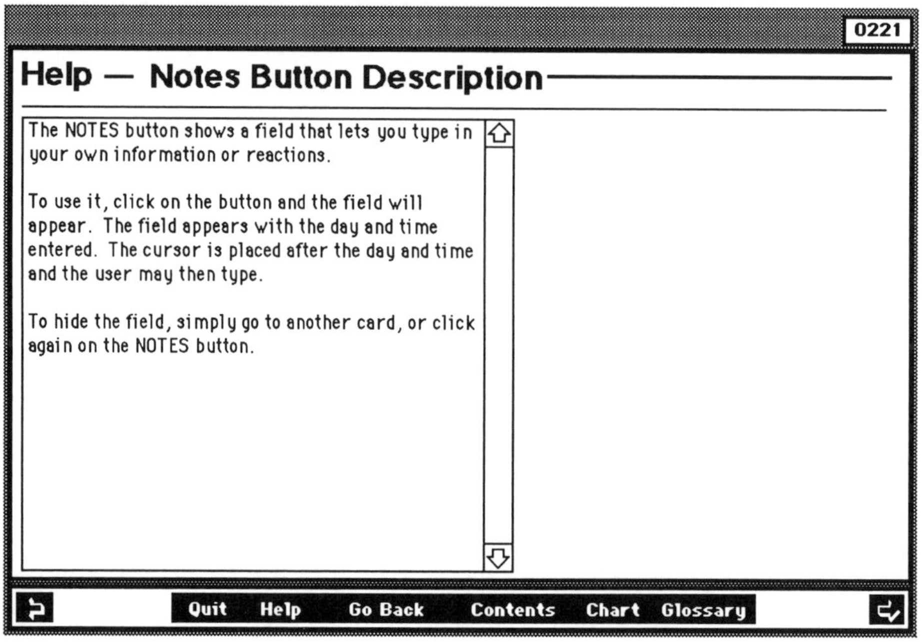

```
                                                              ┌────┐
                                                              │0210│
                                                              └────┘
  Help — Main Help Menu ──────────────────────────────

              Help topics are listed below.    Click on the topic for
              which you need help or more information.
  ──────────────────────────────────────────────────────

    ○ PEOPLE SECTION — How to Use        ○ DOCUMENTS SECTION — How to Use

    ○ EVENTS SECTION — How to Use        ○ PLACES SECTION — How to Use

    ○ POLITICAL MAPS — How to Use        ○ INDICES SECTION — How to Use

    ○ TIME LINE SECTION — How to Use     ○ Page/Card Design — Descriptions

    ○ GLOSSARY SECTION — How to Use      ○ Control Buttons — Descriptions


  ┌─┐     Quit   Help    Go Back   Contents   Chart  Glossary    ┌─┐
  └─┘                                                            └─┘
```

```
                                                              ┌────┐
                                                              │0221│
                                                              └────┘
  Help — Notes Button Description ───────────────────────

  ┌──────────────────────────────────────────────────┐┌─┐
  │The NOTES button shows a field that lets you type in││⇧│
  │your own information or reactions.                  │├─┤
  │                                                    ││ │
  │To use it, click on the button and the field will   ││ │
  │appear. The field appears with the day and time     ││ │
  │entered. The cursor is placed after the day and time││ │
  │and the user may then type.                         ││ │
  │                                                    ││ │
  │To hide the field, simply go to another card, or click││ │
  │again on the NOTES button.                          ││ │
  │                                                    ││ │
  │                                                    ││ │
  │                                                    ││ │
  │                                                    ││ │
  │                                                    ││ │
  │                                                    │├─┤
  │                                                    ││⇩│
  └──────────────────────────────────────────────────┘└─┘
  ┌─┐     Quit   Help    Go Back   Contents   Chart  Glossary    ┌─┐
  └─┘                                                            └─┘
```

CHAPTER 9

Evolution and Maintenance

Rose Marra

Chapter Objectives It is wishful thinking to believe that any application you create will not require further updates after it is finished. Just as a live lecture evolves as the lecturer gains new information and refines the old, so a computer-based environment evolves through revision and maintenance. It is the product team's responsibility to consider the environment's evolution and maintainability during the program's inception. The recommendations in this chapter are likely to produce a more usable product. If maintenance and evolution are not considered, then the shelf life of the product may be too short. This chapter addresses

- what a product team can do during product development to create an environment that meets the changing needs and desires of the customer with minimum expense and upheaval in a timely fashion, as well as

- design and implementation factors in software products that make maintenance and evolution as easy as possible.

DEFINITIONS

Product We begin the discussion with some definitions, starting with product. A product includes the software and the entire set of supporting materials and accompanying documentation, training, installation instructions, marketing and distribution strategies, and processes for product updates. Marketing is an important part of the product because it makes potential and existing customers aware of the existence of the product and updates.

All aspects of the product are part of the maintenance and evolution process. It may be true that the software creation requires most of the effort, but it cannot be isolated from the other parts of the product. For example, you discover a bug in a learning environment you have just made available to users. Although not a major problem, it cannot be ignored. The bug must be fixed and new software distributed to the customers. Your software development team fixes the problem and produces another set of diskettes or CD-ROMs for customers. If the team views the product strictly as the software, they may think that this is ready to ship out to customers-who on receiving it may have the normal, confused reaction of "Why did they send me another copy of this?" The team must realize that addressing the problem in the software portion of the product is not always enough. In this case, a release letter or installation instructions describing to the customer why they are receiving a product update may also be necessary.

Evolution Evolution takes advantage of new technology and design improvements to update functionality. Technology improvements include features offered in a new operating system or authoring software release. For example, if your hypermedia environment is authored in HyperCard and a new version of HyperCard is released that greatly decreases stack search times, you may want to redesign your application to take advantage of the new functionality.

Design improvements update functionality to better satisfy customer needs. Part of releasing a product is getting customer feedback and responding to that feedback appropriately. Inevitably there will be some portion of that feedback that engenders product changes; design improvements address these changes.

Maintenance Product maintenance includes changes in the product due to bugs or other needs for operation changes. A bug is usually thought of as being in the software, but it could also occur in product documentation or training materials. Other maintenance product changes may involve any other updates necessary to keep the product functioning for the customers. These could include software updates to support newly available hardware.

Note that both of these definitions have implications for product distribution as well as product change. Although it this may seem obvious, product redistribution — especially for a bug fix that the entire customer base needs to receive — is not a trivial process and involves considerable expense. On the other hand, updates made of minimal changes may be included in a new version release to new customers and as a value added update to existing customers.

The chapter proceeds with a section discussing reasons for considering maintenance and evolution issues, guidelines for designing products that are more easily evolved and maintainable and, finally, a summary of maintenance and evolution issues.

RATIONALE FOR EVOLUTION AND MAINTENANCE

The guidelines and activities associated with developing a maintainable and evolvable product may seem like additional effort; however, one of the goals of this section is to convince you that following the guidelines is worth the effort. Why, then, is the job not complete once your team has completed the design, development, and delivery of your product? There are both external and internal reasons for developing a continuing evolution and maintenance strategy.

External Needs   No matter how good you are, bugs will still show up in the product and are the most frequent reason for changing your product. Furthermore, serious bugs require a fix and redistribution to achieve and maintain customer satisfaction. Bugs often appear in the software, but there may also be problems in other parts of your product such as documentation or training-nothing is immune. Some bugs may be found by customers, whereas others may be discovered internally by your organization after the product is released. Although not all bugs have to be fixed-some can just be explained-part of having a maintainable and evolvable product is to have a plan in place for deciding how to deal with them.

Procedures for making changes in the product, whether to correct bugs or for any other reason, ultimately makes you more responsive to customers or learners. If customers want a change in the software, and your team has already acknowledged this possibility by developing a procedure for making changes and distributing them, you are more likely to go ahead and make that change.

An even more obvious reason for updates is that customers need and expect change. Even if your design and implementation process was very thorough in getting customers' input, their needs and expectations are likely to change. If the product is to be successful both in terms of customer satisfaction and sales, then the product must evolve as the desires of the customers evolve. We are not suggesting that you have to keep up with the customer's every whim (one of the guidelines deals with how to appropriately filter customer feedback). You must, however, be in touch with those whims so that you can make informed decisions on how to satisfy customer needs with the product.

Internal Needs   While customer-based reasons are certainly good ones for wanting to build an evolvable and maintainable product, there are reasons internal to your own organization that are also important. Although "keeping up with the Jones" may seem to be a bad reason for doing anything, in this case it is valid to suggest that instructional designers learn from what computer scientists know regarding product development (Bruce & Pederson, 1982; AT&T GBCS, 1993).

One benefit learned from computer scientists is that the same processes that make code more maintainable (i.e., commenting code, expert review of code, modular code, and so on) also help you to discover bugs earlier in the development cycle. Discovering a problem sooner means that it is both cheaper to fix and more likely to be fixed. If a problem is found later in the cycle, then more parts of the team are involved in fixing it and therefore the fix is more expensive.

For example, imagine that *Desert Shield* is almost ready to be shipped to customers. In fact, the software disk is actually being duplicated when suddenly someone discovers that all the find routines search only forward. Although finding the problem this late is still better than finding it after it has been shipped, it nevertheless requires scrapping all the duplicated disks, fixing the bug, testing (perhaps by an external organization), and duplicating the disks again. If the bug had been found earlier, only the software developers would have been involved, thus making it cheaper to fix.

Another internal reason for planning on evolution and maintenance is that there simply are not enough project resources to put all the desired functionality into the first release of a product. Just as Tessmer and Wedman's (1990) Layers of Necessity model applied to instructional design cautions designers that they may have to pick and choose which portions of the instructional design process to implement because of resource limitations, so it also applies to product development. Perhaps because of these limited resources, the first release of the learning environment does not meet all of the learning objectives. Perhaps the documentation is sufficient, but not completely satisfactory. These sorts of constraints are *likely* to occur, and all of them may lead your team to a planned evolution of the product.

A final internal reason for planned evolution and maintenance is that a product team cannot count on the same individual developers to be around to maintain and evolve their product. In a worst-case scenario, a portion of a product is designed by one person who does not follow commonly known team guidelines. If that person leaves, his or her portion of the product may be incomprehensible by anyone else on the team. It may be necessary to start over in order to update that portion of the product. The guidelines, which include suggestions for placing some level of procedures on your development process, can help your team avoid this situation.

To summarize, there are two types of reasons to design a product that is easily evolvable and maintainable. External reasons focus on satisfying customer needs and keeping up with other products and technology changes. Internal reasons make it clear that ignoring these guidelines can result in a poorly developed product that can be quite costly to maintain.

CREATING PROCEDURES

Before proceeding to the guidelines, we discuss the need to define procedures for product development that help to create a high-quality product that is also easier to evolve and maintain. The purpose of this section is to look at two things: first, how procedures are used in product development, and second, the level of procedures necessary for various products based on factors such as product size and the amount of new territory being covered.

People tend to have an innate reaction against procedures, which they associate with words such as red tape and bureaucracy. However, procedures also provide a structure for efficient product maintenance and evolution. They provide a formal structure to insure that the necessary communication and interactions take place to develop a successful product in an efficient manner. The procedures recommended in the following guidelines provide mechanisms for team members to use to get customer feedback during development and to check and balance each other's work.

Check and Balance By check and balance we mean that there must be a least some minimal procedures to insure that

- the sum of the pieces each team member contributes cover all aspects of the product and do not leave anything out (e.g., "Oh, I thought *you* were doing that!"),

- and that these pieces are consistent with one another in content, look, and feel.

For example, the consistency issue might show up in the documentation in which two writers contributing to the same user guide may independently decide to use different terminology. One writer may refer to navigation controls and the other to navigation buttons. This may seem minor to some readers, but it could confuse novices. Procedures can provide checkpoints at which the chapters are reviewed as a whole and thus prevent such inconsistencies.

Procedures help program development in several ways. First, procedures provide standards for coding styles. Second, procedures insure programmers' code compiles (unit testing). Third, procedures insure that a programmer's code can be combined with the other programmers' code (integration testing). Finally, procedures insure that all modules can be assembled to create the final product.

Several factors affect how many procedures your team has and the nature of the procedures. These factors include size of the team, expectations for revised releases, previous release history, and the amount of new territory being covered by the release.

Generally, smaller product teams may not require as many formal procedures as do larger teams. In such product development teams, much of what is accomplished via detailed documented procedures in a larger development team is done through informal communication. Even so, we argue that some documented process for designing and implementing the project, even at a high level, should exist if only for the purpose of getting the team to agree and adopt a process. Larger product teams, because of their size and inability to informally communicate project status, need more carefully detailed procedures set forth in writing.

A couple of exceptions to the above exist. The need for procedural changes may be uncovered during project retrospectives. A project retrospective occurs at the end of a development cycle at which time the team examines what went wrong (and right) with the development process and then decides how to change development procedures to prevent the same problems from occurring again. For example, a small team may have had prior experience with product development and run into particular problems. Perhaps documentation team members were having difficulty interviewing subject matter experts in order to obtain information needed for the product documentation. This caused the documentation portion of the product to be delivered late and in a less than complete state. In the next round, the team should consider putting procedures in place to insure that the interface between documentation team members and subject matter experts is agreed upon and that expectations from both parties are known. Note that this prior experience caveat would apply to all teams and not just to small ones. The same is true of the next exception.

More detailed procedures may be necessary when the team is covering new territory in the product development. This new territory may consist of new technology that the software must utilize (e.g., new hardware or a new operating system), a new set of customers to satisfy, or a new product development cycle that requires the entire development process to happen much more quickly than originally planned. Any time the team is facing a major new aspect to their development, they should think through and document via procedures how the new aspect(s) will affect the team and how to best proceed to produce a quality product.

The point of this discourse is not to delineate all the potentially necessary procedures. In addition to our brief example, you should refer to any one of the following sources for details on suggested procedures for software product development (Bruce & Pederson, 1982; Softky, 1983).

GUIDELINES

9.1 Create documented procedures for product design and development, product introduction, and new releases and versions.

A set of documented procedures put into place at the onset of a product development may reduce the amount of evolution and maintenance needed because of bugs and failure to meet important customer needs. These procedures formalize, to whatever degree your project deems necessary, the way the product is developed and put together, the frequency and means of documenting customer feedback, and the internal checks and balances for the components of the product. For instance, there may be a procedure that describes mandatory review of programming code by other developers or experts to make sure it follows certain software guidelines and practice. These types of activities can catch mistakes *before* they go out the door and thus reduce some product maintenance.

These same procedures can be applied toward product updates done for maintenance and evolution reasons. After all, maintenance and evolution activities may occur during a subsequent release of the product, and even if that release requires less work than the prior one, procedures are most likely still necessary to insure good product quality.

9.2 Create plans and procedures for new releases to ensure that software releases are available to satisfy customer needs.

Although it is nice to imagine that success and perfection are your only paths, you will have to evolve or maintain your program. When you plan your project, you should dedicate time after the initial release to evolution and maintenance. Some software houses call this field support, meaning that the product requires continued support once it is in the field and being used.

Whereas the maintenance aspect is unavoidable (i.e., if a problem surfaces in the product, then it must be addressed), the evolution of the product is more of a choice. Note that product maintenance does not always mean a new product release. A bug could be addressed via a minimal software patch (i.e., an isolated fix for just the problem and not any other code) or simply with a work-around document that describes the way to avoid the problem and what to do if the user does encounter the problem. Determining whether the team wants to issue a new release of the product may be based on current product sales, customer feedback, the competition's plans, and whether your team has future plans for another product to take this one's place.

However, the point of this guideline is that even if your team does not plan on a major new release of the product, plans for addressing at least minimal product changes must be in place in preparation for the possibility of having to perform product maintenance. Whether you are updating all of your customers with an entirely new improved product or simply distributing a software patch or work-around for an isolated bug, your team still must have the processes in place to contact and distribute to all customers.

9.3   Design and write code and all other aspects of the product so that it can be picked up and maintained by another person at any time.

Although it may seem easier to do so, it is not a very practical or safe idea to assume that the individual that starts designing or developing a portion of the product will be the one that finishes and maintains it. Thus, it is a good idea to proceed with the job in such a fashion that it can be picked up by another person. Several suggestions listed below can aid in such a transition and help to create product elements that are easier to read and maintain.

9.4   Comment computer code with explanations.

Although the developer may feel that the intent and action of the code is clear, another individual who has to take over, or possibly the same developer 6 months later, may not see it that way. Including code comments takes little time and avoids lots of confusion. Figure 9.1 depicts comments in a script from *Desert Shield*. Comments are preceded by double dashes (--).

9.5   Use descriptive names for variables.

Use names in your software that are descriptive. Although most programming languages allow cryptic variable names such as "x" and "y", names that describe the purpose of the variable, as in "feedback_score" have the same benefits as the comments described above. Code is easier to read and subsequently easier to maintain or evolve.

Figure 9.1 shows examples both of descriptive names and the use of letters including "x" and "y." Letters are used as counters or for short-term calculations or operations. Names such as "LogLine," "lastname," and "firstname" are used in operations that help explain the purpose of the code.

Fig. 9.1. Code comments in *Desert Shield* script.

```
-- TargetRecord tracks the buttons and fields clicked on and
-- cards opened. It is used solely as a research device to
-- see how people use the program. It slows the operation of
-- the program down a bit, so the default value is
-- disabled. The "Program Controls" card
-- in the help section lets you enable/disable this command.

on TargetRecord
    global LogLine        -- line number for fld TargetRecord
    global LName          -- last name of student
    set lockmessages to true
    put LogLine & ". " & the short name of the target & ", " ¬
    & the id of the target & ", ? ¬
    & the date & ", " & the long time into line LogLine ¬
    of fld Log of cd LName
    add 1 to LogLine
    set lockMessages to false
end TargetRecord

-- HideArrows is used to hide the left arrow on the first card
-- of a section and the right arrow on the last card of a
-- section.

on hidearrows
    show bg btn "left"
    show bg btn "right"
    put the short name of the first cd of this bg into firstname
    put the short name of the last cd of this bg into lastname
    put the short name of this cd into thisname
    if thisname = firstname then hide bg btn "left"
    if thisname = lastname then hide bg btn "right"
end hidearrows
```

9.6   Include a short document describing the purpose of all components included with the program.

All aspects of the product, code, accompanying documentation, and training should have a document or set of documents that give a high-level description of what that part of the product is intended to do and what it contains. For example, the documentation portion of the team may have a coverage plan that describes all documents delivered with the product and what they contain.

Although this may not seem like a significant document to describe, the coverage plan insures that anyone taking over the documentation for evolution and maintenance knows exactly what documents already exist and will not have to wonder if they are missing any.

For the software, such a document may include several things including a functional description of the code that describes what the code is supposed to do and how the interface for that functionality is supposed to look. A document that describes a high-level flow of the code is useful for providing information on how the code is structured to anyone who has to maintain the code. This information can be used later to verify that the code actually does and looks as it was defined.

9.7   Design and write modular code to make software updates less error prone, easier to implement, and less disruptive to the rest of the software.

Modular code is a chunk of programming code used for multiple purposes. The chunk is usually placed in one location and called on when needed. This usually makes the program run faster and more efficiently and saves memory by cutting down on repetitive operations.

Modular code performs two main functions. First, blocks of code are not duplicated throughout the body of the software because the same piece of code performs the same function for all of its parts. Second, the links between portions of the code are clearly defined so that each code portion or routine (sometimes called a function in various programming languages) has a clear definition of its inputs and outputs. For example, a code routine designed to sort a HyperCard stack defines its inputs as being the stack to be sorted and the field from the card to sort on (i.e., student ID number, or student age). Further, it defines its output as the sorted stack. The advantages of these aspects of modularity are described in the following discussion.

Modular code has several advantages. First, it is parsimonious. An example from *Desert Shield* regarding how the various *Find* menus are implemented illustrates these benefits. Although the program gives you the ability to "find" many different kinds of objects, each find does not have a totally separate section of code (Fig. 9.2). One section of the code implements a general search and find routine; other routines call it or ask it to do a find and provide it with the type of object to find and the particular name. In this fashion, only one piece of code actually has to implement this find function (versus five or six if they were all implemented separately). This also provides product consistency, because all the find functions work the same way.

Second, modular code makes updates (for bug fixes or other evolution) easier. If, for example, the design team wanted to change how the Find command works, they would only need to change one routine that does the find; if the code is not modular, then they may have needed to change many more lines and also run the risk of missing some of the changes and introducing an inconsistency or bug into the product.

Third, modular code makes concurrent or phased development possible, which may be a benefit when project managers are figuring out how to staff a product development team. The second aspect of modularity described previously, in which input/output interfaces between modules of code are clearly defined (even

Figure 9.2. Modular code: *Desert Shield* **"Find" operations.**

```
create menu "Find"
put "People" into menu "Find" with menuMessage "doFindPerson"
put "Word/Phrase" after menu "Find" with menuMessage¬
"doFindGlossary"
put "Date" after menu "Find" with menuMessage "doFindDate"
put "Place" after menu "Find" with menuMessage "doFindPlace"
put "Document" after menu "Find" with menuMessage ¬
"doFindDocument"
put "Anything" after menu "Find" with menuMessage ¬
"doFindAnything"
```

The following example shows one of the scripts, doFindPerson,
which is basically similar to the others created in the previous
routine.

```
on doFindPerson
  global PersonWord  -- temporary container for name searched

  -- The next routine checks to see if "help" is needed if the
  -- optionkey is pressed.
  if the optionkey is down then
    push cd
    lock screen
    go to cd "findhelp"
    unlock screen with visual effect wipe left

    -- If no optionkey, then the program looks for the name.
  else
    Ask "Enter the person you wish to find."
    put it into PersonWord
    if it is empty then
      exit doFindPerson
    else
      lock screen
      Find PersonWord in fld MainPerson

    -- If no one is found, then options are presented.
     if the result is not empty then
       answer "Sorry. Nothing matched your search. " &¬
       "Please try another synonym, use the arrow keys, ¬
       "or use " & the index." with "Try Again" or ¬
       "Exit Search"
         if it is "Try Again" then doFindPerson
         if it is "Exit Search" then exit doFindPerson
     end if
     unlock screen with visual effect wipe left
   end if
 end if
end doFindPerson
```

before they actually are completed), facilitates this concurrent development. Once each code module or routine is clearly defined in terms of its inputs and outputs, different software developers can actually implement the code. Developer A does not have to know exactly how the routine that Developer B is writing works internally so long as Developer A knows what that routine needs as inputs and what it provides as outputs. Thus, software modules can be written independently from others, which allows for increased flexibility in initial software development as well as in subsequent releases.

9.8   Design and write code so it does not depend directly on unique hardware and operating system details.

The purpose of this guideline is to produce code that is more easily portable to another hardware or operating system environment. Hardware comes and goes-it becomes obsolete very quickly. For your environment to continue its usefulness, it may be necessary to have other hardware platforms as possibilities. This may be as simple as making sure that your environment runs on several different Macintoshes or having an environment that works on both MS-DOS-based and Macintosh platforms.

9.9   Put in place and follow a procedure for getting customer feedback both during the design and development cycle as well as after the product is released.

If one of the main reasons for doing program maintenance is to increase customer satisfaction, then it is probably no surprise that you'll need to solicit customer feedback both along the way with formative evaluation during product development and after the product is released. The feedback you gather during the development cycle may influence and make changes to the product under development, but it is also possible that you may discover items that the customer would like to have that you cannot include in this release because of scheduling or some other resource issue. These items can be recorded and considered for a future release.

These evaluations and feedback-gathering sessions that occur while the product is in its formative stages are all variations of formative evaluation strategies and methods described by Tessmer (1993). (See chapter 13 for a thorough description of formative evaluation processes.) Once the product is released, some sort of summative evaluation should be performed to find out if the product is meeting its intended needs and if the customer desires any other improvements .

The formative and summative evaluations are likely to produce a lot of data, but gathering the data, as Tessmer pointed out, is only part of the task. No matter what mechanism or procedure your product uses, it must include a method to summarize the improvements or bug fixes and have them ready for consideration for the next release of the product. There may be yet another procedure for determining which changes actually go in the product. This is discussed in the next guideline.

9.10 Before adding new functionalities, make sure that these additions fit in with the overall product purpose, design, and style.

The process of deciding which items to include in the next release begins once customer feedback is gathered and synthesized. These suggestions can then be added to any items that the product team was not able to include in the prior release. Generally, items considered to be bugs must be included in plans for a subsequent release, but beyond that how do you decide? As in almost any product development, resources are likely to be limited, so you will not be able to do everything. Even if you had the resources to do all the updates you would like, the point of this guideline is to warn you against adding an improvement without first scrutinizing how it fits in with the overall product.

A suggested improvement may seem like a good idea initially, but each suggestion must be considered within the context of the entire product. The product, whether a hypermedia learning environment or computer-aided-instruction (CAI) program, has a purpose or a set of objectives it is designed to meet. Customers may realize this implicitly, but may not limit their suggestions to the defined product purpose. Although the team may decide to expand the product's purpose if they feel that it would be beneficial and blend well with the current design, such a change is likely to be quite an extensive undertaking. For example, in *Desert Shield*, perhaps a user requested that the program be expanded to include the ability to predict munitions supplies necessary for a particular conflict. Although this may be good for this user's needs (perhaps such an application would fit in well with the math unit this user teaches), it does not fit the overall goal of the environment which is to provide a database of information about the political process toward war. On the other hand, a suggestion to include transcripts of President Bush's press conferences does fit the environment's purpose and may be considered more seriously.

Once these types of decisions are made, the team may choose a variety of methods to place priorities on the remaining items and then determine which can be included in the release. A couple of possibilities might be to assign priorities based the number of customers who requested the improvement or determine priorities by the amount of revenue such a feature might generate. Of course each of these priorities must be compared to the cost of its development, and that cost must include all aspects of the product, not just the software.

CONCLUSION

This chapter discusses the need for developing a product that is both evolvable and maintainable. We make the argument that no matter how good your product is, there is always some aspect that could be improved and certainly always the possibility that some problem or bug is discovered and needs to be addressed. In either case, a product designed to be more easily maintained and evolved can respond to either of these situations more effectively.

Although we recommend the guidelines from this chapter as sound practice, we recognize that arguments might be brought against them. Just as instructional designers often meet resistance from upper management toward following all the steps in a particular model for developing instruction, product teams may also meet resistance toward implementing the guidelines suggested in this chapter. Interestingly, resistance in this latter case may come from both management and individual team members. Management may argue that these guidelines add cost to the product that is not necessary. Team members may feel that following the guidelines' procedures is too much trouble (i.e., the "bureaucracy" we referred to above) and does not add to the final product.

While we realize that a functional product *could* be built without following this set of guidelines, we do argue that over time the costs of maintaining and evolving such products will outweigh the up-front costs of developing and following the suggested procedures and guidelines. Products, no matter how high quality you may think they are, do have problems. If your team intends to be responsive to customer needs and satisfaction, then these problems must be addressed. Following the guidelines from this chapter can reduce the upheaval and expense of dealing with these issues.

Furthermore, we have argued that following these guidelines can in fact reduce the number of problems that surface in the product after it is released. Procedures facilitate finding product problems earlier in the development and make these problems cheaper to fix. In spite of these reasons, you may find yourself having to ease into some of these guidelines. If your team or some subset has prior experience in developing products, you may wish to examine what problems occurred previously and thus decide the which procedures from which your product could most benefit.

REFERENCES

AT&T. (1993). GBC System development process platform: Overview of the SDP. Privately available within AT&T (COMPAS ID 29446).

Bruce, P., & Pederson, S. (1982). *The software development project.* New York: Wiley.

Ege, R. K., & Stary, C. (1992, November). Designing maintainable, reusable interfaces. *IEEE Software.*

Softky, S. (1983). *The ABCs of developing software.* Menlo Park CA: ABC Press.

Tessmer, M. (1993). *Planning and conducting formative evaluations.* London: Kogan Page.

Tessmer, M., & Wedman, J. (1990). A layers-of-necessity instructional development model. *Educational Technology Research and Development, 38.*

CHAPTER *10*

Formative Evaluation

Martin Tessmer

Chapter Objectives This chapter is about formative evaluation of multimedia systems. In this chapter, I

- describe some basic front-end evaluation guidelines that should be followed by decision makers at the project's outset; and

- outline some formative evaluation guidelines that should be used early in the development of applications.

FRONT-END AND FORMATIVE EVALUATION PURPOSES

Evaluation Evaluation is the appraisal of an entity's worth. People evaluate multimedia to make decisions about its instructional worth. Evaluators may make these decisions, or the information may be given to decision makers. In many classic evaluation models evaluators furnish information to the decision makers (Tucker, 1993). In multimedia development the evaluator is often part of the design team that plans or produces the multimedia program, and thus is one of the decision makers.

Multimedia front-end and formative evaluation are two complementary evaluation measures because they help multimedia developers make two separate but related decisions about multimedia projects. Front-end evaluation occurs at the planning stage of a project, before it is seriously undertaken. Formative evaluation occurs in the developmental stages of the project, as multimedia systems are being both designed and produced. Its purpose is to identify changes that must be made to improve the multimedia program while it is still being developed. Front-end evaluation logically precedes formative evaluation.

Front-end Evaluation Front-end evaluation is a *process* evaluation. The development process itself is evaluated to determine if multimedia development should be undertaken and how it should be done. The evaluation weighs organizational and instructional factors to determine the worth of pursuing multimedia development.

Product Evaluation
Formative evaluation is more of a *product* evaluation in which the product, the multimedia program, is evaluated in its formative stages to determine how to improve it (Tessmer, 1993). Front-end evaluation asks the question " Should we do multimedia? " whereas formative evaluation asks " How can we revise it? " Front-end evaluation is for risk-management; formative evaluation is for quality control.

MULTIMEDIA EVALUATION NEEDS

Multimedia development has special evaluation needs because of its novelty and complexity. Multimedia development can be time and resource intensive. It may cost as much as $200,000 to develop a program (Hoekema, 1992), or it may take a design team several years to complete a project (Jones, 1990). Developing a multimedia project make take 200 to 500 programming hours for every hour of instruction (Merrill, Li, & Jones, 1990; Stone, 1993). While new multimedia prototyping tools such as *Authorware Professional™* have reduced programming complexity, there are other issues that make multimedia development a resource-intensive process:

- Many multimedia projects are new to a design team. They have never developed a multimedia product before.

- Multimedia development makes instructional design more complex than with other media (Jaffe & Lynch, 1989) because multimedia development offers an ever-expanding array of media, information, and instructional strategy options to incorporate.

- The integration of multiple-media formats in a logical and user-friendly interface is complex and challenging.

Multimedia can then be difficult to develop because it is a "cutting edge " technology that embodies a wide range of instructional and audiovisual features. Its cost and complexity mean that front-end and formative assessments are critical. The potential development costs mean that front-end analysis of project feasibility is especially important. The complexity and unfamiliarity in developing a multimedia program means that the product should be formatively evaluated early and often to insure its instructional success.

Techno-Love
Because multimedia is a cutting edge technology, some clients are interested in multimedia development for that very reason: They want to be on the cutting edge. Multimedia is sought for its current appeal rather than its instructional potential (Tessmer & Jonassen, 1993). Developers such as Rand Spiro have objected that most multimedia work has been driven by the power of the technology instead of learning or research goals (Jones, 1990). This motivation can lead to what Hannafin and Phillips (1987) called "technocentric" design in which the media features and presumed technological capabilities rather than instructional needs or outcomes guide the instructional design. Multimedia then becomes a solution in search of a problem. This "techno-love" creates another need for careful front-end

analysis. Instructional projects may be conceived rather to utilize technological features than to satisfy instructional needs.

FRONT-END EVALUATION QUESTIONS

As the previous section indicated, multimedia development can be time and resource intensive. As such, the importance increases that such expensive projects be successful if they are undertaken. This increases the need for a careful front-end evaluation of a multimedia project.

Multimedia front-end evaluation is an assessment of the feasibility of developing a *successful* instructional product, one that is both instructionally effective and practically workable in learners' environments of use (Tessmer & Harris, 1992). At the project's outset, decision makers should answer some questions about instructional intentions, learner and instructor expectations, and organizational support.

The instructional evaluation criteria concern the general and specific goals of the multimedia project: What do we expect students to acquire from using the multimedia?

10.1 Define the learning outcomes to be acquired from the program.

Learning outcomes are the learned capabilities acquired by learners from the instruction (Gagné, 1977). These include cognitive outcomes such as factual recall, concepts, procedures, or problem solving. Attitudinal outcomes may also be part of the project goals: interest in the topic, motivation to learn more, and reduced computer anxiety. The learning outcomes are the specific skills or knowledge that the developers or instructors hope students will acquire from the program and are part of a goal-directed multimedia learning environment (Hannafin, 1992) as opposed to a purely exploratory one without specific learning goals.

Problem-Solving Outcomes Although multimedia may facilitate the learning of any cognitive or attitudinal outcome, it is best used for complex, open-ended problem solving. Jaffe and Lynch (1989) found multimedia and multimedia applications to be particularly suitable for such ill-structured problem solving. Problem-solving outcomes often have no specific answer or procedure and require learners to investigate different data sources and create their own solution procedures. As such it may better to use multimedia's capability of creating a knowledge exploration environment to guide learners in creating their own knowledge. Thus, multimedia may well suit problem-solving outcomes such as developing a small business' budget or critiquing an editorial on an environmental issue. It may be less well suited for teaching procedural or verbal information outcomes.

Concept Learning Outcomes Integrated concept learning may also be a viable multimedia outcome. Knowledge integration involves the learner's synthesis of a wide variety of knowledge or perspectives around a single concept (Cognition and Technology Group at Vanderbilt, 1992). For example, learning the concept of abortion may involve investigating a variety of historical and professional opinions on the topic and experiencing audio and film footage of demonstrations and confrontations. The concept outcome involves independently synthesizing a variety of information from different audiovisual sources. As such, the concept outcome is a worthy candidate for multimedia formats. However, if the goal is for the learner to understand the basic concept and issues of abortion (i.e., how it is done, why it is politically sensitive) then a simpler textual or graphic medium may be a less expensive choice than multimedia.

Factual recall, concept learning (simple example identification) or procedure learning may be better achieved through video, text, or computer-based tutorials. The project planners should decide if another medium could accomplish the same learning with a smaller time and money investment. The question is not "can multimedia teach this?" but rather "could some simpler, less expensive media teach this?" As Janda (1992) indicated " Given the considerable costs associated with multimedia applications, educators should evaluate their use compared with alternative methods of teaching" (p.341).

For example, Tessmer and Jonassen (1993) evaluated a computer tutorial on insurance policies for its viability for being repurposed into a multimedia format. The content required little media other than words and simple graphics. The learners were to acquire specific factual and rule-based skills. Tessmer and Jonassen concluded that the program should not be repurposed into multimedia, but that it would be cheaper and more effective to invest in print job aids and a redesign of the practice and feedback segments of the tutorial. In this program, the intended addition of sound, color and animation would do little more than add some cosmetic appeal to the program that might sustain the learners' attention but add little to the explanation or practice. A hypertext system would not be needed for the program's linear teaching sequence, so multimedia development was not warranted in this case.

To determine the intended program's multimedia outcomes, project planners should convene to specify the project's learning outcomes. This may necessitate a preliminary task analysis of the topic by interviewing subject matter experts and instructors upon the topic. Above all, a specific outcome list must be specified in print, including both attitudinal and cognitive outcomes. Questions such as the following should be asked:

- Are learners to acquire skills in addition to verbal information?

- If learners are to acquire skills, are they open-ended problem-solving skills that require that learners to generate their own definition of the problem, method for solving, or solution?

- Are learners to acquire attitudinal outcomes such as interest, confidence, or independence in controlling their own learning?

- Should learners acquire metacognitive skills as part of the instruction? Is learning how to learn one of the goals of the learning experience?

If the answer is "no" to all of these questions, there may be more cost- or learning-effective alternatives to multimedia for the project.

10.2   Specify intended learning experiences.

Learning outcomes should be complex enough to justify multimedia investment. However, the learning experience may be the most important target of multimedia development. Although learning outcomes are the products of learning, experiences are derived from the learning process: They represent the journey more than the destination. Multimedia programs have targeted learning experiences such as

- helping students become independent thinkers (Cognition and Technology Group at Vanderbilt, 1992, p. 66),

- having students become editors and authors of their knowledge (Wilson & Tally, 1991, p. 1),

- enabling learners to create their own multimedia representations in order to experience knowledge construction (*Technology and Learning*, 1993), and

- making the learner integrate the knowledge of diverse disciplines and media (Trumbull, Gay, & Mazur, 1991)

Learning experiences aim at personal intellectual development over specific knowledge acquisition, at the process of learning over its products (outcomes).

The intended multimedia learning experience is often exploratory or generative in nature. As such it is contrary to didactic or direct instructional methods (i.e., drill and practice, tutorials) by which knowledge is given to the student. Such direct instruction can be incorporated into multimedia and may profit from its animation, database, video, or hypertext systems. However, direct instruction may be more economically achieved through means that involve other media or instruction. For example, a computer-based tutorial with a direct practice and feedback system may be better suited for a direct instructional experience, as may instructor-guided instruction or peer tutoring.

Focus Group   The planners must specify the program's intended learning experiences in deciding if they are worth the development effort or if the experiences should be revamped to exploit multimedia capabilities. To this end, front-end evaluators should survey decision makers and users about their perceptions of the learning experience.

A focus group may be used to evaluate the intended learning experiences by involving all project stakeholders (Morgan & Krueger, 1993). Hypermedia users are important components of the focus group. The users are the students who learn from the program along with the instructors who use it for teaching. Both learners and instructors have expectations for the instruction. If those expectations cannot be met in the multimedia product, the project may fail through lack of use of its product (Tessmer & Harris, 1992).

In a focus group, the decision makers and users compare perceptions, voice disagreements, and achieve consensus about intended experiences. The group determines if the users and planners have different perceptions of the intended learning experiences. For example, school administrators may commission a multimedia lesson for stand-alone objectives-based instruction, whereas the teachers may see it as a knowledge exploration supplement to regular classroom teaching. If there is a divergence of learning experience expectations, the difference should be resolved before serious development work is undertaken. If the differences cannot be resolved, the project should be abandoned.

10.3 Examine instructors' intended use of multimedia and hypermedia applications.

Instructors will have both learning goals and learning roles for the multimedia product. The learning goals are the outcomes and experiences described in the previous sections. The learning roles concern the type and amount of instruction the instructor will delegate to the hypermedia. Instructors' perceived roles determine if and how they will use multimedia (Tobin & Dawson, 1992). They may expect the program to complement their role as authoritative providers of knowledge (Cognition and Technology Group at Vanderbilt, 1992), or to supplement their traditional instruction (Zahner, Reiser, Dick & Gill, 1992).

If instructors see the multimedia program as an occasional supplement to classroom "business as usual", it may not be worth the development effort unless these expectations can be changed. If the multimedia program offers knowledge exploration and the instructor expects skill-based or didactic instruction, it may not be used at all or will be adapted to suit instructor needs (Apple & Juncyk, 1990). If instructor role expectations are not managed, the interest in technological innovation may subside (Aust, 1993).

As part of the front-end analysis, the evaluator must identify the instructors' expectations for multimedia use. This can be done by holding a meeting or focus group sessions with instructors who will be potential users. If a large number of instructors may be using the multimedia, a questionnaire should be used as a complementary data gathering device (Fig. 10.1) to precede the focus group. Based on the data gathered, the evaluator can then construct a user model of how teachers intend to use the multimedia (Silverman, 1992). The user model would outline the users' purposes and expectations. This depiction can then be used to compare it to the planners' intended learning experiences and roles for the multimedia product. It also can be used as the focal discussion point for the focus group session.

10.4 Examine student expectations for use of media.

Student expectations are often ignored in assessing multimedia feasibility, but their expectations may be as valid as teacher expectations for project success. Judging from prior computer-based-training use, students may expect multimedia to be intuitively easy to use or to be read in a linear fashion like a text (Horney, 1992). They may expect that they are to memorize the multimedia information they access, not integrate it (Marra, Tessmer & Jonassen, 1993). Unless encouraged or trained to explore multimedia resources, they may revert to simple reading or browsing strategies (e.g. Anderson-Inman & Horney 1993; Horney, 1992). As with instructors, student expectations counter to the multimedia

---

Fig. 10.1. Instructor intentions questionnaire excerpt.

I intend to use Exploring Weather! to (circle all letters that apply)

    A. supplement my classroom lesson

    B. replace my classroom lesson

    C. provide remedial learning

    D. provide enrichment learning

    E. be a free time option for students

    F. show audiovisuals to the class

    G. be a reference resource for me

    H. I do not intend to use it.

    I. I don't know at this time.

Comments:

---

program mean that the project must budget for training and orientation to proper multimedia strategies, or the program strategies must be redesigned to accommodate these divergent expectations.

Selected students can be interviewed to determine their multimedia expectations (Fig. 10.2). For example, several multimedia enthusiasts and skeptics might be chosen, or a combination of media sophisticates and illiterates. Because students may be unaware of their expectations from the program, a better strategy may be to observe students using a similar multimedia program.

Students' usage behaviors indicate their program expectations by showing what multimedia features they consult and how long they spend on them (Inman-Anderson & Horney, 1993). As with instructors a " user model " or synopsis of student use can be sketched out. The evaluator can then compare the expectations of instructors, learners, and project planners for discrepancies.

Development Support Even when the project goals and roles are appropriate for multimedia development, the project cannot be undertaken without an evaluation of the organizational support structure for it. As the director of a university multimedia laboratory, Jones (1990) indicated that "The most brilliant, original idea is helpless without infrastructure support" (p.20). The determination of organizational support should be part of the preliminary front-end analysis to determine how much time and money the providers will devote to multimedia development and user training.

Fig. 10.2. Sample multimedia expectations questions for students.

(See also Fig. 10.4, Learner Expectation Questions)

Answered through interview

1. How do you like to learn?

2. How do you expect to use this program?

3. (While using) Why did you make that choice?

4. (After using) What did you gain from this?

5. (After using) What problems did you encounter?

Answered through observation of use

1. Are students using the program linearly?

2. Are they using it randomly?

3. Do students seem lost?

4. What multimedia features do they utilize?

5. Do learning products or behaviors reflect a purposeful use of the program?

10.5 Examine institutional support for cost and development overruns.

Multimedia projects are frequently subject to time and cost overruns, often as much as two or three times the original estimates (*New Media*, 1994; Whitten, 1992). In particular, the first multimedia project for a development team may take a long time to define and implement (Biggie, Buchanon, Hazan, & Kossiakoff, 1989). Overruns may mean that a project even comes to a standstill (Knight, 1992). As one computer developer said, "A computer-based instruction project takes three times as long as you planned. A carefully planned project only takes twice as long!"

Evaluators must determine whether extra time and resources may be available if the project requires it. Unless the degree of overrun tolerance is identified, developers run the risk of becoming involved in a project that may never be completed because of overruns or one that must later be drastically scaled as a result. This scaling down may result in reducing quality control tasks such as formative evaluation and product revision (Fig. 10.3).

If the overrun tolerance is minimal or ambiguous, the development team should consider abandoning the project. As another alternative, the project design may be revised by using the Layers of Necessity instructional design approach (Tessmer & Wedman, 1990, 1992). That is, the design plan specifies an basic layer of multimedia features for multimedia development. This initial layer is

Fig. 10.3. Diminishing resources effect upon multimedia development.

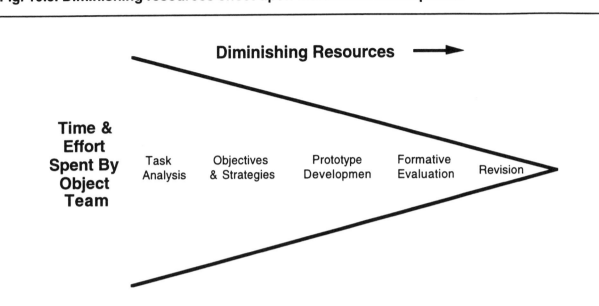

Diminishing Resources →

Time & Effort Spent By Object Team

Task Analysis   Objectives & Strategies   Prototype Developmen   Formative Evaluation   Revision

certain to be completed within project deadlines. Then, time and money permitting, a second layer of multimedia features are added to the multimedia program. Multimedia's modular organization of features and media suits such a layered approach, because a basic program can be embellished with additional features without drastically reprogramming the original components. To plan such a layered approach, however, the degree of overrun tolerance must first be identified.

The project evaluator should identify the support level of the people who control the project resources: time, money, staff, and services. If only one or two decision makers are involved, the evaluator can interview them together to obtain consensus. Steer clear of vague endorsements by avoiding such questions as: "Do you support multimedia development?" or "What is your attitude toward multimedia development?" Instead the evaluator should pose specific questions to the resource providers: "If the team director tells you that the project will go over budget by 3 months (or $20,000), what would you do?" Without making the providers feel that they are committing themselves to new time and money, the evaluator must determine their time and money tolerances.

10.6   Provide time and money for user training.

Multimedia technology may be alien to both the instructors and learners who will use it. The media, strategies, interface, and goals of multimedia may all run counter to the users' previous instructional experiences. Users may lack skills, motivation, or attitudes for using the system effectively (Trumbull et al., 1991). For example, a multimedia program's user control concept may be unfamiliar to users, who then will require training in self-directed learning strategies to effectively use the program. For all of its importance, user training may be undervalued or overlooked. In one survey of school districts, 42% of the managers surveyed "planned not to spend a single dime on training the teachers who were to effect changes through technology" (Editors, 1993, p. 30).

Multimedia projects often need to have extensive user training resources allocated to them. User training often requires more than a standard workshop or orientation session, particularly if the multimedia developers are interested in continued implementation of their product in the real world. Knight (1992) indicated that teachers require three training days to overcome technology fears and learn classroom media integration strategies. If the multimedia project cannot provide the resources for planning and implementing user training, it may not be worth pursuing. If resources are minimal or unknown, a Layers of Necessity project design may become necessary. The Layers approach would dictate that fewer multimedia features are built into the first layer of product development so that more resources are available for user training. Resources permitting, a second layer of multimedia features can then be added.

As part of the project feasibility evaluation, the evaluator must determine the time and resources allocated for user training. What do instructors and learners need to know to use the system effectively? What training should be provided? Will that training be supported? As with overrun support, the providers must be directly queried on the specific levels of training support that will be provided. Different from overruns, however, the evaluator should at least have a general training plan or approach in mind. This plan should involve interviews with the potential users to determine their levels of multimedia literacy.

For larger user populations a training needs survey can be distributed, but it may not provide the depth and clarity of responses that user interviews might provide. Either way, the evaluator must confirm not only users' technology use experience, but also their familiarity with being independent and constructive learners on the computer (Fig. 10.4). If a user survey cannot be conducted, it may be best to assume that the users are unfamiliar with multimedia learning.

FORMATIVE EVALUATION QUESTIONS

After the preceding front-end questions are answered, the evaluator and other decision makers should be able to evaluate the feasibility of the multimedia project. Is it worth pursuing, and if so, in what form? If the project is not rejected, the front-end analysis should inform the development team about

- learning experiences and outcomes that should be targeted,

- resources and support that are available,

- multimedia features that can be included within project limitations, and

- training strategies that can be feasibly implemented

At this point multimedia development begins, initiating the formative evaluation process.

Fig. 10.4. Learner questions to determine multimedia training needs.

---

1. Have you used a CD-ROM system for learning? If yes, describe how you used it.

2. Have you even used a hypertext system for learning? How did you use it?

3. What is the best computer-based lesson you have ever used? Why did you like it?

4. Have you ever been trained by someone to use an instructional computer program? How were you trained?

5. What do you like best about computer learning? What do you like least?

6. Have you used any instructional programs where you chose what you would learn? Describe how you used it.

Generally, multimedia is formatively evaluated the same as other media. That is, learners and experts are used in individual and group evaluations of rough drafts of the final product (Tessmer, 1993). However, as a novel, complex, and resource-intensive development medium, multimedia demands some unique formative evaluation questions and techniques.

Because of the costs and complexity of multimedia development, it is important that a *prototype* be evaluated as part of the initial multimedia design phase. A prototype is a working model that contains critical elements of the program. It is often an operating sample of the system's functions and interface. The representation of critical features is more important than the inclusion of all content or modules. In some cases, alternative prototype versions of the multimedia instruction are created. The alternative versions allow designers to compare different strategies or interfaces, and to prevent bias toward one version (Aust, 1993). At later stages, check-discs can be developed for the evaluation of a fuller, more finalized version of the instruction.

The prototype can be used to design the program as well as revise it (Tripp & Bichelmeyer, 1990). For example, a design team may build a working version of the instruction to help them visualize the interface and hypertext features they have discussed and to redesign these features via design group criticism, a practice common to architecture and engineering design (Zeisel, 1984). Along with the design team, instructors and students can be valuable participants in the prototype evaluation.

As with all formative evaluations, the prototype evaluation should investigate questions of clarity, ease of use, feedback quality and content accuracy. However, multimedia also contains certain attributes that are more indigenous to its symbol system and functions. Evaluation questions about these attributes constitute distinct and important evaluation criteria. Multimedia should be evaluated in terms of its interface, integration, and learning experience.

Interface Evaluation Chapter 8 discusses the concepts behind designing human computer interfaces. Here we discuss evaluating the effectiveness of the interface. The interface is the "boundary between the computer and human" (Reisner, 1987), the "location of communications and metacommunications" between the user and the system (Van Der Veer, Wijk, & Felt, 1990, p.133). Different types of interfaces can yield vastly different results in student learning (Palumbo & Lidwell, 1992). As the communications link between computer and user, the interface is a critical feature of multimedia usability and leaning effectiveness. Raskin (1987) indicated that one of the primary obstacles to successful multimedia development has been the failure to give adequate attention to the interface.

There are a wide variety of interface criteria. For an extensive list the reader is referred to Rauden and Johnson (1989). This chapter describes four interface evaluation guidelines that are critical to multimedia usability: interface transparency, metaphor, forgiveness, and informativeness.

10.7 Make sure the interface is transparent.

Interface *transparency* refers to the intuitiveness of the interface to its user. A transparent interface enables users to operate the program with minimal training and to navigate with less use of help systems. When using computer technologies, learners must divide their cognitive load between learning the content and using the software (Orey & Nelson, 1991). Consequently, effective interface design helps to reduce cognitive load on the learner (Oren, Salomon, Kreitman, & Don, 1990; Norman & Draper, 1986). The more transparent the interface is to users, the more users can concentrate on the multimedia content.

To evaluate transparency, users may be observed, tracked, and interviewed while using the multimedia prototype. Apple's Kathleen Gomoll (1990) evaluated interface prototypes via user think-aloud protocols and software use. A learning task was set for the learner; then his or her usage patterns, comments, and trouble spots could be recorded. For example, learners are required to write editorials on free trade agreements, using a hypertext database. As the learners use the program, the evaluator encourages them to voice their thoughts ("Now where is the photo file?" "All right, how do I compare that video to this speech?"). The evaluator notes the comments and also observes the learners' choices and behaviors (e.g. learners went back to the main menu instead of directly branching to what they wanted, they continually made choices and immediately exited from them, they spent a long time studying each screen's options).

For any interface evaluation, several transparency questions are important:

- How well can the learner use the program without training or helps?

- How well can they use the multimedia after training or orientation to the system?

- What helps are accessed?

- Where do learners feel lost or confused, and why?

- Are there too many features on the screen?

- Can some screen options be masked at a given point?

- Does feature placement reflect predicted frequency of use?

- Do icons depict the functions they allow and match the interface metaphor (Cates, 1993)?

10.8 Make the interface metaphor match the learner and learning experience.

Lakoff and Johnson (1980) defined a metaphor as "understanding and experiencing one kind of thing in terms of another" (p.5). The interface metaphor is an important determinant of system usability (Richards et al., 1990; Mitsch & Dubberly, 1990). The metaphor provides a mental model for the user of the multimedia system (Erickson, 1990) depicting how it is organized, how to proceed through it, and what activities it allows (Chiou, 1992). The interface metaphor is the theme by which the entire multimedia system is organized and represented. Using a familiar metaphor allows the user to bridge the gap between the unknown of program structure and content and the known of their own experience. Conversely, an inappropriate metaphor can be misleading or uninformative and hamper multimedia usability and effectiveness. For example, a museum interface may imply that the learner is free to search and explore information. A book metaphor may imply a more linear and structured search strategy, an office metaphor a nonlinear but task-oriented one.

For an interface metaphor to be successful, it must be both usable and informative. It can be usable only if its imagery matches both the learner's prior knowledge of the metaphor and the multimedia system's functionality. For example, Fig. 10.5 shows a multimedia program that has a video cassette recorder metaphor embedded in the overall HyperCard stack metaphor. The controls are designed to resemble VCR controls in form and function. For the VCR metaphor to be successful, the buttons must reflect all the speed and play capabilities of this card. At the same time, the speed and play functions should be obvious to users who have VCRs.

Both experts and learners may be used to evaluate the interface metaphor. Experts may be asked if the metaphor mimics the way the system actually works. Does it match the functionality of the system? Is the metaphor easy to represent with iconic or auditory representations (Erickson, 1990)? Is the metaphor consistently represented across different media formats? Is there a more appropriate metaphor?

Learners can be observed and interviewed on their reactions to the metaphor. Do learners understand the metaphor? Does the metaphor match the learner's experience? When shown the interface, what do learners say it suggests or implies about how they can use the instruction? Does it contain any misleading connotations? Does the metaphor match their visual/spatial skill levels? Does the metaphor capture the intended organization of nodes and media? When using the prototype, where do learners have problems using the system, and why?

Fig. 10.5. Multimedia program with HyperCard and VCR metaphors.

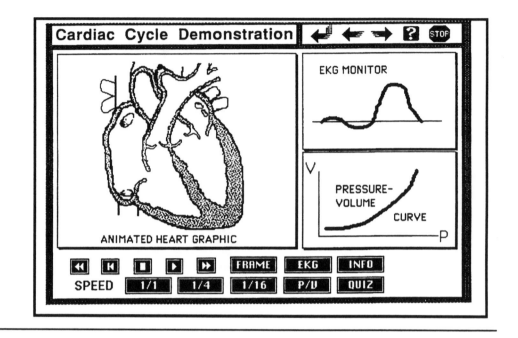

To evaluate the system metaphor, experts can be interviewed while using the prototype, or surveys may be sent to distant experts (Tessmer, 1993). Learners should be observed and interviewed while using a multimedia prototype. Because several plausible metaphors may be posed for any multimedia system, alternative prototypes can be constructed, each with a different metaphor for evaluation.

10.8 The interface should be flexible and forgiving.

Multimedia learners tend to jump back and forth across multimedia nodes (*Syllabus*, 1992). Forgiving interfaces allow learners to correct mistakes or (for multimedia) reverse directions in the program. The "forgiveness" is built into the command structure of the interface (e.g. its buttons or pull-down selections). The use of such forgiving interfaces has its precedence in forgiving commands such as "undo", "home", or "revert". Multimedia may be new to most users, and the aim of many programs is user exploration or experimentation. The confidence to experiment or explore is facilitated by forgiving interfaces.

To evaluate interface forgiveness, there are several questions to be answered. Can users undo what they create or choose? Do they feel free to explore or experiment with the program, or do they interact tentatively? Observing learner use can inform the evaluator on tentativeness. Audit trails can indicate the presence or absence of experimentation (Horney, 1992). User interviews will elaborate observations and audit trail data. CBT design experts can also be used to anticipate user problems that would require forgiveness functions.

10.9 Make the interface informative.

Whereas a forgiving interface allows users to eliminate navigational mistakes, an informative interface prevents them, providing learners with valuable information to help them maintain their orientation and sense of direction as they navigate through the program,. At its best, it is a feedback system on learners' navigation at any given point in their use of the multimedia program. Multimedia users may require considerable orientation and reminding during their program use. Informative interfaces alleviate such problems as being "lost in hyperspace." An informative interface often contains an advisory system and at least one map of learner choices.

Evaluating informativeness is determined by learners' use of informative features and the absence of navigational problems. Can learners tell where they are, where they have been? Can the program advise them on what topics or media they might consult next? Can it inform them of how they have done so far on exercises, questions, or projects? Does the feedback resolve learners' needs when they look for help or guidance? The more the multimedia system allows learner exploration and control, the greater the need for system informativeness.

Evaluating Multimedia Integration

"Integration" is a term that defines hyper- and multimedia technologies (Gayeski, 1992; Jaffe & Lynch, 1989). It is also a necessary feature of performance support systems and integrated learning systems (Carr, 1992; Sherry, 1992). Nevertheless, this crucial multimedia concept is rarely defined in the literature.

What is integration? It is the *seamless organization* of multimedia attributes within the program. It is a degree term more than a success term, meaning there are degrees of media integration. As the definition implies, there are two critical attributes to integration: seamlessness and organization. Multimedia's content and media should be evaluated by both of these attributes.

Seamless technologies are those that allow for transitions from major media or content areas with little user difficulty. From a holistic systems perspective, a seamless technology is one without the seams of discrete (and artificial) categories (Hughes, 1986). The effect of seamlessness is to minimize extraneous user thought or effort while using the multimedia system. This seamlessness allows for easier assimilation of multimedia information.

Seamlessness is a property of multimedia content, media, and interface. A seamless user interface is transparent and contributes heavily to navigational ease. Seamless content and media contribute to user knowledge integration, and thus are worthy evaluation targets.

An integrated multimedia program will resemble an integrated society: Its members maintain their individual characteristics but are not organized or isolated by them. Instead, they become part of a "neighborhood" of a common task, pursuit, or topic. To formatively evaluate multimedia integration, three aspects can be investigated: content seamlessness, content organization, and media seamlessness.

10.10 Make the content seamless.

Multimedia knowledge bases should be "deeply intertwingled" with multiple interconnectedness (Nelson, in Jones, 1990). The multimedia's content integration should be as seamless as its interface. A seamless interface allows the learner to access different knowledge components of the program with little labor or mental adjustment. Similarly, the content of the program should have a degree of seamlessness to it to allow for easier knowledge integration.

Seamless content is a characteristic of the connection between content areas, be they nodes, networks, or topics. The effect of seamless content is to allow the learner to absorb different content areas with as little confusion as possible, so that the learner may concentrate upon learning the content. For example, a learner who moves from an economics to a history text node about New York might benefit from a "bridge" (a short explanation of differences) between economic and political perspectives. Common terminology, writing style, and screen formatting across content domains are also helpful. Over and above interface design, these content aspects contribute to seamless transitions.

Software design experts may evaluate the program's content structure, but users evaluations are critical. Users should be observed and interviewed while they are using the prototype. The evaluation of content seamlessness will focus upon learners' understanding of disparate content areas as they access them. Do learners understand the similarities and differences between content domains accessed? Do they synthesize different content areas into their solutions or products. Can learners easily access different content domains or nodes (events)?

Test performance and tracking patterns may provide necessary but not sufficient information for evaluating content seamlessness. In addition, learners should also be probed in a one-to-one evaluation as they use the program. They should be queried as they make content transitions to determine whether they understand the similarities and distinctions between contents. Learners can also be encouraged to comment about why they made a choice and (after leaving it) what they gained from it. For example, Frau, Midoro, and Pedemonte (1992) have videotaped students using the system and analyzed their choices and other usage behaviors.

10.11 Organize the content for the desired learning experience.

The external content organization is the way central ideas are linked in the program. Content can be physically linked in a variety of ways (Parunak, 1989): as a line, hierarchy, or hypercube (Fig. 10.6; see also chapter 5 for a more detailed discussion of links). Each linking pattern may support a different learning experience. A hypercube lattice encourages open exploration and

Fig. 10.6. Content links (after Parunak, 1989).

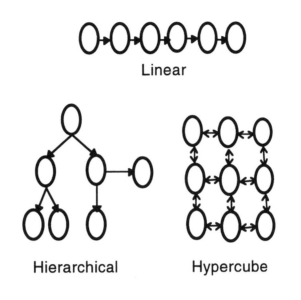

comparison of knowledge. A hierarchical organization suggests more specific access paths, but may maintain task focus or reduce user confusion. A linear content organization may encourage a more didactic or tutorial approach, but may suppress knowledge construction.

For example, a program designed for student information exploration could display choices of economic, political, and historical information in photos, audio, and text formats for each. If these nine options are all cross-linked to each other, the learner is accessing more of a hypercube structure. If the program first has the learner choosing between economic, political, or historical information in the first screen, then displays the media formats for the choice made on the next screen, a more hierarchical structure is being used, particularly if the student must return to the first screen to make further choices.

The physical content links should be determined by the program's purpose. If the learning experience is aimed at having the learner construct an expert's ideational schema, the content may be organized in the same way as an expert's ideational structure, which may be a hypercube or hierarchy with multiple cross connections. A thematic or topical organization encourages learner access to a restricted network within the multimedia, more like a hierarchy. A task orientation (the learner has a specific performance task) encourages learners to access whatever will help them accomplish the task, so a hypercube may be most suitable. Thematic and task organizations are used to avoid the problems of undirected searches (Richards, 1990).

Several content organization questions are paramount:

- Does the content organization facilitate the intended learning experience?

- Do learners engage in the intended information search patterns?

The design team can be the first source of content organization review. Upon construction of the prototype, the team compares the links between content areas with the intended instructional experiences. For example, the team can manipulate a prototype with a hypercube structure to determine if it allows for knowledge exploration. They can determine if the program structure allows them to access diverse information and media without backtracking through several other nodes.

The design team should first self-evaluate the prototype by comparing its functions with the learning experience design derived from the front-end analysis. This self-evaluation can include role-playing user actions, decisions, and confusions. If users are part of the design team, they should try out the prototype.

After design team review, the prototype can be used by learners to help designers evaluate the organization–experience match in the program. The multimedia lesson can be programmed to track learner's access paths and times (Beasley, 1992). Pathfinder programs such as *KnotMac* (Interlink, 1992) can trace learners' acquisitions of a mental model by measuring and illustrating changes in their conceptual network as the move through the multimedia program. Learners can be "posttested" by having them construct a concept map of their ideational associations to assess the degree of conceptual change and correspondence to a presumed "expert" structure (Nelson, 1992; Jonassen, 1987; Frau et al., 1992). Programs such as *SemNet* can be incorporated into the prototype to allow learners to develop these concept maps.

10.12 The media should be seamless in transition.

Content seamlessness helps the multimedia learner integrate different knowledge bases. Media seamlessness helps them to integrate different symbol systems. Media can be seamless in program navigation or cognition. A seamless navigation means that media can be accessed without learners having to use special commands or software to access it, and thus maintain concentration upon integrating program content. For example, a seamless multimedia program would allow users to move from audio to video components of the same content node by clicking on similar icons for each. A less seamless program might require several commands for accessing a video " player " program to see the video. The transparency and uniformity of the interface will contribute to the seamless transition.

A cognitively seamless transition helps learners to integrate such diverse information sources as photos, video, animation, and text. The seamless effect is encouraged by a program that stimulates integrative thought. Different media possess different symbol systems, which in turn tap different physical and mental processing capabilities (Kozma, 1992; Salomon, 1979). Many multimedia programs intend for learners to access different media while building their own knowledge base. Unfortunately, easy access to diverse media does not automatically lead to easy integration of the different symbol systems. Learners may require helps in understanding the information in a given media source and in relating it to previous information. For example, an on-line "notebook" that learners must complete encourages learners to extract ideas from the media and relate it to previous information, whatever the media source. A private database for learners to store their own audio and visual information encourages them to relate diverse media by task, topic, or learner need.

To determine physical seamlessness, learners should be observed while accessing different media in the prototype. Learners' mistakes in accessing the media or using it after it is accessed can indicate needed revisions in programming logic, interface design, or instructions in how to use the program. An on-line message button for comments can be used to record comments about access problems (Tessmer, 1993). Programming experts can review an interface prototype to determine if users could accomplish node transitions in a simpler manner if the program were redesigned.

To evaluate cognitive seamlessness, several questions arise:

- Can learners process each different media format offered in the program (video clips, hypertext, sound bites)?

- Can learners integrate information from different media into a common schema?

These questions can be answered in a one-to-one evaluation. Learners are interviewed while they use different multimedia sources in the prototype. During the evaluation learners are asked questions about what they derive from the media accessed, and how it relates to knowledge from other media sources. As a "posttest" learners can be given a task or question that requires the use of diverse media sources accessed, to determine if information was derived from the media accessed and if it was related to other media information. The lack of understanding or synthesizing diverse media sources may necessitate program revisions to encourage the extraction and integration of media information.

EVALUATING THE MULTIMEDIA EXPERIENCE AND OUTCOMES

As indicated earlier, multimedia development may be driven by both experience and outcome. One of the hallmark multimedia experiences is exploration; multimedia is designed for learners to explore the content and develop their own knowledge base (Linn, 1991). In other cases, multimedia may contain tutorials or other more didactic instructional experiences (Misanchuk & Schweir, 1992; Schweir & Misanchuk, 1993). As part of either kind of learning experience, the program may teach outcomes from problem solving or concept learning (Jaffe & Lynch, 1989).

The design team should have identified the learning experience in the front-end evaluation of the project, because it determines multimedia feasibility as well as its design. The subsequent formative evaluation of the multimedia prototype should determine if learners obtained the desired experience, and if the experience enabled learners to achieve the desired learning outcomes. For example, learners may choose more linear paths through the most exploratory networks (e.g. Horney,

1992; Marra et al., 1993), indicating that they may not achieved the desired learning experience even though the content and media integration structures allowed it. Then again, learners may access a wide variety of media and content areas in a wide-open fashion, only to subsequently demonstrate that they did not integrate the knowledge in a problem-solving manner. This lack of integration could mean that the exploratory experience did not enable problem solving learning outcomes.

The learning experience evaluation then has two main questions:

• Which learners are not deriving the intended experiences, and why?

• What learners are not achieving the desired outcomes, and why?

In a formative evaluation, the purpose of measuring learning gains is not to verify program success, but to identify program defects that inhibit learners from deriving the intended experience and outcome. The formative evaluation questions are intended to *improve* the success of the program by identifying weaknesses, not to *prove* its worth (Markle, 1989).

Learners should be observed and interviewed about their use of navigational aids, because aids such as maps and metaphors can actually hinder learning (Cates, 1993; Stanton, Taylor, & Tweedie, 1992). Audit trails can track learners' routes through the program to determine if their choices reflect the intended learning experience. Interviewing learners can clarify their perceptions of the learning experience and the outcomes they derived. Observing learners' job performance can determine if the knowledge or attitudes gained from the program have transferred to the workplace. Evaluation questions can be interposed into the program to assess learners' progress in integrating ideas, solving problems, understanding content relationships (Tessmer, 1993). Learners can construct knowledge maps that indicate if and how their knowledge structures evolved through the program (Frau et al., 1992; Jonassen, 1987; Nelson, 1992). Use of these divergent sources and careful evaluation of learner products and behaviors will indicate if and how learners failed to achieve outcomes as well as how the multimedia program can be revised to enable their achievement.

CONCLUSION

No instructional design project should be undertaken without a front-end evaluation of its feasibility, nor should any instruction be produced without expert and learner formative evaluation. Given its state of the art, multimedia necessitates a more thorough investment of each evaluation measure. Multimedia is a complex, if not bewildering, resource-intensive instructional medium to develop and use. As Mueller (1991) noted, there is a broadening gap between the capabilities of interactive computer systems and the ability of people to use these capabilities.

As with video, computers, and text, the technology was not *developed for* instruction as much as it has been *applied to* instruction. As an infant technology, multimedia development is still in search of its own research-based design paradigms. Multimedia development may be more art than craft or science, because there are too few case studies to create a craft's experience base and even fewer research-based principles than needed to make it a science.

Multimedia developers must be wary of commitment to development projects with severe time or resource constraints or traditional didactic goals. They must also depend on the comments and behaviors of their users to help them design as well as revise multimedia prototypes. The use of front-end and formative evaluation is not a drain of project development resources. It is a part of project development for instructional success, as determined by the risk management benefits of front-end evaluation and the quality control of formative evaluation.

REFERENCES

Anderson-Inman, L., & Horney, M., (1993) Profiles of hypertext readers: Results from the ElectroText Project. Paper presented at the annual convention of the American Educational Research Association, Atlanta.

Apple, M. W. & Juncyk S. (1990). 'You don't have to be a teacher to teach this unit': Teaching, technology and gender in the classroom. *American Educational Research Journal, 27*(2), 227-251.

Aust, R. (1993). Wide-area network resources for instructor education. Paper presented at the annual convention of the American Educational Research Association, New Orleans.

Beasley, R. (1992). A methodology for collecting data using IBM's *Linkway*: A multimedia authoring language. *Journal of Educational Multimedia and Hypermedia, 1*(4), 465-470.

Biggie, A.V., Buchanon, W. E., Hazan, P., & Kossiakoff, A. (1989). A multimedia rapid prototyping tool for the development of computer-assisted instruction. *Johns Hopkins APL Technical Digest, 10*(3), 246-254.

Browne, D., Totterdell, P. & Boyle, E. (1990). The evaluation of adaptive systems. In D. Browne, P. Totterdell & D. Norman (Eds.). *Adaptive user interfaces* (pp. 141-194). London: Academic Press.

Carr, C. (1992). Performance support systems — the next step? *Performance and Instruction, 31*, 23-26.

Cates, W. (1993). Making the most of imagery: Theoretical issues in selecting metaphorical images. Paper presented at the annual convention of the American Educational Research Association, Atlanta, GA.

Chiou, G. (1992). Situated learning, metaphors, and computer-based learning environments. *Educational Technology, 32*(8), 7-11.

Cognition and Technology Group at Vanderbilt. (1992). The Jasper Experiment: an exploration of issues in learning and instructional design. *Educational Technology Research and Development, 40*(1), 65-80.

Editors. (1993). Update: The latest technology in the schools. *Technology and Learning, 13*(5), 28-32.

Erickson, T. (1990). Working with interface metaphors. In B. Laurel (Ed.) *The art of human-computer interface design* (pp. 65-73). Reading MA: Addison–Wesley.

Frau, E., Midoro, V. & Pedemonte, G. (1992). Do multimedia systems really enhance learning? A case study of earthquake education. *Educational Training and Technology International, 29*(1), 42-51.

Gagnè, R. (1977). *The conditions of learning* (3rd ed.). New York: Holt, Rinehart & Winston.

Gayeski, D. (1992). Making sense of multimedia: Introduction to special issue. *Educational Technology, 32*(5), 9-10.

Gomoll, K. (1990). Some techniques for observing users. In B. Laurel (Ed.) *The art of human-computer interface design.*(pp. 85-90). Reading MA: Addison–Wesley.

Hannafin, M. (1992). Emerging technologies, ISD, and learning environments: Critical perspectives. *Educational Technology Research and Development, 40(*1), 49-63.

Hannafin, M., & Phillips, T. (1987). Perspectives in the design of interactive video: beyond tape versus disc. *Journal of Research and Development in Education, 21*(1), 44-60.

Hoekema, J. (1992). Hypercard and CD-I: The 'Mutt and Jeff' of multimedia platforms. *Educational Technology, 32*(5), 28-34.

Horney, M. (1992). Authoring hypertext: Issues and problems from experience. Paper presented at the annual convention of the American Educational Research Association, San Francisco, CA.

Hughes, T. (1986). The seamless web: Technology, science, et cetera, et cetera. *Social Studies of Science, 14*, 281-292.

Interlink. (1992). *Knot-Mac. Knowledge network organizing tool for the Mac.* Las Cruces NM.

Jaffe, C., & Lynch, P. (1989). Multimedia for education in the life sciences. *Academic Computing, 1(1)*, 10-13.

Janda, K. (1992). Multimedia in political science: Sobering lessons from a teaching experience. *Journal of Educational Multimedia and Hypermedia, 1*(1), 341-354.

Jonassen, D. (1987). Assessing cognitive structure: Verifying a method using pattern notes. *Journal of Research and Development in Education, 20*(3), 1-13.

Jones, R. A. (1990). To "criss-cross in every direction"; or, why multimedia works. *Academic Computing, 1(1)*, 20-23.

Knight, P. (1992). Factors to consider in evaluating multimedia platforms for widespread curricular adoption. *Educational Technology, 31*(5), 25.

Kozma, R. (1992). Learning with media. *Review of Educational Research, 61*(2), 179-211.

Lakoff, G., & Johnson, M. (1980). *Metaphors we live by.* Chicago: University of Chicago Press.

Linn, M. (1991). Multimedia as a personalized knowledge tool for knowledge organization. Paper presented at the annual meeting of the American Educational Research Association, Chicago.

Markle, S.M. (1989). The ancient history of formative evaluation. *Performance and Instruction, 29*, 27-29.

Marra, R., Tessmer, M., & Jonassen, D. (1993). Human computer interface and instructional design. Paper presented at the annual convention of the Association for Educational Communications Technology, New Orleans.

Merrill, M. D., Li, Z., & Jones, M. (1990). Limitations of first generation instructional design. *Educational Technology, 30*(1), 7-11.

Misanchuk, E., & Schweir, R. (1992). Representing interactive multimedia and multimedia audit trails. *Journal of Interactive Multimedia and Hypermedia, 1*(1), 355-372.

Mitsch, D. and Dubberly, H. (1990). Muddy media, or the myth of the intuitive. In *Multimedia use interface design*. Santa Clara CA: Multimedia Computing Corporation.

Morgan, D. & Krueger, R. (1993). When to use focus groups and why. In D. Morgan (Ed.). *Successful focus groups* (pp. 3-20). Newbury Park CA: Sage Publications.

Nelson, W. (1992). Adaptive multimedia systems: Possibilities for learner modeling. Paper presented at the annual meeting of the American Educational Research Association, San Francisco.

New Media (1994) Tips from the New Media INVISION Award of Excellence winners. *New Media, 8*(4), 16.

Norman, D. A., & Draper, S. W. (Eds.) (1986). *User centered system design*. Hillsdale NJ: Lawrence Erlbaum & Associates.

Oren, T., Salomon, G, Kreitman, K. & Don, A. (1990). Guides: Characterizing the interface. In B. Laurel (Ed.) *The art of human-computer interface design* (pp. 367-374). Reading MA: Addison-Wesley.

Orey, M., & Nelson, W. (1991). Using intelligent tutoring design principles to integrate cognitive theory into computer-based instruction. Paper presented at the annual convention of the Association for Educational Communications and Technology, Orlando FL.

Palumbo, D., & Lidwell, W. M. (1992). A computer-based environment to promote knowledge construction: The problems and promises of multimedia. Paper presented at the annual conference of the American Educational Research Association, San Francisco.

Parunak, V. D., (1989). Multimedia topologies and user navigation. *Hypertext '89 proceedings* (pp. 43-50). New York: Association for Computing Machinery.

Raskin, J. (1987). The hype in hypertext: A critique. *Hypertext '87 proceedings* (pp 325-330). New York: Association for Computing Machinery.

Rauden, S., & Johnson, G. (1989). *Evaluating the usability of the human-computer interface*. New York: Halsted Press.

Reisner, P. (1987). HCI, what is it and what research is needed? In J. Carroll (Ed.). *Interfacing human thought* (pp. 337-352). Cambridge MA: MIT Press.

Richards, T. (1990). Integrated multimedia: Bridging the missing links. *Academic Computing, 1*, 24-25, 44.

Salomon, G. (1979). *Interaction of media, cognition and learning*. San Francisco: Jossey-Bass.

Schweir, R. A., & Misanchuk, E. R. (1993). *Interactive multimedia instruction*. Englewood Cliffs NJ: Educational Technology Publications.

Sherry, M. (1992). The new ILSs: branching out. *Technology & Learning, 12*, 14-29.

Silverman, B. (1992). *Critiquing human error*. London: Academic Press, p. 79.

Stanton, N. , Taylor, R. , & Tweedie, L. (1992). Maps as navigational aids in hypertext environments: An empirical evaluation. *Journal of Educational Multimedia and Hypermedia, 1*(4), 431-444.

Stone, D. L. (1993). Personal communication.

Syllabus (1992). Using computers in instruction. *Syllabus, 21*(2), 4-5.

Technology and Learning (1993). Multimedia tools. *Technology and Learning, 13*(5), 38.

Tessmer, M. (1993). *Planning and conducting formative evaluations*. London: Kogan Page.

Tessmer, M., & Harris, D. (1992). *Analysing the instructional setting: Environmental analysis*. London: Kogan Page.

Tessmer, M., & Jonassen, D. (1993). Evaluating computer-based training for repurposing to multimedia: A case study. Paper presented at the annual convention of the Association for Educational Communications and Technology, New Orleans.

Tessmer, M., & Wedman, J. (1990). A layers of necessity instructional development model. *Educational Technology Research and Development, 38*(2), 77-85.

Tessmer, M. & Wedman, J. (1992). Decision-making factors and principles for selecting a layer of instructional design activities. *Performance and Instruction, 31*(4), 1-7.

Tobin, K., & Dawson, G. (1992). Constraints to curriculum reform: Teachers and the myths of schooling. *Educational Technology Research and Development, 40*(1), 81-92.

Tripp, S., & Bichelmeyer, B. (1990). Rapid prototyping: An alternative instructional design strategy. *Educational Technology Research and Development, 38*(1), 31-44.

Trumbull, D. Gay, G., & Mazur, J. (1991). J. Charting the complex: Research on the use of a multimedia system. Paper presented at the annual meeting of the American Educational Research Association, Chicago.

Tucker, S. (1993). Evaluating interactive instructional technologies: A cognitive model. Paper presented at the annual meeting of the Association for Educational Communications Technology, New Orleans.

Van Der Veer, G., Wijk, R., & Felt, M. (1990). Metaphors and metacommunications in the development of mental models. In P. Fallon (Eds.). *Cognitive ergonomics* (pp. 133-145). New York: Academic Press.

Whitten III, W. B. (1992). The hurdles of technology transfer. *Educational Technology, 32*(5), 19-24.

Wilson, K., & Tally, B. (1991). Looking at discovery-oriented multimedia. *News from the Center for Children and Technology, 1*(1), 1-2.

Zahner, J. E., Reiser, R., Dick, W. & Gill, B. (1992). Evaluating instructional software: a simplified model. *Educational Technology Research and Development, 40*(3), 55-63.

Zeisel, J. (1984). *Inquiry by design*. Cambridge MA: Cambridge University Press.

PART III

Rich Environments for Active Learning

CHAPTER 11

Encourage Student Responsibility

Scott Grabinger
Joanna C. Dunlap

Chapter Objectives Picture a typical classroom assignment such as worksheets, essays, papers, homework, problems, and so on. The assignment, developed by the teacher with considerable time and effort provides students with the following information:

- what they will learn;

- how they will learn it, including the activities they must do to complete the assignment;

- the questions that have to be answered;

- what classroom and library resources need to be used; and

- when the assignment is due.

In other words, everything the students must do is mapped out for them in significant detail; leaving nothing left to speculation or the imagination. Then, when students have completed the assignment, the teacher evaluates them on how well they were able to follow the rules of the assignment. With learning considered in this light, we need to ask: Who, in fact, is doing the major cognitive processing and learning on the assignments?

Usually, we think of the student as doing most of the work on assignments, and hopefully learning in the process. However, in analyzing more deeply, it is apparent to us that the teacher is doing most of the work and most of the learning. When developing assignments for students, teachers customary set the goals, plan the objectives, select the strategies, ask the questions, and evaluate the work. The irony is that these tasks are all high-level cognitive activities involving analysis, synthesis, and evaluation. Are those not the same kinds of activities that we want students to perform? Unfortunately, in the many classroom settings, students take less active roles, often simply receiving information and reacting to selected activities in teacher-determined ways. Students engage in low-level rote or algorithmic activities that leave little room for analysis, synthesis, or evaluation tasks. In fact, students are usually not allowed to engage in these types of activities because teachers believe that students lack the skills needed to initiate and take on the responsibility for their own educational process.

In this chapter we take the view that the student should be doing this work. Therefore, we

- discuss ways to give students control and responsibility for their learning and

- recommend ways to involve students in making their own decisions about learning.

REALs

As instructional hypermedia designers, how do we create classroom settings that engage students in the types of activities usually reserved for teachers? How can we provide opportunities for students to take on the initiative and responsibility for their own learning? This chapter discusses the use of rich environments for active learning (REALs) in the classroom and how hypermedia instructional systems can be used to support these types of learning environments.

Definition of REALs
Rich environments for active learning are comprehensive instructional systems that

- encourage student responsibility, decision making, and intentional learning in an atmosphere of collaboration among students and teachers;

- promote study and investigation within meaningful, authentic, and information-rich contexts; and

- utilize participation in activities that promote high-level thinking processes, including problem solving, experimentation, original creations, discussion, and examination of topics from multiple perspectives.

REALs encourage students to develop initiative and responsibility for their own learning within active and meaningful contexts. If we want our students to become lifelong learners and capable problem solvers, then the high-level activities that have typically fallen solely within the domain of the teacher must become an integral part of each student's educational process and experience.

The following guidelines, inspired in part by Vygotsky's (1978) zone of proximal development and Bereiter and Scardamalia's (Scardamalia & Bereiter, 1991; Scardamalia, Bereiter, McLean, Swallow, & Woodruff, 1989) work on intentional learning, focus on strategies that instructional designers and teachers can use to make students more responsible for their own learning. This is not an easy task because it involves significant changes in the roles of both students and teachers. Therefore, those role changes are also discussed within the guidelines.

GUIDELINES

11.1 Allow and teach students to determine what they need to learn through questioning and goal setting.

Questioning and Goal Setting

In REALs, students should work to identify their knowledge and skill deficits and to develop strategies in the form of personal learning goals for meeting those deficits. They should learn to compare what they know to what they do not know and ask questions to guide their quest for new knowledge. This is traditionally the role of the school district, teacher, or training manager. However, this does not absolve school or training personnel from the responsibility of determining what is needed. Instead, it recognizes that the learner too must agree with what is needed in order to create a sense of ownership (i.e., buy-in) in the learning process.

One of the advantages of encouraging students to identify their own knowledge and skill deficits is that it treats knowledge gaps and mistakes in a positive way. Most instructional activities require students to display their knowledge. Students are rewarded for demonstrating knowledge gains and for hiding knowledge deficits. For example, a teacher may ask students to respond to a set of questions. If students provide the correct answers to the questions, then they have been successful and are rewarded with praise from the teacher and peer recognition. But, if a student does not know the correct answers, then his or her lack of knowledge emerges as a form of failure: The teacher may provide negative feedback (e.g., "No that is incorrect") and immediately call on another student to answer the question. As a consequence, the student may feel punished, embarrassed, or stupid. Instead of allowing students to feel this way, teachers need to place an equal emphasis on rewarding students for honest analysis and self-assessment in identifying what they do not know.

For example, one REAL we have implemented in a classroom setting prompts students to answer questions about what they already know about a new subject and what they need to learn more about. Figure 11.1 shows a screen from the program *InfoAgent* that helps students ask questions in thinking about what they may not know.

Another advantage in encouraging students to identify their own knowledge and skill deficits is that it is very difficult for one teacher in a classroom to consistently assess what each student knows and does not know for each new concept covered. If teachers can guide students in the identification of what they already know and what they need to learn, then students can assume more responsibility in addressing their learning needs during an instructional unit.

Fig. 11.1. *InfoAgent* screen promoting goal setting.

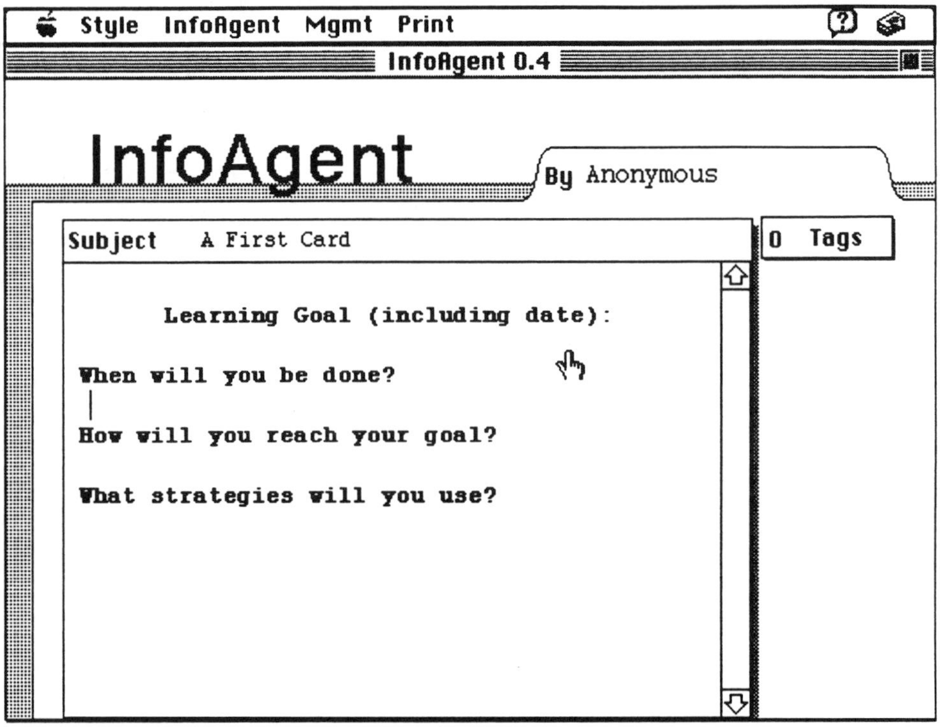

Students must also be able to relate what they do know to what they do not know. They must learn to realistically appraise and explicate their skill and knowledge areas that require improvement. Part of this involves the ability to ask questions because asking insightful, meaningful questions that will guide subsequent learning requires a lot of consideration and effort.

The art of questioning is a skill that needs to be taught and consistently practiced over time and within a variety of instructional contexts. Scardamalia and Bereiter (1991) found in two studies with fifth- and sixth-grade students that they could be taught to ask intelligent high- and low-level questions about topics about which they knew little or nothing. Low-level questions focus on verbal and factual information that helps to provide the conceptual base for the construction of high-level questions. For example, low-level questions formulated in a social science class may be, "What is culture?" or "What is a population?" Low-level questions can usually be answered with definitions or "yes" or "no" answers.

In contrast, high-level questions focus on relationships, predictions, and conjecture. In the same social science class, high-level questions asked may include, "How do different cultures with the same societal structure interact? "What is the historical experience of the United States with multicultural interaction: in schools, politics, and so forth?" "How does a country's population size affect import and export relationships with other countries?" or "How does population size affect environmental issues such as reforestation, waste disposal and landfills, air and water pollution, and loss of open space?" High level questions need explanation, longer answers, and analysis and synthesis.

11.2 Provide sufficient scaffolding in the environment to help students with prompts, examples, modeling, and collaborative support.

To help students determine what they need to learn, the teacher in the classroom must provide considerable support. This type of support may include

- modeling behavior with think-alouds so students can see what types of processes their teacher goes through to determine his or her knowledge deficits (e.g., "When I approach this new content, the first thing I do is ask myself...");

- engaging students in think-alouds to provide appropriate feedback and coaching;

- guiding students in the development of lists that present what they already know about a subject;

- providing prompts to students to help stimulate their thinking, such as "I don't understand..." "I always believed that..." "Someone told me that..." or "How does X work?"; and

- letting students help each other develop questions.

The amount of support necessary depends, in part, on the sophistication of the students. Students who have had little experience with taking responsibility for their own learning need much more support and instruction in the metacognitive skills necessary to identify what they need to learn. Teachers can write and select appropriate pretest questions and model this skill for students so they learn to write their own pretest questions. Teachers need to ascertain whether students' self-assessments about what they know and do not know are grounded in reality as well as whether their goals are too broad or narrow. As students become stronger in the area of self-assessment, teachers can help them learn how to provide each other with feedback regarding goal and deficit determination. It is important to remember that students often need to be guided and supported by the teacher during higher-level learning activities.

Finally, teachers must help the students to prioritize their goals. Students may be too ambitious or have too many trivial goals. They can help each other sort through the goals and determine which are trivial and which are important. This is also an important role for the teacher because students may need help in establishing a manageable set of goals in a subject area they know little about. Again, prioritizing and limiting learning goals can be modeled for the students by their teacher.

Computer support in a learning environment can help students determine what they need to learn by providing some structured reminders of the determination process they need to go through. Basically, computer programs can help students to identify what they do not know and encourage students to be curious, to look at knowledge deficits as opportunities rather than failures. For example, a computer program could provide students with reminders on how to determine what they know and do not know about a subject by presenting think-aloud scripts that they could use themselves. Computer programs can also encourage and guide serious question formulation by providing students with examples of the types of questions they may want to investigate along with instruction and examples of both high- and low-level questions. Alternatively, a computer program could present students with a series of open-ended questions such as

"I want to compare how _____ relates to _____."

or

"If _____ is true, how does it affect _____?"

If even more structure is needed, pretests can be administered via a computer. Based on the students' pretest outcomes, areas of deficit could be presented to them as interesting content areas to investigate.

Computers can be used to help the teacher with the process of individual student guidance and coaching. For example, questions and goals can be recorded on a networked computer system for later referral by the teacher. The teacher can then make appropriate comments to support each student's effort. Students can also use a computer network system to provide feedback to each other or to collaborate on alleviating common knowledge deficits and in pursuing common learning goals. We have made extensive use of electronic mail (e-mail) to help students during the writing process. Instead of waiting until the students have completed a paper, feedback is provided during every step of the process by using e-mail as a way to send the instructor summaries or examples of progress and to get feedback the same day. In this way, the teacher and student are able to focus more on the process of writing than on the product.

11.3 Enable students to manage their own learning activities.

After setting goals, students need to develop plans to achieve those goals. Ordinarily, the selection of strategies and tactics falls within the province of the teacher, but to develop as independent learners, students must also learn to perform these functions. A student's learning plan should describe priorities, instructional tactics, resources, deadlines, roles in collaborative learning situations, and proposed learning outcomes, including presentation and dissemination of new knowledge and skills, if applicable.

This is a place where the traditional roles of both teachers and students change radically. Remember, students are used to being told what to do. Their involvement in the planning and development of learning activities is minimal. Teachers are used to telling students what to do via assignments (e.g., what to read, write, study, or memorize), tests, and in-class activities. Teachers arrange the instructional events that occur during a semester or school year to achieve a specified set of predetermined objectives—this has always been a major aspect of the teacher's role. Simply stated, teachers are used to being obeyed by students.

The teacher tells, the student does. It is a time honored role. However, a complex society demands members who are better able to act flexibly and take initiative when facing a problem. Unfortunately, years of being told what to do by others does not foster the initiative nor the ability to solve problems and make decisions with any range of flexibility or innovation. As teachers, it is our responsibility to create learning environments in the classroom that foster students' ability to fulfill the demands of our increasingly complicated and complex world.

It is not easy, however, for students to learn to take the initiative. They cannot suddenly be told to start planning their own learning activities because it is a new role for which they have little prior experience, practice, or training. If left on their own, students may continue to choose the same learning strategies over and over again, even if these are inappropriate, ineffective, or inefficient. One role of teachers in a REAL is to help students learn new strategies. Because of the difficulty involved in taking initiative in the learning process, students must be guided and supported by the teacher, slowly taking on more and more control of their zones of proximal development. It is a progressive process beginning with small steps.

It is important to recognize that teachers have a difficult time adapting to this role. One mistake teachers make is turning over some responsibility to students, but continuing to maintain a controlling structure. Consequently, the transfer of responsibility from the teacher to the students is nothing but an illusion. Students pick up on this and become disgruntled and confused as to their roles. Even though teachers recognize the need to improve students' higher-level thinking and problem-solving skills, they are reluctant, or simply do not possess the skills to change any of the tried and true teaching methods of the past. To implement this kind of change requires considerable negotiation and flexibility between students and teacher.

In contrast, teachers may make the mistake of providing students with more responsibility for the learning process than the students are prepared to handle. Students are left confused and aimless when they are abandoned to their own devices but do not know how to begin to set their own schedule or identify strategies or resources.

One way to avoid such difficulties is to begin to turn responsibility over to the students by having them determine how they will meet the learning goals they have established. A good classroom strategy is to use small and large group discussions so students can learn from each other and from modeling the teacher's behavior. During group discussions students can share ideas about strategies and tactics that can be used to meet goals. They should be encouraged to write down their plans to serve as a referent during the learning activities. Their plans can be used during evaluation to see if students have in fact met their goals. Depending on the age level and sophistication of the students, teachers may provide varying levels of support, from no help at all to extensive lists of options (e.g., go to the library, interview an expert, access an online encyclopedia, conduct an experiment, etc.) for the students to use as thought stimulators.

To manage their own learning activities, students need to utilize basic project management skills. In a traditional operating mode, teachers tell the students how much time they have and when they must be finished. Everybody finishes at the same time. Students, however, should be taught to estimate their own time requirements. This can be done within a structure developed by the teacher. Perhaps a block of time or a terminal point can be assigned by the teacher. But students should begin to get a concept of time, try to monitor how their learning progresses, and estimate how much time each step takes.

Computer programs can support these activities in a variety of ways. First, a project management program can help set deadlines and monitor progress. A computer can provide students opportunities to record their plans, as shown in Fig. 11.1. It could also provide a database of suggestions for strategies to use. Telecommunications options can provide links to resources that can be used to access more information. For example, students can access online knowledge bases and encyclopedias or can contact experts and professionals in the content areas they are studying.

11.4 Enable students to contribute to each other's learning through collaborative activities.

Collaborative Learning

A *sine qua non* for any kind of REAL is the integration of cooperative and collaborative learning techniques. An old aphorism is that a person learns more by teaching than by studying. Every student should also be a teacher and learn to make the decisions that a teacher makes. A successful REAL uses cooperative learning techniques to help students set goals, develop plans, manage time, and study information. For cooperative learning to occur, students must recognize what they are trying to learn, value it, and wish to share that value with others.

Cooperative learning has found new emphasis in education in the last five years. It is a frightening proposition for most teachers because it raises questions about evaluation (i.e., one student performing all the work for other members of the cooperative group while the others do nothing at all). Another concern for teachers is that when cooperative learning is occurring, the classroom is noisy and can appear chaotic. Teachers fear that they have lost control and students are "goofing off" instead of staying on task.

The biggest challenge for teachers is that there is more to collaborative learning than simply telling students to go work together. In a true collaborative setting, each student in a group has a defined role for making that group a success. Collaboration involves more than just creating a group and then dividing up the work. Successful and productive collaborative learning requires training, practice, and significant time and effort. Therefore, when students are first starting out, teachers need to be responsible for providing a structure to make collaborative learning work. To teach about collaborative learning is beyond the scope of this text. However, the following guidelines offer some suggestions on how to go about using collaborative learning in a classroom setting.

11.5 Keep collaborative groups small.

Small groups, three to five people, are the most successful. When groups are too large, it becomes easier for people to hide or minimize their participation and contribution.

11.6   Make sure each student in the group has a role. Rotate the roles.

In addition to collaborating on the task, each student should be assigned a role in group activities. For example, a three-person group might include these roles: "recorder" to keep track of comments, ideas, and plans; "organizer" to watch the time and make sure the group stays on task; and "participation monitor" to make sure everyone participates. Large groups may include roles such as "clarifier," a person who tries to repeat in different words what someone says to make sure everyone understands; "questioner" to ask questions and stimulate discussion; "devil's advocate" to argue against ideas; or "brainstormer" to make sure that everyone brainstorms without making value judgments. The purpose of the group may suggest other tasks.

Finally, roles should be rotated on a daily basis. Leaders, recorders, questioners, and any other roles must go to different people. Everyone must get a chance to perform in each situation to bring their unique style to the group. This can be hard to maintain with strong students who always want to be the leaders, but it is the teacher's responsibility to make sure that rotation occurs and that everyone gets opportunities to be group leaders. In this way not only do the students get the benefit of multiple perspectives and experiences because of their ever-changing roles, but students are also protected from having to be a role that they do not like, such as recorder, everyday.

11.7   Provide continuing training in being part of a collaborative effort.

The tasks cannot be assigned without training. Learning to collaborate is difficult for any age group. In order for REAL implementation to be successful, therefore, students must be trained in each group role so they know what to do when they are assigned a specific role. Job aids may be useful as reminders, providing lists of suggestions on how to perform the roles.

11.8   Vary the learning activities. Do not rely solely on group activities.

Working in a group is time consuming and can be exhausting. Moreover, sometimes it is inappropriate, especially if students need to pursue individual needs and objectives. Therefore, it is often appropriate to give students individual assignments, so they have a chance to perform some tasks on their own and get the individual space that they need.

11.9   Group projects should be assessed by both the teacher and group members. Maintain individual accountability.

Individual accountability should not go out the window with a group project. Each group member should be asked to assess and evaluate his or her own role in accomplishing the task. Individuals should also be asked to assess and evaluate the roles of other group members. Making a collaborative environment work means that the group must be aware of their individual and group responsibilities. Group members need to learn to deal with problems rather than ignore and hide them out of fear of conflict. Teachers can provide this sense of accountability by structuring the group work to include both individual and group assessments. The group dynamics of the situation make it more complex, but it can be dealt with through proper planning and structure.

The computer can provide a myriad of ways of supporting collaborative learning. A networked system may help one group collaborate with another. There are programs that help students read and comment on each other's work when group meetings are not possible. The computer could be the focal point of a collaborative effort by presenting a scenario or case for a small group of students to study. Figure 11.2 shows a screen used in a program whose purpose was to help group members interact with each other in a collaborative fashion.

11.10 Help students develop metacognitive awareness skills.

Metacognitive Awareness

Metacognitive awareness means that learners are thinking about the effectiveness of the learning strategies they are using during learning activities. For example, if students are memorizing the order of the planets from the sun, they could be asked to describe how they did it. If the students are metacognitively aware, then they would know whether they used a repetition strategy or a mnemonic strategy to memorize the order of the planets.

Metacognitive awareness is a skill associated with successful learners. Successful learners are able to analyze what they are doing — what strategies they are employing — and evaluate its value. Less successful learners may not try to use different learning strategies because they do not realize that the techniques they are using are not be appropriate or effective for the task they have undertaken.

The process of assessing metacognitive strategies should be made overt to help students become aware of what they are doing. Teachers can model this process by using think-aloud protocols (e.g., "When I started to work on this problem, the first thing I did was break it down into its subproblems. Then, I looked at each subproblem in order to figure out how I should go about learning what I need to know to solve that subproblem.").

To support the development of this ability, students should be expected to produce records about the processes and strategies they use, as well as products reflecting their knowledge. It is just as important to reflect on the process of learning as it is to consider the resulting products. Associative memory tasks should provide strategies for memorizing: mnemonics and drill-and-practice. Problem solving should record overt evidence of participation in the problem-solving steps.

Students should be frequently encouraged to reflect on the processes they are using during the learning process, to compare one strategy to another, and to evaluate the effectiveness of a strategy for the particular learning activity they have chosen. They should be stopped and asked, "What are you doing? Is it working? If it is not, what are your other options?" The teacher needs to help students think about learning strategy options. It is not enough for students to think about whether something they are doing is working or not. The process they are using should be labeled, and alternatives need to be considered. Students may not have these alternatives at their fingertips, but teacher guidance and job aids may help them consider all other possibilities.

Fig. 11.2. 5180 collaborative screen.

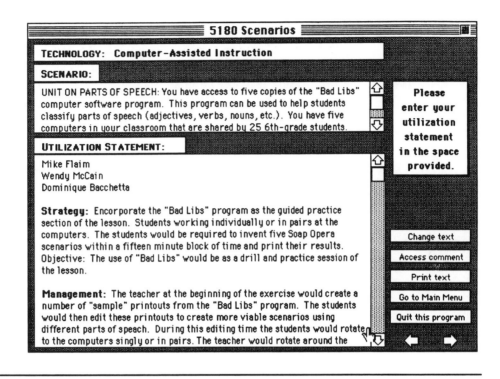

To assess the effectiveness of various strategies, students should be asked to rate the difficulty of a task. This helps with time management and may provide motivation for identifying simpler subtasks and appropriate strategies for attacking those subtasks.

The success of strategies can be monitored by using self-ratings or ratings by others on how much is learned. In addition, self-ratings or ratings by others within a collaborative group on how much effort went into the learning process encourages students. Students should keep track of their effort to stay on task and meet self-imposed deadlines.

Students should be encouraged to recognize frustration and blocks in the learning process. They should be taught to identify the source of that frustration and encouraged to seek help from other students and teachers. Teachers should keep a watchful eye for signs of frustration, but must avoid telling students what to do next. Instead, teachers need to guide the students through the frustrations by helping them understand both the causes and the processes they are using. Students should be taught to discriminate between frustration caused by problems and frustrations caused by inappropriate strategies.

Computer support could begin with an online database of information so students can begin to rely less on the knowledge of the teacher and learn to seek other sources, or perspectives, of information. The computer can also provide students with a structure for journal writing that includes space to record personal reflections on new knowledge gains and the ways (good and bad) in which that new knowledge was acquired. Lessons presented on the computer can include embedded questions about metacognition itself. A computer program can also incorporate an expert system that suggests specific strategies for specific learning objectives. Computer support can provide students with time, opportunity, and a nonthreatening environment in which to think about what they are doing and why. This means that the program should refrain from bombarding students with stimulation and from always controlling what students think about. This is not so much an alternative to classroom learning as it is an environment for quiet, reflective thinking that precedes class discussion. It provides anonymity in posing and answering questions, as well as private, computer-managed interchanges during which students can reflect on ideas and consider their views and responses.

11.11 Create a safe climate for learning.

This guideline is crucial to all aspects of REALs. Students are not going to be willing to take the risks necessary to assume responsibility if the environment punishes them for making mistakes. The teacher needs to encourage students to experiment and try different options. When a mistake is made, teachers need to emphasize an understanding of what went wrong rather than focus on the creation of a mistake-free product. When students ask for help, teachers have to hold back from telling students the correct answer; Instead, teachers need to ask students to perform the analysis themselves by guiding them through the analysis process.

Again, students must be trained and encouraged to take risks. This is a new element in learning for most students. The teacher is the primary person to encourage this kind of risk-taking by providing positive and constructive feedback and encouragement, as well as by modeling risk-taking behavior.

The computer provides a number of options for helping create an non-threatening environment. A networked system can provide an open forum for communication by protecting the anonymity of respondents. Computer-assisted instruction (CAI) programs can provide instant feedback and help students work in a step-by-step manner to arrive at the correct response or solution. Examine the screens in Fig. 11.3. These screens show the students' process of learning and decision making. They also show how students receive feedback by comparing their answers to the ones provided by the CAI program. CAI can also provide more access to informative feedback (see Fig. 11.4) to help students learn from mistakes.

The computer can provide an environment that is nonjudgmental. Students can use simulations and games to try new strategies without fear of retribution from the teacher.

CONCLUSION

Student responsibility is the most crucial aspect of creating a rich environment for active learning (REAL). The primary idea behind a REAL is to create an environment in which students create complex, rich knowledge structures that will apply to a variety of problems. However, to become capable problem solvers, students must know how to learn and be willing and able to take responsibility for identifying learning deficits, setting goals, managing the learning process, and monitoring the learning strategies they use.

REFERENCES

Heath, S. (1994). *InfoAgent.* Columbia MO: Hypermedia and Instructional Software Clearinghouse.

Scardamalia, M., & Bereiter, C. (1991). Higher levels of agency for children in knowledge building: A challenge for the design of new knowledge media. *The Journal of the Learning Sciences, 1*(1), 37-68.

Scardamalia, M., Bereiter, C., McLean, R. S., Swallow, J., & Woodruff, E. (1989). Computer-supported intentional learning environments. *Journal of Educational Computing Research, 5*(1), 51-68.

Vygotsky, L. S. (1978). *Mind in society.* Cambridge MA: Harvard University Press.

Fig. 11.3. Decision making while receiving feedback (from "Platelets in Transfusion Medicine"

Blood Spots: Determine Cause of Bleeding

Based on the patient's symptoms and signs so far, what is the apparent cause of the patient's bleeding? If needed, order labs before making this determination. Click on your hypothesis below to continue.

[Anatomic]

[Platelets]

[Plasma Procoagulant Activity]

What do I need to know?
- Consult Textbook
- Review Case History
- Review Physical Exam
- Review Labs Ordered

What do I do?
- Order Labs

Where am I?
- Help

Blood Spots: Select the degree to which the following case findings support platelets as the cause of bleeding.

Case Findings	No Support	Possible Support	Probable Support	Definite Support
Bleeding was not markedly prolonged.	E	○	●	○
The bleeding was not associated with medications.	E	○	●	○
Petechiae and purpura were present and diffuse.	E	●	○	○
Bleeding occurred spontaneously without trauma or surgery.	E	○	○	○
Platelet count was very low.	○	E	●	○
Screening coagulation studies were normal.	○	○	●	○

What do I need to know?
- Consult Textbook
- Review Case History
- Review Physical Exam
- Review Labs Ordered
- Review Your Decisions

What do I do?
- See Expert's Summary

Where am I?
- Help

Blood Spots: Select the degree to which the following case findings support platelets as the cause of bleeding.

Case Findings	No Support	Possible Support	Probable Support	Definite Support
Bleeding was not markedly prolonged.	○	○	●	○
The bleeding was not associated with medications.	○	○	●	○
Petechiae and purpura were present and diffuse.	○	●	○	○
Bleeding occurred spontaneously without trauma or surgery.	●	○	○	○
Platelet count was very low.	○	○	●	○
Screening coagulation studies were normal.	○	○	●	○

What do I need to know?
- Consult Textbook
- Review Case History
- Review Physical Exam
- Review Labs Ordered
- Review Your Decisions

What do I do?
- See Expert's Selection

Where am I?
- Help

Blood Spots: Select the degree to which the following case findings support platelets as the cause of bleeding.

In summary, this is a child with diffuse symptoms and signs of bleeding, (epistaxis, petechiae, and purpura). She has no other symptoms of disease or physical findings.

Screening clotting studies were normal, but her platelet count was extremely low. She had no specific anatomic lesion to serve as a major cause for bleeding.

What do I do?
- If you want to review the expert's choices then click on the "**Review Selection**" button.
- If you have selected the incorrect cause of bleeding in this case, click on the "**Change Cause**" button to change your choice.
- If you are ready to proceed, click on the "**Determine Etiology**" button to proceed to the next step.

What do I need to know?
- Consult Textbook
- Review Case History
- Review Physical Exam
- Review Labs Ordered
- Review Your Decisions

What do I do?
- Review Selection
- Change Cause
- Determine Etiology

Where am I?
- Help

Fig. 11.4. Feedback screens.

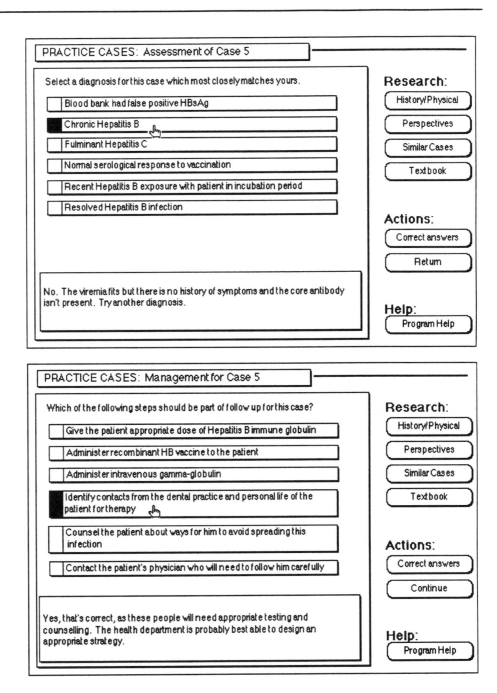

CHAPTER 12

Make Learning Meaningful

Joanna C. Dunlap
Scott Grabinger

Chapter Objectives

"Why do I have to learn this stuff?"

"I'll never have to do this in the *real* world."

"What does this have to do with anything?"

How many times have you heard students make these types of comments or ask similar questions during instruction? Such student questions typically accompany one specific instructional activity: the introduction of new content presented out of context, such as introducing sentence structuring and diagramming without involving the students in writing activities, or introducing computer programming concepts without putting the students in front of computers.

In many situations, content is often presented to learners in simplified, decontextualized, isolated chunks that promote memorization and near transfer rather than problem solving or higher-level thinking. Due to the constraints of the environment, it is difficult to help students see interrelationships among content areas, the inherent complexity of the content, or the content's application to realistic situations.

We have tried to address this problem in the past is by integrating computer-based applications in the classroom. Many people believed that the introduction of computer-based instruction (CBI) programs and videodiscs in the classroom would help present an authentic nature of content and, therefore, make learning more meaningful. Unfortunately, these media applications have not lived up to their initial promise. Except for a few isolated instances (e.g., the Jasper series), these applications are too much a part of the traditional classroom, helping us do what we have always done by presenting content via simplified, decontextualized, isolated presentations and activities. The main problem is that we have tried to integrate decontextualized computer-based applications into the classroom without changing other parts of the environment: the roles of teachers and students, student activities, and learning goals and objectives.

How then can we structure the learning environment so that learning is more meaningful for students? What are the alternatives, and how do we implement and support them in the classroom? In this chapter, we discuss

- the use of rich environments for active learning (REALs) in classrooms to make learning more meaningful for students,

- ways to make the need and reason to learn content apparent, and

- how to use hypermedia/multimedia instructional systems to support these more meaningful activities.

REALs are based on constructivist assumptions about learning that encourage the use of generative learning strategies that anchor instruction in realistic, contextualized, cross-disciplinary situations. This rationale for REALs is consistent with goals stated by educators attempting to restructure the way in which students learn (American Association for the Advancement of Science, 1989; National Council of Teachers for Mathematics, 1989; Resnick & Klopfer, 1989). These organizations and educators believe that our schools should move away from teaching quantities of information and move toward teaching students to become independent thinkers and creative problem solvers. REALs help to provide structure and guidelines that facilitate meeting these new instructional goals.

To understand the rationale behind the use of REALs in a classroom in order to support activities that help make learning more meaningful for students, it is important to know a little more about the theoretical foundations of constructivistic learning environments. A leader in the area of constructivistic learning environment development is the Cognition and Technology Group at Vanderbilt (CTGV). According to the developers of the Jasper Woodbury series of videodisc-based learning materials, environments for science and mathematical problem solving can be created that are based on three building blocks: generative learning, anchored instruction, and cooperative learning (CTGV, 1993).

GENERATIVE LEARNING

The first required element of constructivistic learning environments, as described by CTGV (1993), is that learning must be generative. Generative learning requires students to "engage in argumentation and reflection as they try to use and then refine their existing knowledge as they attempt to make sense of alternate points of view" (CTGV, 1993, p. 16). In general, this requires a shift in the traditional roles of students and teachers. Students become investigators, seekers, and problem solvers. Teachers become facilitators and coaches, rather than presenters of knowledge. For generative learning to occur, students must work with information, manipulate it, change it, relate it to existing knowledge structures, and use it to support problem solving. This is a higher-level thinking activity, as opposed to simply copying down information and memorizing it for an upcoming exam. In other words, students learn how to actually *use* or *apply* the information they learn; Generative learning activities require students to take static information and *generate* fluid, flexible, usable knowledge.

Note: The use of generative learning strategies is a pervasive theme in REALs. These strategies are discussed in this chapter in terms of their ability to make learning meaningful. They are also discussed in more detail as a major theme in the next chapter in terms of promoting active knowledge construction.

ANCHORED INSTRUCTION

Anchored instruction is the process of "anchoring or situating instruction in meaningful problem-solving contexts that allow one to simulate in the classroom some of the advantages of apprenticeship learning" (CTGV, 1993, p. 17). In anchored or authentic learning situations, students develop component skills and objectives (e.g., computational skills, definitions of concepts, and so on) in the context of meaningful, realistic problems and problem-solving activities. This is in direct contrast to the way students develop component skills and objectives in a more traditional classroom environment. In the traditional environment, students work on simplified, decontextualized problems using the same strategies and arriving at the same answers. Simply stated, it is the difference between providing meaningful learning activities and "I'm never going to use this" activities.

Context plays a major role in teaching students to be independent thinkers and creative problem solvers. Authentic learning environments present students with meaningful activities that lead to far transfer: defining problems, identifying resources, setting priorities, addressing subsets of the problem, exploring different approaches to problems, and generating a variety of appropriate solutions. These are the same skills and abilities that are required during realistic, outside-of-the-classroom problem solving and decision making activities.

COOPERATIVE LEARNING AND GENERATIVITY

CTGV and other researchers argue that cooperative learning and problem-solving groups facilitate generative learning. Working in peer groups helps students to refine their knowledge through argumentation, structured controversy, and reciprocal teaching. In addition, students are more willing to take on the additional risk required to tackle complex, ill-structured, authentic problems when they have the support of others in the cooperative group. Related, cooperative problem-solving groups also address students' need for scaffolding during unfamiliar learning and problem-solving activities. With the support of others in the group, students are more likely to achieve goals that they may not have been able to meet on their own.

Often, as soon as you mention cooperative groups in a classroom, the response is, "Ah, do we have to?" or "Oh, not again." Unfortunately, many students have had negative experiences in cooperative groups because of the unfair division of labor. However, we emphasize that true cooperative learning is not about the division of labor. There are techniques for providing the appropriate amount of structure and scaffolding necessary for less-skilled groups to work together — equally, fairly, and in a way that permits everyone gets something out of the experience. For generative learning to work, all students must be active learners, not only when they are working individually, but also when they are working with others in a cooperative group. To use cooperative groups to support and enhance generative learning activities, teachers need to apply appropriate facilitating techniques to make sure that all students are active learners.

GUIDELINES

The following guidelines focus on strategies that instructional designers, teachers, or both can use to help make learning more meaningful for students. Some of these ideas will be revisited in the next chapter. The purpose of these guidelines is to describe some of the instructional techniques that can be used to get students intentionally and enthusiastically involved in the material, and to show how multimedia/hypermedia instructional systems can be used to support these techniques. The next chapter focuses more on learning strategies and tactics to be used within a unit of instruction. Again, the adoption of these techniques is not an easy task because it involves significant changes in the roles of both students and teachers. Those role changes are discussed within the guidelines.

12.1 Make maximum use of existing knowledge.

Knowledge is a continuous process of construction: building on what is already known in order to elaborate on existing knowledge structures. In a constructivistic view of learning, the learner's knowledge representations "are constantly open to change, its structure and linkages forming the foundation to which other knowledge structures are appended" (Bednar, Cunningham, Duffy, & Perry, 1991, p. 91). Therefore, the learning of new material is facilitated by calling upon existing knowledge to serve as a point of reference and as a foundation from which new knowledge structures are built.

One question often asked in a classroom is, "What does this have to do with what I already know?" Students want to understand and make the connections between existing and new knowledge. Such connections facilitate new learning because students are more comfortable with what they know. Unfortunately, we often do not take the time to allow students to explore and determine these connections on their own. To address this issue, it is necessary to engage students in activities in the classroom that allow them to consider how their new learning is related to and supported by their existing knowledge. We need to build opportunities into learning activities for students to reflect on what they already know.

Teachers, programs, or texts can do this by making direct references to what students already know based on the context of the situation and on the learning sequence they are following. Students also should be taught to pause and think on their own initiative about what they know.

12.2 Ask students to explicitly describe relationships of new information to existing information through text, visuals, analogies, or oral discussion.

Students must generate the relationships between new and existing knowledge. In this way, they explicitly create a link, or many links, between new and existing knowledge. If students are not asked to describe these relationships, it is possible these important connections will not be made. It is simply not enough to make students aware that something new is similar to something old. Instead, students must become active learners and generate overt representations of the relationships.

A variety of tactics may be used for this: text, visuals, metaphors, analogies, and oral discussion. For example, a number of computer programs, such as *SemNet* and *KNOT-Mac*, allow students to generate graphic representations of their knowledge structures. Figure 12.1 shows an example of a *KNOT-Mac* screen describing the relationships among concepts related to the topic of learning environments. It is through the generation of these descriptions that the students identify points of similarity and difference that encourage thoughtful reconciliation and subsequent modification of existing knowledge structures.

This is not a particularly difficult principle to implement. Mostly, it is a matter of taking the time to get it done. This reflects one of the role changes involved in using this strategy. Teachers must avoid the traditional practice of telling students what the relationship is between old and new knowledge by such statements as, "Remember last week when we were talking about _____? Well this subject is just like that because..." It is necessary to allow students to generate these relationships and to redirect them if they are on the wrong track. This method is based on constructivism theory (Bednar et al., 1991). Constructivists believe that each student constructs an individual and independent view of the reality being discussed. This does not deny the existence of common knowledge, but proposes that common knowledge is developed through social interaction and negotiation. If this is the case, it is not very effective for teachers to relate a common view of new and old knowledge to students. Instead, students are better off relating their own understandings of the concepts and problems, while teachers assist with misunderstandings and misrepresentations.

Hypermedia and multimedia instructional systems can support the implementation of this guideline by reminding students that they should consider the connection between old and new knowledge. Hypermedia support for this practice could include programs that provide opportunities for learners to reflect upon these relationships as they use the program. For example, a program may provide a place for learners to write out their comments in text or to draw graphically the relationship between old and new knowledge. One REAL-like knowledge-base system used in an advanced hypermedia instructional development class presented students with a screen that asked a series of questions focusing on the relationship between existing and new knowledge. In this way, students were prompted to reflect. Figure 12.2 shows an example of a program intended to help students reflect on existing knowledge.

Fig. 12.1. KNOT-Mac representation of concept connections.

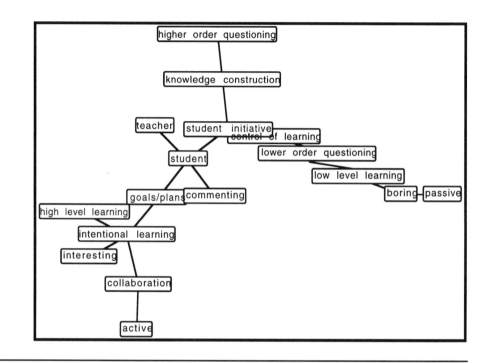

Fig. 12.2. InfoAgent screen to stimulate thinking.

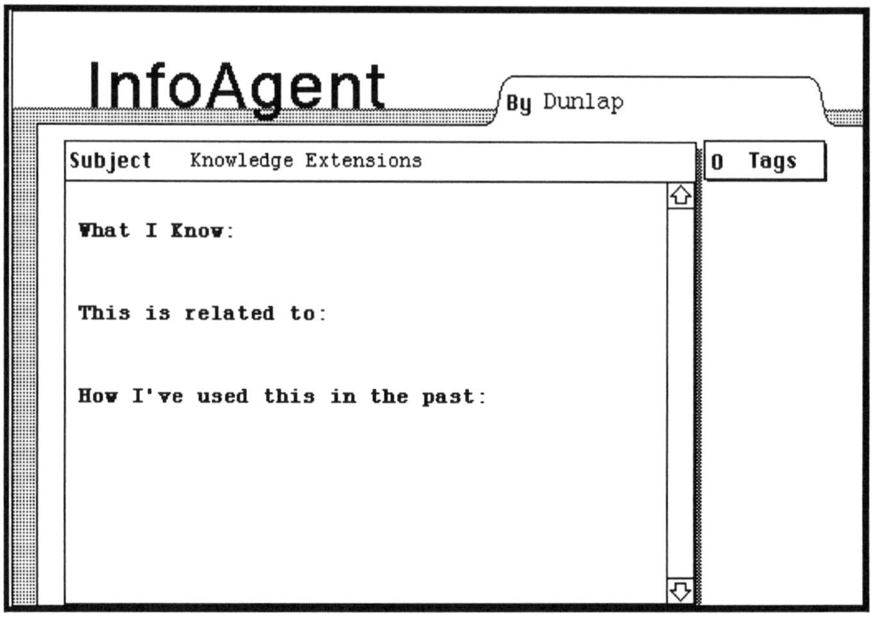

A more structured program could direct the learners to make these connections. Along these same lines, a knowledge base built by the learners should include opportunities to build in active links between new parts of the knowledge base and older parts of the knowledge base. For a class in instructional message design, students were asked to enter information regarding message design principles. The program then provided ways for students to link their new knowledge with knowledge they had entered into the program before (see Fig. 12.3).Another way to encourage this activity involves asking students to develop metaphors or analogies for the new learning. For example, in learning about a computer, a student might consider how the computer is like a human brain or like a tree. A hypermedia/multimedia system can provide structure for this type of activity by presenting questions that the student can complete, such as "A _____ is like a _____ because _____ ."

12.3 Anchoring instruction in realistic situations enhances the meaningfulness of the content.

Anchored instruction refers to instruction based on realistic, complex situations. Rather than separating new content into its component skills, the skills are taught together with their links and interrelationships within a meaningful problem-solving context.

This guideline is based on an apprenticeship learning model (Brown, Collins, & Duguid, 1989). For example, in colonial America, a young man would learn the craft of silversmithing through apprenticeship. He would be attached to a master for about seven years working within the context of the shop. He actually learned by doing because he worked on realistic tasks. There were no classes in the component skills, such as hammering, smelting, cutting, shining, or welding. Rather, the apprentice learned by working on real problems and tasks, seeing how each component fit with other parts to create a whole. The preceding guideline directly addresses students' objections: "Why do we need to learn this stuff?" and "I'm never going to do this in the *real* world." When instruction is anchored in a meaningful and realistic context, the answers to these questions become obvious

Anchored instruction does not imply 100% fidelity to reality. The nature of both the learners and content must be taken into consideration when creating a context for the instruction. The role of the teacher is contingent on how much complexity and reality is necessary to make the learning activities meaningful. Students must learn to deal with a variety of stimuli within the context. Unfortunately, this is often a difficult leap for students. Their previous classroom-based problem-solving activities may have required them to deal with only a limited set of stimuli in a decontextualized situation. Students are used to solving simplified, decontextualized problems in the same way, over and over again. But in anchored instruction, the students must learn to handle authentic problems that have the natural complexity of real problems intact. Therefore, the amount of scaffolding

Fig. 12.3. Making learning meaningful.

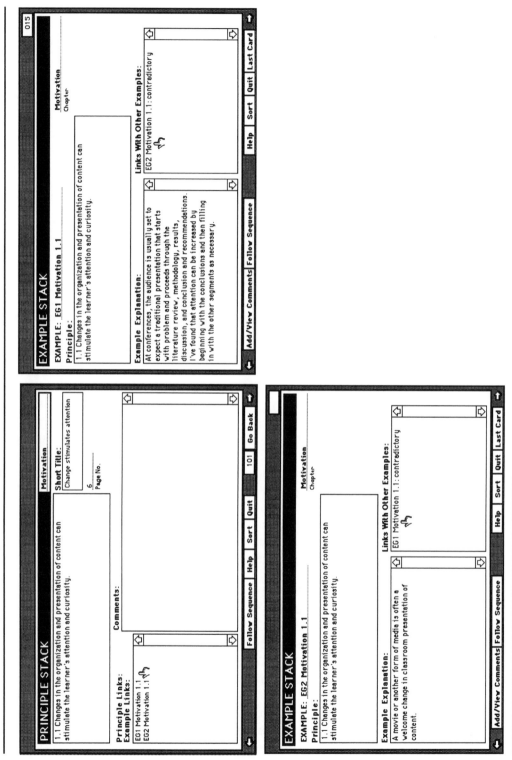

that the teacher must provide varies, depending on the problem-solving experiences to which students have been exposed previously and the complexity level of the problems they now have to tackle.

Complex problems provide a great deal more information than teachers and students are used to handling. This information makes the environment richer and more complex with multiple solutions. Both students and teachers, therefore, must become comfortable with a certain level of ambiguity: multiple ways to approach problems, multiple solutions, and multiple correct answers.

Hypermedia and multimedia applications are strong candidates for providing and supporting anchored instruction, ill-structured problems, and multiple solutions. Multimedia provides realistic representations using images, audio, and text to set up situations. For example, the Jasper Woodbury series developed by the Cognition and Technology Group at Vanderbilt uses videodiscs to present complex, realistic mathematical problems to fifth- and sixth-grade students. The Jasper series is a set of video adventures that provide realistic and motivating contexts for problems-solving and higher-level thinking skills. Rather than focusing on procedural or computational aspects of problem solving, the Jasper series emphasizes problem and task identification, exposure to multiple approaches and solutions to problems, and the identification of relevant information and materials. The computational and procedural aspects of problem solving are directly applied to the solution of the problem.

Hypermedia provides unique opportunities for anchored instruction. Hypermedia applications permit learners to pursue a chain of thought much as they would in a real-life situation. They are not tied to an artificial linear sequence based on someone else's knowledge structure. They are free to pursue supplemental information and to link together disparate pieces of information. For example, a series of hypermedia programs developed for third-year medical students presents them with authentic clinical problems that they must assess and manage (see Fig. 12.4). Because the students require some structure and scaffolding to help them deal with the complex and ill-structured problems presented, the programs provide them with opportunities to get advice from experts and other sources. In this way they can check their decisions with others before they proceed.

12.4 Provide multiple ways to learn content.

A third way to promote meaningful learning is to provide variety in the learning activities. Given that students are accepting more responsibility and that they are working in authentic contexts that relate to things they know, students must be free to pursue a variety of ways to learn. Some students learn better individually; others learn better in groups. Some like to read; others like to listen. Some take notes; others sit passively. Some like to talk things out with others, whereas others like to sit and reflect. If we believe that we must give students more responsibility, then the responsibility must carry over into the ways they gather information and learn content. Yet, at the same time, when students are learning content, they should also be learning lifelong skills for finding and using information.

12.5   Provide access to a variety of experts, databases, and libraries.

The use of the Internet and other online databases is growing faster than even Malthus could predict. It is clear that an important lifelong skill is the identification of appropriate resources and the practice of effective searching strategies. Students should use telecommunications to access worldwide resources. These should include electronic mail and information gathering resources. Students should contact professionals and other students in the fields they are studying. They should also use the wide variety of reference services and knowledge bases to access information. The use of library media centers and online reference systems should be an important part of most learning environments.

12.6   Provide a variety of symbol systems in the learning environment.

An important element of hypermedia and multimedia systems is that the use of multiple modalities is part of the definition of the concepts. Multimedia systems can help teachers reach all kinds of learners. Students can be encouraged to use text, illustrations, audio recording, videotaping, and computer-based technologies to find and learn content. Not only should teachers make multiple symbol systems part of the learning environment, but students should use multimedia to present their information to become fluent in a variety of communication methods.

12.7   Provide learning options that reflect the ability and maturity of students.

One of the most important things the teacher, trainer, or facilitator can do is tailor the REAL and supplementary programs to the ability and maturity of the students. Although one of the goals of hypermedia and multimedia environments is the representation of realistic complexity, this must be tempered by the previous experience and maturity level of the students.

However, when first adopting the REAL system, you must be careful to avoid oversimplifying things. Remember, one of the reasons for creating REALs is to motivate students with realistic situations. If too much decontextualization occurs at the beginning, then that goal is forgotten.

A multimedia/hypermedia instructional system can easily support different ability and maturity levels of students. Scaffolding that slowly disappears can be created as part of the hypermedia program. Students with higher skill levels can be given an option to access additional activities, exercises, or elaborations. Students can also be asked to work together in collaborative groups until they begin to feel comfortable with the content and are able to tackle some of the problems on their own.

Fig. 12.4. Medical program screens showing information sources (from "Handling Transfusion Hazards" © Daniel Ambruso, MD).

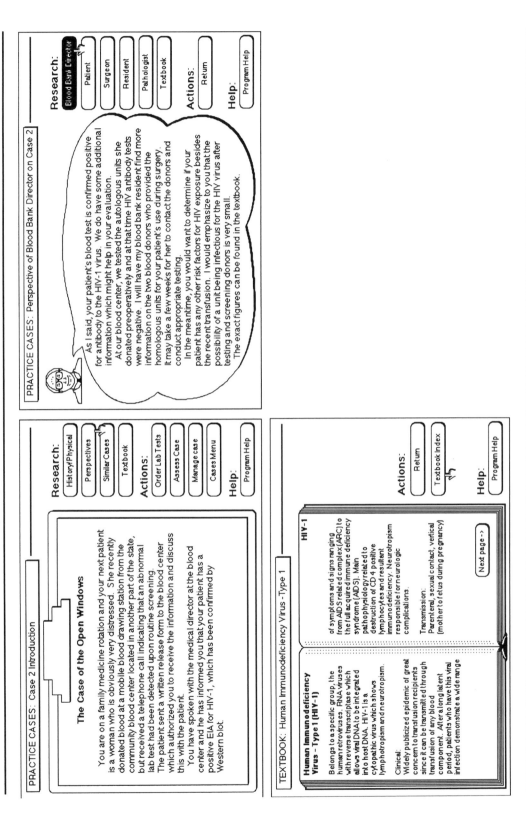

PRACTICE CASES: Case 2 Introduction

The Case of the Open Windows

You are on a family medicine rotation and your next patient is a woman who is obviously very distressed. She recently donated blood at a mobile blood drawing station from the community blood center located in another part of the state, but received a telephone call indicating that an abnormal lab test had been detected upon routine screening.

The patient sent a written release form to the blood center which authorized you to receive the information and discuss this with the patient.

You have spoken with the medical director at the blood center and he has informed you that your patient has a positive EIA for HIV-1, which has been confirmed by Western blot.

Research:
- History/Physical
- Perspectives
- Similar Cases
- Textbook

Actions:
- Order Lab Tests
- Assess Case
- Manage case
- Cases Menu

Help:
- Program Help

PRACTICE CASES: Perspective of Blood Bank Director on Case 2

As I said, your patient's blood test is confirmed positive for antibody to the HIV-1 virus. We do have some additional information which might help in your evaluation.

At our blood center, we tested the autologous units she donated preoperatively and at that time HIV antibody tests were negative. I will have my blood bank resident find more information on the two blood donors who provided the homologous units for your patient's use during surgery. It may take a few weeks for her to contact the donors and conduct appropriate testing.

In the meantime, you would want to determine if your patient has any other risk factors for HIV exposure besides the recent transfusion. I would emphasize to you that the possibility of a unit being infectious for the HIV virus after testing and screening donors is very small.

The exact figures can be found in the textbook.

Research:
- Blood Bank Director
- Patient
- Surgeon
- Resident
- Pathologist
- Textbook

Actions:
- Return

Help:
- Program Help

TEXTBOOK: Human Immunodeficiency Virus - Type 1

Human Immunodeficiency Virus - Type 1 (HIV-1)

Belongs to a specific group, the human retroviruses. RNA viruses with reverse transcriptase which allows viral DNA to be integrated into host DNA. HIV-1 is a cytopathic virus which shows lymphotropism and neurotropism.

Clinical:
Widely publicized epidemic of great concern to transfusion recipients since it can be transmitted through transfusion of any blood component. After a long latent period, patients who have this viral infection demonstrate a wide range

HIV-1

of symptoms and signs ranging from AIDS related complex (ARC) to the full acquired immune deficiency syndrome (AIDS). Main pathophysiology related to destruction of CD 4 positive lymphocytes and resultant immunodeficiency. Neurotropism responsible for neurologic complications.

Transmission:
Parenteral, sexual contact, vertical (mother to fetus during pregnancy)

Next page ->

Actions:
- Return
- Textbook Index

Help:
- Program Help

CONCLUSION

Making learning meaningful has always been recognized as a critical element in education. The primary idea behind a REAL is to create an environment in which students create complex, rich knowledge structures that will apply to a variety of problems. This cannot be done through decontextualized, lower-level activities. To encourage the development of capable problem solvers, teachers must provide students with environments that are anchored or situated in realistic problems.

REFERENCES

American Association for the Advancement of Science. (1989). *Science for all Americans. A Project 2061 report on literacy goals in science, mathematics, and technology.* Washington DC: American Association for the Advancement of Science.

Bednar, A. K., Cunningham, D., Duffy, T. M., & Perry, J. D. (1991). Theory into practice: How do we link? In Anglin, G. J. (Ed.). *Instructional technology: Past, present, and future* (pp. 88-101). Englewood CO: Libraries Unlimited.

Brown, J. S., Collins, A., & Duguid, P. (1989). Situated cognition and the culture of learning. *Educational Researcher, 18*(1), 32-42.

Cognition and Technology Group at Vanderbilt (CTGV) (1993). Designing learning environments that support thinking: The Jasper Series as a case study. In T. M. Duffy, J. Lowych, & D. H. Jonassen, (Eds.). *Designing environments for constructive learning.* Berlin: Springer-Verlag.

National Council of Teachers of Mathematics. (1989). *Curriculum and evaluation standards for school mathematics.* Reston VA: National Council of Teachers of Mathematics.

Resnick, L. B., & Klopfer, L. E. (Eds.). (1989). *Toward the thinking curriculum: Current cognitive research.* Alexandria VA: Association for Supervision and Curriculum Development.

CHAPTER 13

Active Knowledge Construction

Joanna C. Dunlap
Scott Grabinger

Chapter Objectives Chapter 12 describes the need for students to engage in generative learning in which they are asked to take action deliberately to create meaning from what they are studying (Wittrock, 1974, 1978). Students, instead of having knowledge transferred to them, are engaged in a continuous and collaborative process of building and reshaping mental structures as a natural consequence of their experience and interaction with the world (Forman & Pufall, 1988; Fosnot, 1989; Goodman, 1984). In this chapter, we build upon generative learning and emphasize the importance of making knowledge building visible or overt. Most of what successful learners — learners who are able to engage in complex problem-solving and higher-level thinking activities — do is hidden. One of the main goals of the following guidelines is to make the knowledge construction process overt. Additionally, the guidelines reflect the current emphasis in learning theory — constructivism.

In a typical classroom, teachers often play a structured role that focuses on conveying knowledge. Much of what happens in classrooms involves telling students what they should know about some aspect of the world. The instructional strategy of telling creates a learning environment in which students take word-for-word notes while listening to a teacher's lecture or reading from texts. Students spend a lot of time memorizing information for multiple-choice and fill-in-the-blank questions on upcoming exams. Inevitably students forget most of the information they learned because they have not put the knowledge to active use in an authentic situation.

Does this sound familiar? It should. Educators, economists, and employers express a growing concern regarding the future economic stability of the United States that stems from an ever-widening gap between the capabilities of high-school and college graduates and the skills, knowledge, and problem-solving abilities that employers require. A recent report by the U.S. Department of Labor

(1991) stated that "More than half of our young people leave school without the knowledge or foundation required to find and hold a good job." Due to the ever-changing complexities and competitiveness of the global marketplace, businesses need employees who can adjust to the demands of the moment and tackle problems that are inherently ambiguous, ill-structured, and complex.

Unfortunately, this is not a simple request. To bridge the classroom-workplace gap, students have to be involved in problem-solving and higher-level thinking activities — referred to as *active knowledge construction* — while they are still in the classroom. Therefore, instead of being told what to know about specific content areas, an act that Bruner (1990) refers to as *imposing* understanding on someone, students must engage in their own active construction of knowledge in order to be prepared for the demands of the workplace. To appropriately address this need, we need to develop strategies for creating learning environments that are structured to allow and promote active knowledge construction by students.

The strategies inherent in rich environments for active learning (REALs) address this need. In this chapter, we

- describe the elements of active knowledge construction;

- emphasize the importance of making knowledge building overt; and

- provide guidelines for teachers and instructional designers to involve learners in high level thinking activities such as problem identification, problem solving, reflection, analysis and synthesis, and reasoning.

GUIDELINES

13.1 Engage students in complex, open-ended problem-solving activities that require creativity and flexibility.

Teachers who use REALs must develop activities that promote reasoning, analysis, synthesis, evaluation, and problem solving. Whereas more successful students seem to be able to initiate these activities on their own, less successful students need a structure or scaffolding to help them learn and use higher-level thinking strategies. REALs call on students to identify and work with

- authentic, open-ended problems with natural uncertainty, complexity, and ill-structuredness intact;

- controversy, discussion, and collaboration; and

- judgments and decision making.

13.2 Engage students in exploration and experimentation by having them make predictions and form hypotheses.

One way to engage students in higher-level thinking is to present them with an open-ended scenario and ask them to describe what they think will happen. Students must be required to support their predictions through oral and written argumentation that includes evidence presented in the scenario that led them to form particular hypotheses. These types of activities can be conducted with students working individually or in small collaborative groups. Either way, students need to present their predictions and hypotheses. Overt articulation is important because it allows teachers and other students to learn how others approached a problem and to identify the source of faulty reasoning.

Another way to encourage students to become involved in higher-level thinking activities involves giving them opportunities to explore content based on their own individually determined needs and desires and allowing them to experiment with new concepts. Students need to be encouraged to explore, alter, and manipulate the parameters of the content, problem, or environment, and to discover and examine all possible outcomes, solutions, or both. Exploratory and experimentation learning activities provide opportunities that allow for the "rearranging or transforming [of] evidence in such a way that one is enabled to go beyond the evidence so reassembled to additional new insights" (Bruner, 1961, p. 22). Students become explorers discovering what needs to be figured out and then figuring it out on their own (Schank & Jona, 1991).

Support Technology for Problem-Solving Activities

A hypermedia system can support these types of activities by presenting students with realistic scenarios via video, videodisc, and computer-based case simulations and then exhibiting computer displays that ask specific questions and prompt students to take action. For example, *Interactive Physics*, a program designed to help students explore physics, presents students with a series of screens that prompts them to describe Newton's laws of motion. Students are asked to think about what will happen to objects based on what they know about Newton's laws. Predictions and hypotheses are handled in one of two ways:

- If there is limited computer support in the classroom, class, or small group discussions, allow students an opportunity to articulate their ideas.

- Peer commenting can be done within the computer program itself. Comments are examined in the programs by using a computer network that gives all students access to the comments.

It is important to note how the teacher's role changes to support activities of this sort. In addition to managing the activity to ensure complete and equitable student participation, the teacher must emphasize that there are many possible predictions that can be derived from one scenario. Students must be encouraged to experiment and develop alternative plans to avoid being locked into a single algorithmic pattern.

For example, the *Geometric Supposer* is a hypermedia/multimedia system designed to encourage students to be makers of mathematics (Schwartz & Yerushalmy, 1987). The *Geometric Supposer* environment provides students with a wide range of tools that support student-centered exploration and manipulation of geometric structures so they can make their own discoveries of existing theorems. Using the *Geometric Supposer*, students discover for themselves many attributes of triangles (Schwartz & Yerushalmy, 1987):

- If they draw a median in a triangle, the median bisects the area of the triangle.

- A midsegment in a triangle is parallel to the third side of the triangle.

- The three midsegments of the triangle partition the triangle into four triangles that are congruent to one another.

Additionally, students use the *Geometric Supposer* environment to discover new theorems (becoming makers of mathematics), which demonstrates that students are developing critical thinking skills and problem solving abilities by engaging in this type of environment.

13.3 Provide scaffolding to help students manage the complexity of ill-structured problems.

How do we get students started if they are not accustomed to engaging in ill-structured problem-solving activities? Complex problems require scaffolding, support, and guidance to prevent students from being overwhelmed by the complexity and solution options. Scaffolding involves providing the support and guidance appropriate for the learners' ages and experience levels. Authentic environments balance realism with learner ability, experience, maturity, age, and knowledge.

Scaffolding involves guidance in the forms of hints, questions, and materials that lead learners through a process of solving problems. However leading does not mean telling. Teachers must set up the environment to help students identify what they need to do rather than tell them which steps to perform in an algorithmic manner. Students must learn ways to solve problems and overcome obstacles in addition to learning to arrive at problems. Most important, they must learn to be comfortable with a trial-and-error approach.

Support Technology for Questions and Hints

Technology in the form of hypermedia can provide guidance and support by supplying questions that prompt students through the problem-solving activity. For example, at different points in the activity, a program (or teachers or other students) can stop students and ask questions to help learners activate higher-level thinking activities:

- A literature program may ask, "What is the main problem facing the characters?"

- A mathematics program can provide a process hint by asking, "Can this problem be broken down into smaller, more manageable problems?"

- A social sciences program may ask, "What pieces of information must you find to solve this problem?"

After they have completed a problem, students can be given time to reflect on the process by questions, such as these:

- Which problem-solving strategies did you use? Which ones worked? Which ones did not work?

- What would you do differently the next time?

- What would you do similarly the next time?

- What was the single greatest difficulty in solving the problem?

- Did you start by looking at the overall problem, or did you immediately break the problem down into smaller chunks?

- What resources did you use? Which were most helpful?

13.4 Provide a coaching structure.

Because complex, open-ended problem solving is a new and unfamiliar activity for most students, teachers must change their role from controlling all activity in the classroom to coaching the activities in the classroom. A coach helps to guide students in the right direction, although ultimate performance is up to the student. The teacher must learn to ask questions rather than tell students what to do. For example, some general questions might include the following:

- What is causing the source of your frustration?

- That's a good solution. What if "X" was not available to you? How would that affect your solution?

- Do you think that your assumption is true? How would you find out?

- Who do you think could help you with this part of the problem?

- What do you think would happen if you tried using "Y"?

- Where would you go to find the information you need?

- What do you need to know before you can continue?

- Why don't you try your idea out? If it doesn't work, we'll try another.

Students need time to get used to the coaching relationship. They will require a lot of encouragement. They must learn to enjoy the problem-solving process and believe that multiple solutions are OK. At first, students want the teacher simply to tell them how to get to the right answer. Therefore, they need time to get comfortable with making decisions on their own and simply experimenting with different approaches and solutions. Teachers must let students make incorrect decisions and then allow them to see the consequences of their decisions so they can understand what went wrong or right.

Support Technology for Coaching

Supporting hypermedia and multimedia programs can help coach students by suggesting strategies and processes for them to consider during specific problem-solving activities. For example, a program developed for third-year medical students that requires them to solve complex problems related to transfusion medicine provides students with a "What can I do?" option at all times (see Fig. 13.1). By clicking on the "What can I do?" button, students are provided with suggestions on what possible problem-solving steps may be appropriate at that given moment in the problem-solving process.

Fig. 13.1. Accessing suggestions on next course of action (From "Transfusion Management of the Surgical Patient" © Daniel R. Ambruso, MD).

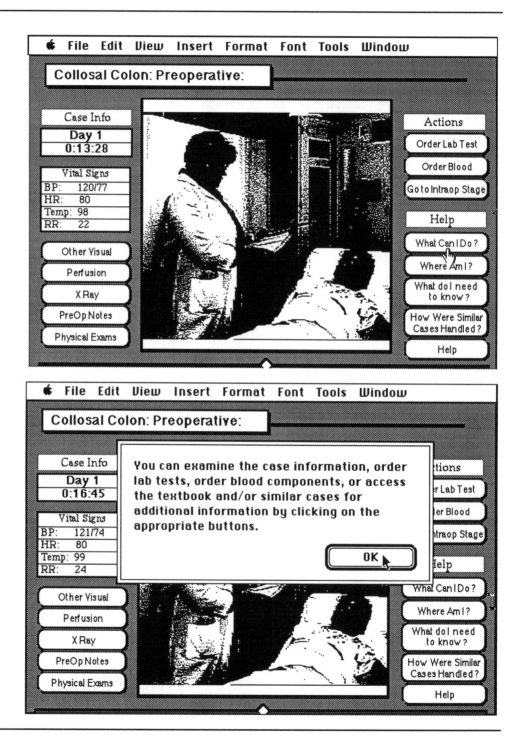

13.5   Student activities and products must reflect the process as well as the solution.

Complex problem solving involves working with ill-structured information (i.e., information that has multiple approaches and more than one acceptable solution). However, students typically engage in simplified, segmented, and decontextualized problem-solving activities. When tackling these types of problems, students are often evaluated by a single correct answer reached by using a single correct procedure. Often they must come up with the answer on the first attempt, and if they arrive at the wrong answer or use the wrong procedure, they are not encouraged to reflect on what they would do differently the next time because they are already moving on to the next subject.

Emphasize Process   The essence, then, of most higher-level thinking skills is the process that leads to the solution of a problem. REALs are often based on solving problems in a realistic context. But realism or authenticity adds complexity that is usually reflected in multiple processes and solutions. This means that knowledge about the solution process is as important as the solution. Teachers must emphasize skills including analysis, synthesis, problem definition, and hypothesis setting. The teacher must create an environment conducive to students approaching problems from different directions and with different resources and strategies. In other words, students must be taught to learn as well as to follow directions.

13.6   Provide a safe learning environment.

Complex, open-ended problem solving can be encouraged in a variety of ways. But first and foremost, teachers must provide an environment that is safe for the students. Many students' previous experiences with problem-solving activities may have included hearing comments such as "Boy, that's a dumb answer." "Don't you know how to do this?" and "WRONG!" A certain level of fear, therefore, may be associated with problem solving due to what peers and teachers have said in the past. Students believe that mistakes are "bad" and should at all times be avoided, disguised, or hidden if at all possible.

When learners tackle anything new, mistakes are to be expected. REALs encourage students to feel free to make mistakes. Problem-solving activities in REALs reflect the reality that solving problems is often a trial-and-error operation. A REAL enables students to try new things without being punished or downgraded, and to reflect on what they are doing.

Support Technology for Safe Learning   Hypermedia can help by providing opportunities for students to record and reflect on information and their learning. For example, the questions listed in Guideline 13.3 could be presented in an online computer format because they are in a program called *InfoAgent* (see Fig. 13.2). Students can enter their responses to these questions and then revisit them in the future before tackling another problem.

Fig. 13.2. *InfoAgent* screen promoting reflection on the learning process.

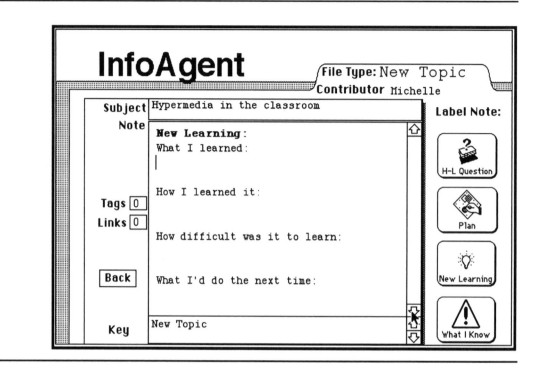

In this way, students not only get an opportunity to reflect on their problem solving, but also maintain an ongoing record that can be used as a resource to remind them of strategies they want to try again, refine, or avoid using altogether.

Peer commenting is another factor involved in creating a safe environment. If students are commenting on each other's problem solutions or approaches, then it is important to recognize that students may be uncomfortable in honestly critiquing their peers. A REAL addresses this issue by allowing students to provide comments, observations, critiques, and suggestions to their peers anonymously. Also, students receive scaffolding through built-in suggestions or guidelines on the kinds of comments that are appropriate and how to phrase those comments. For example, peer commentators can be prompted to use open-ended questions, such as

- I liked the way you handled _____. The only thing I would add to what you have already done is _____.

- I think you answered this question very well. However, I am also curious about _____. Was there a reason why you chose not to look at that aspect?

By allowing anonymous peer commenting and providing scaffolding for structuring comments, a lot of the risk involved in critiquing peers is removed, helping students to become more comfortable with and less fearful of honest peer commenting.

13.6 Promote collaboration among students.

(Note: Although collaborative learning is discussed in both chapter 11 and chapter 12, it is so important to REALs, that it is visited again here within the context of active learning.) Collaboration is an integral part of the problem-solving process for four main reasons.

First, collaboration gives students an opportunity to see and hear how other students approach and solve problems. Because the students in a collaborative group work closely together, they are able to share ideas and perspectives and help each other clarify issues.

Second, when problems are complex, students working collaboratively together can often successfully tackle problems that individual students working alone would not be able to handle. Collaboration gives rise to unique insights and solutions (Brown, Collins, & Duguid, 1989).

Third, collaboration encourages students to help each other grow as thinkers and problem solvers by providing constructive, individualized feedback to each member of the collaborative group. The development of complex problem-solving abilities requires individualized feedback, an activity teachers in the classroom are not always able to do successfully because of time constraints and the number of students in the class. Students working collaboratively can help each other through the complex problem-solving process by taking on the responsibility of providing constructive, individualized feedback to all members of the group.

Finally, collaboration allows students to share the risk involved in problem solving. Complex, open-ended problem solving involves a lot of risk because complex problems often require students to try new or unorthodox approaches and consider creative solutions. It is risky because there is the potential for failure. Because students do not want to take sole responsibility for mistakes or failures, collaboration provides students with a mechanism for spreading out the risk.

Support Technology for Collaboration Hypermedia and multimedia programs also provide mechanisms for self-coaching. For example, as discussed previously, a program can allow students to record their problem-solving processes so they can be used as a resource during future problem-solving activities. This gives students a chance to do their own fault analysis, or self-coaching, by showing them what they did during previous problem-solving activities, including what strategies worked and what strategies were not effective or useful.

13.7 Encourage students to revisit content and problems from different perspectives, given a variety of different constraints.

Another way to promote active knowledge construction is to encourage students to revisit previous content and problems from a variety of different perspectives, given different variables or twists.

To be effective higher-level thinkers and complex problem solvers, successful students revisit new information/content by repeatedly considering how it can be applied in a number of different situations from a variety of perspectives (Spiro & Jehng, 1990). When successful students work on problems, they constantly refine their decisions to come up with more effective and efficient strategies, approaches, and solutions. They enjoy making revisions and have confidence in their own solutions. Less successful students tend to stop at one pass through information and usually examine only one viewpoint. They are reluctant to make revisions or to seek more efficient and effective solutions to problems. They have little confidence in their own ability and look for ways to give the teachers exactly what they think the teachers expect.

Support Technology for Crisscrossing

Computer support can play an important role in operationalizing this guideline. Computer databases and hypermedia programs permit easy manipulation of vast amounts of data, allowing students to review the data from a variety of different organizational structures. Hypermedia programs provide students with the ability to rearrange data to represent different perspectives, and reflect on how the reorganization affects their original conclusions.

Most educational software or classroom activities have access to a limited body of knowledge, and students must work within the confines of that limited knowledge base. However, activities that occur outside the typical classroom setting are open to many kinds of knowledge and usually several alternative solutions. REALs should make large databases available to students, and should also support more open-ended tasks in which students build their own databases. Students that construct databases can interrelate, label, sort, and perform periodic reorganizations and house cleanings to enhance the quality of the community knowledge base. Performing these actions encourages students to constantly reexamine existing knowledge in new ways. Some of the activities that hypermedia programs can support in REALs include the following:

- Organization tasks including multiple arrangements, labeling, sorting, editing, prioritizing, timelines, iconic and digital images, outlining, hierarchical lists, concept maps, causal chains

- Generation tasks including the creation of knowledge bases to examine data and its components

- Cross-referencing tasks including the examination of relationships among different nodes of information by looking for links with other subject areas

- Multiple perspective tasks including examination of an issue or problem from several positions, either current or historical, and the examination of the same problem from different value systems or through different resources.

Another hypermedia program developed for third-year medical students, called "Handling Transfusion Hazards," operationalizes this guideline by presenting students with a transfusion problem and then providing them with a variety of sources that present different viewpoints on the problem. Students can gather information by looking at a variety of experts' perspectives on the problem. For example, the student can look at what the surgeon, attending physician, patient, nurse, resident, or blood bank director has to say about a particular problem, with each individual's perspective on the case differing on some point (see Fig. 13.3). Another source of information is the file of similar cases. This file presents how similar problems were handled given different time and resource constraints. In this way, students take multiple passes through the information, seeing it from many people's points of view and examining how those different points of view change their perspectives on the problem.

13.8 Encourage students to reflect on the processes and outcomes of knowledge construction activities.

This process of reflection is just as important as engaging in the high-level thinking activities themselves. Reflection gives students opportunities to think about how they answered a question, made a decision, or solved a problem. It allows students to consider what strategies were successful or unsuccessful, what issues need to be remembered for next time, and what could be done differently in the future. In other words, reflection gives students a chance to evaluate their high-level thinking performance and take mental notes that can be used to adjust and refine subsequent performance.

13.9 Encourage students to record their learning processes through a variety of evidence.

To reflect on the processes and outcomes of knowledge construction activities, students need to make their learning processes overt. One way to help students do this is by suggesting particular learning strategies that encourage planning and make the studying process overt.

REALs help students make their learning processes overt by providing a structure that helps students keep track of goals, objectives, chosen resources, strategies used, and timelines. Students who keep track of this type of information are planning for knowledge construction and, therefore, can use their plans to monitor their progress.

Students should be able see that they are making progress and that the strategy is a valuable tool for attaining the ultimate objective. To guide multistep processes, students should be asked to record steps within their strategy. An emphasis on the process and how a particular strategy is working teaches students that their thinking process is more important than a right or wrong final product, thus making it more acceptable to make errors.

Support Technology for Recording Learning

Hypermedia/multimedia programs can operationalize this guideline by

• asking students to add a new fact to the database,

• recording the steps involved in solving a problem,

Fig. 13.3. Different expert perspectives on a problem (From "Handling Transfusion Hazards").
© Daniel R. Ambruso, M.D).

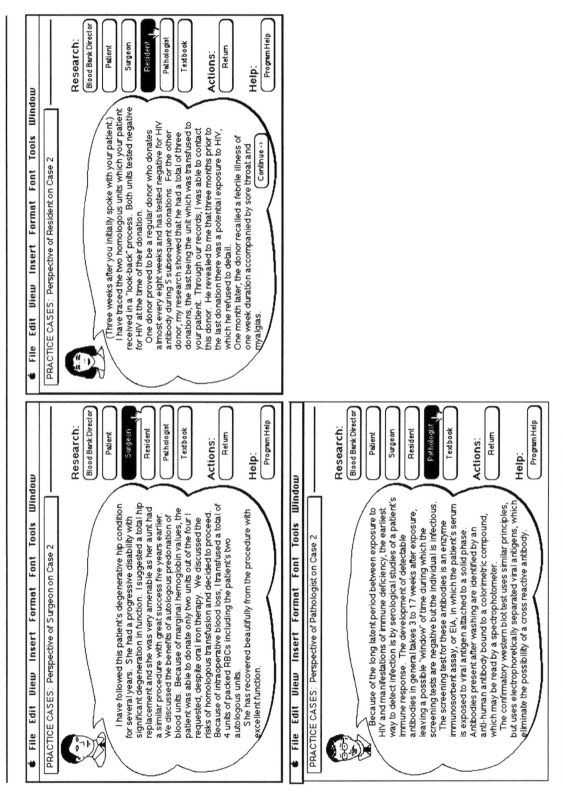

- encouraging students to describe their intentions in pursuing a particular answer or solution or developing a particular product,

- adding personal notes that argue against a standard position; or

- asking students to record hypotheses or predictions.

For example, a hypermedia system requires students to take a position on an issue and then defend that position. Other students are required to respond to the different positions and add notes stating their own

positions and arguments. The hypermedia program records all positions and notes so students can go back and look at earlier entries to see how their positions and ability to effectively defend positions changed and developed over time. In this way, their argumentation process is made overt so they are able to reflect not only on the outcomes of the argumentation, but on the process of argumentation itself.

Multimedia systems can make students' learning processes overt in other ways as well. *InfoAgent* asks students to record the questions they want to research and the steps needed to answer the questions (see Fig. 13.4). When the students have researched their questions and come up with answers, *InfoAgent* then prompts them to add the new information to a knowledge base.

13.10 Promote student articulation and presentation of ideas through multimedia products.

Articulation is a very important part of the knowledge construction process. Articulation means that students must make their ideas, perspectives, solutions, products, and so on available to others for reflection, review, criticism, and use. In other words, students must present what they have learned — their knowledge construction — to others. In fact, students have not really completed the knowledge construction process until they have presented what they have learned to others.

The notion of presentation helps bridge the classroom-workplace gap. In on-the-job situations, people are constantly making presentations to their employees and employers, colleagues, and customers in public forums (e.g., board meetings, company meetings, project development meetings, brainstorming sessions, manager retreats, salesroom presentations, training classes). Yet, in a typical classroom setting, students are asked to present their ideas privately via a paper handed in to the teacher. Instead, REALs require students to demonstrate what they have learned in ways that authentically represent what they will have to do on the job. Because REALs place an emphasis on formal methods of articulation, student presentations of knowledge construction outcomes should be part of the student assessment and/or evaluation process (for more on student assessment and evaluation, see chapter 14).

Students live in a multimedia world. They should, therefore, be encouraged to present their ideas, perspectives, positions, problem solutions, and projects in

Fig. 13.4. Prompting for information.

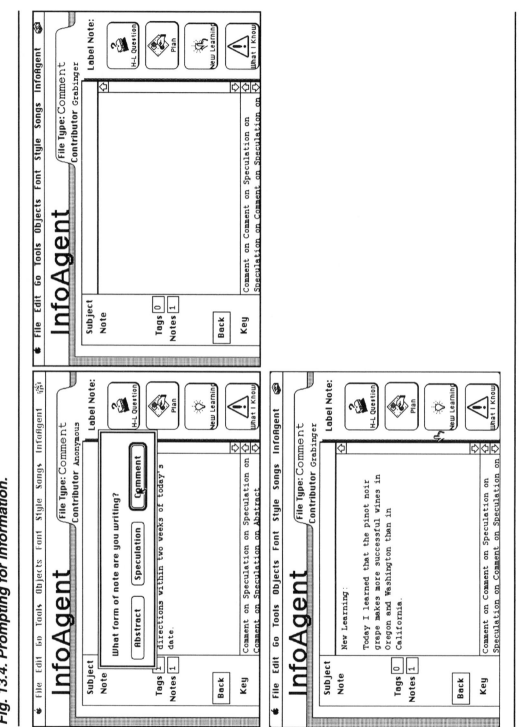

multimedia formats. Hypermedia/multimedia programs can support student presentations by allowing students to create presentation systems — systems that display students' work in a linear, sequential manner. By creating a presentation system, students can conduct a formal presentation in front of the class using their presentation system to support the lecture/discussion. A presentation system can also be used like a point-of-sale demonstration program, in which students can access the system when they want to and are then guided through the presentation in a particular way.

An alternative method of presenting students' knowledge construction outcomes is via knowledge bases. Once students have solved a particular problem, they can be required to add their solutions to a commonly accessible knowledge base. Then, the contents of the knowledge base can be used as a resource of information for other students. For example, Scardamalia and Bereiter (1991, 1993; Scardamalia, Bereiter, McLean, Swallow, & Woodruff, 1989) developed an instructional knowledge-base system to support intentional learning activities called a Computer-Supported Intentional Learning Environment (CSILE). One of the many requirements of the system was that once students had researched their questions and articulated their answers using text and graphics, the completed question and answer had to be added to a common knowledge base used as an information resource by other students. In this way, students presented their questions and answers in ways that were understandable and usable by their classmates.

CONCLUSION

Facilitating active knowledge construction has always been recognized as a critical element in learning. The primary idea behind a REAL is to provide an environment in which students create complex, rich knowledge structures that will apply to a variety of problems. This requires complex, contextualized, higher-level activities. To become capable problem solvers, students must be exposed to complex, open-ended problems that are anchored or situated in realistic contexts.

For active knowledge construction to occur, students must be provided with opportunities to engage in high-level thinking, reflection, and articulation activities. REALs provide a structure that supports and scaffolds students in the pursuit of active knowledge construction so they are able to successfully engage in the types of knowledge construction activities (including decision making and problem solving) that are becoming a staple in today's workplace environment.

REFERENCES

Brown, J. S., Collins, A., & Duguid, P. (1989). Situated cognition and the culture of learning. *Educational Researcher, 18*(1), 32-42.

Bruner, J. S. (1961). The act of discovery. *Harvard Educational Review, 31*(1), 21-32.

Bruner, J. S. (1990). *Acts of meaning.* Cambridge MA: Harvard University Press.

Forman, G., & Pufall, P. (Eds.). (1988). *Constructivism in the computer age*. Hillsdale NJ: Lawrence Erlbaum Associates.

Fosnot, C. (1989). *Inquiring teachers, inquiring learners: A constructivist approach for teaching*. New York: Teacher's College Press.

Goodman, N. (1984). *Of mind and other matters*. Cambridge MA: Harvard University Press.

Scardamalia, M., & Bereiter, C. (1991). Higher levels of agency for children in knowledge building: A challenge for the design of new knowledge media. *The Journal of the Learning Sciences*, *1*(1), 37-68.

Scardamalia, M., & Bereiter, C. (1993).

Scardamalia, M., Bereiter, C., McLean, R., Swallow, J., & Woodruff, E. (1989). Computer-supported intentional learning environments. *Journal of Educational Computing Research*, *5*(1), 51 - 68.

Schank, R., & Jona, M. (1991). Empowering the student: New perspectives on the design of teaching systems. *The Journal of the Learning Sciences*, *1*(1), 7-313.

Schwartz, J., & Yerushalmy, M. (1987). The geometric supposer: Using micro-computers to restore invention to the learning of mathematics. In D. Perkins, J. Lochhead, & J. Bishop, (Eds.). *Thinking* (pp. 525-536). Hillsdale NJ: Lawrence Erlbaum Associates.

The Secretary's Commission on Achieving Necessary Skills. (1991). *What work requires of schools: A SCANS report for America 2000*. Washington DC: U.S. Department of Labor.

Spiro, R., & Jehng, J. (1990). Cognitive flexibility and hypertext: Theory and technology for the nonlinear and multidimensional traversal of complex subject matter. In D. Nix, & R. Spiro, (Eds.). *Cognition, education, and multimedia: Exploring ideas in high technology* (pp. 163-213). Hillsdale NJ: Lawrence Erlbaum Associates.

Wittrock, M. (1974). Learning as a generative process. *Educational Psychologist*, *11*, 87-913.

Wittrock, M. (1978). The cognitive movement in instruction. *Educational Psychologist*, *15*, 15-29.

CHAPTER 14

Learner Assessment

Thomas A. Cyr

Chapter Objectives Choosing effective ways to assess learning is a major part of the instructional design process. Appropriate assessment strategies can add to the effects of instruction. Assessments that are closely aligned with instructional goals and embedded within instructional tactics provide effective feedback to both student and instructor. Unaligned and disjointed assessments contribute little to learning, have a demoralizing effect on student motivation, and serve as obstacles to learning. In this chapter I

- compare tests and assessments,

- provide basic definitions and descriptions of the various components of effective performance-based assessment and show how assessment is a critical component in the instructional design of REALs, and

- provide guidelines for developing assessments in interactive multimedia environments.

TESTS VERSUS ASSESSMENT

A widely held assumption by educators is that tests are the main means of assessment and, because of this, determine both instructional strategies and what the student learns (Frederiksen & Collins, 1989; Shepard, 1989). The purpose of this chapter, however, is not to present effective *test* strategies but effective *assessment* strategies. There is a subtle but important distinction. (see Fig. 14.1.)

Tests Tests, in the traditional view, are instruments used to measure achievement. Tests evaluate the quantity and retention of learning following completion of a unit of instruction. The question traditionally asked by tests is usually related to quantity: How much of a particular content does a student know? Tests have summative attributes: They are a final statement about what was

---

Fig. 14.1. Tests versus assessment.

Tests	**Assessments**
• summative in nature	• formative in nature
• often take the form of objective questions	• performance-based analyses
• assess the quantity of learning	• assess the quality of learning
• tend to be competitive	• tend to be collaborative

---

learned and are often reported as values or grades. They frequently take the forms of multiple-choice, true-false, short answer, fill-in-the-blank, or essay. Tests tell how much of a certain subject area learners have retained, but not necessarily whether they can perform with that information in on-the-job situations.

Assessments   Assessments, on the other hand, provide feedback on the quality of performance. Assessments have formative attributes and are part of the developmental process of learning. They examine the strengths and weaknesses of learning as it is developing and have a direct impact on strategies of instruction. Questions asked are usually related to quality of performance: Is the student heading in the right direction in the learning process? If not, what can be done to turn the student in the right direction? Instead of exams, assessments often use complex descriptions of desired performances called rubrics to apply to student products. These rubrics describe the kinds of performance necessary to accomplish a task in a thoughtful manner. Examine Fig. 14.2 for an example of a rubric for a declarative knowledge task.

Finally, tests tend to be competitive; students are compared to each other or a standard. Assessments focus more on the individual, helping each learner to identify strengths and weaknesses. Assessments are more compatible with collaborative behavior because they do not make comparisons to other students, but, only to exemplary products or performance rubrics.

In hypermedia and multimedia learning environments, in which emphasis is placed on learners' self-regulation within authentic and contextualized learning strategies and on the promotion of active knowledge construction (Grabinger & Dunlap, 1995), learning is facilitated by formative assessment strategies in the following ways:

1. They facilitate self-regulation of the learner by providing meaningful feedback to the student regarding progress toward educational goals. Students are able, through these assessments, to make personal judgments about progress and to decide how to redirect their learning.

2. They support the creation and use of authentic environments because assessments occur within the context of realistic problems.

Fig. 14.2. Example of a rubric.

Score	Criteria	Check
4	Demonstrates a complete understanding of the principles, concepts, and facts related to the task; provides new understanding into some facet of the discipline	
3	Displays a complete and accurate understanding of the principles, concepts, and facts related to the task	
2	Displays an incomplete understanding of the principles concepts, and facts related to the task and has some conspicuous misconceptions	
1	Demonstrates serious misconceptions about the principles, concepts, and facts related to the task	

3. Finally, frequent formative assessments promote active knowledge construction in that they require revision. Revising is an active reviewing of one's work. The process of reviewing promotes higher-level thinking in that students analyze what has been done, draw conclusions about the condition of the performance or product, and make necessary improvements. This revision process encourages creative and flexible problem solving that leads to the presentation of the revised performance or product. Self-regulated learners working on projects with depth, complexity, and relevance are more likely to develop the skills necessary for successful out-of-school participation (Berliner, 1992).

Tests are like the mileage or kilometer reading on the odometer. An odometer tells you how far you have gone, but not whether you are going in the right direction or whether you arrive at the correct destination. Tests provide information about what the learner has achieved — how many miles are traveled, but not about the direction the student is going.

Assessments are more like road signs in that they provide information to direct performance and instruction. The difficulty of a journey is greatly increased without road signs. In most cases, getting from one place to another without signs relies heavily on chance. Learning without assessments is similar. Standardized tests, in particular, merely inform about the quantity of right and wrong answers and how a student compares to others in that quantity, but they tell little about how students can apply or perform with what they know in realistic situations. Assessments, on the other hand, are designed in a manner to not only inform the student about achievement but also to reveal what errors were made and where to go next in the learning process.

In rich environments for active learning (REALs), in which emphasis is placed on learners' self-regulation within authentic and contextualized learning strategies and on the promotion of active knowledge construction, formative assessment strategies facilitate learning in several ways:

1. They facilitate self-regulation of the learner by providing meaningful feedback to the student regarding progress toward educational goals. Students are able, through these assessments, to make personal judgments about progress and to decide how to redirect their learning activities.

2. They support the creation and use of authentic environments because the assessments occur within the context of realistic problems needing solutions.

3. Finally, frequent formative assessments promote active knowledge construction because they require revision. The revision process promotes higher level thinking because students analyze what they have done, draw conclusions about the quality of the performance or product, and make necessary improvements. This revision process encourages creative and flexible problem solving. Self-regulated learners working on projects with depth, complexity, duration, and relevance are more likely to develop the skills necessary for successful participation in out-of-school activities (Berliner, 1992).

BASIC PREMISES

Higher-Level Thinking There are two basic premises about hypermedia and multimedia learning environments worth noting before continuing the discussion on assessment. First, learning environments use instructional strategies that engage higher level thinking processes through creative problem-solving activities (Frederickson & Collins, 1989; Resnick, 1987; Shavelson, Baxter, & Pine, 1992; Shepard, 1989; Wiggins, 1991) including analysis, synthesis, application, induction, deduction, innovation, and invention. These processes require students to relate prior learning to new learning and to apply that learning to solve novel problems.

Accessing Information A second premise associated with hypermedia is that it is an effective tool for accessing information. Hypermedia, by definition, means going beyond traditional means of communicating. The effectiveness of hypermedia is rooted in the assumption that students who have multiple means of accessing information at the time they need it will learn more effectively.

Hypermedia is a particularly apt medium for these assessments because student performance is easily collected and examined through various electronic tools. For example, student writing can be collected in electronic portfolios as files in a computer folder. Student performance can be captured on videotape for later viewing or scoring, and computer–adaptive tests with the ability to accommodate to student speed and style can be administered (Bruder, 1993).

Assessment and Context Third, performance-based assessments for learning environments and hypermedia applications have a primary purpose of providing information to learners in a timely manner to improve performance within the context in which it occurs. Assessment feedback provides learners with information about where they are at the moment in the learning journey and what to do next to get to their desired destinations. They are not static nor predetermined. They are dynamic, embedded in the learning process, and reflective of the content.

For learners in hypermedia learning environments, the content is not the end but the means to an end. Learning environments provide activities that require content, but the ultimate goal is not content—it is the ability to use content to reason. The goal is to help learners develop the skills of comparing, classifying, describing, analyzing, inducing, deducing, abstracting, and using information to make decisions in the solving of problems.

In summary, assessments designed to support traditional learning environments and hypermedia learning environments must evolve from equivalent premises.

1. Assessment is a formative method of guiding learning that aims to develop higher-level thinking skills that will serve as lifelong learning skills.

2. The development of hypermedia supports for rich environments for active learning provides many bases from which to help students develop skill in accessing information, a fundamental skill in all higher-level thinking processes.

3. Assessments directed at improving performance must be frequent and embedded in the instructional strategies of the learning environment.

For learning environments, assessments are the road signs of learning. Once a destination is established, assessments provide the feedback guidance necessary to keep learning focused and moving in the correct direction.

ASSESSMENT GUIDELINES

Overall Development of Assessments What are basic criteria for the development of assessments? We suggest several general guidelines to consider in the instructional design process of assessments.

14.1 **Write assessments in terms of the task and performance qualities you want learners to demonstrate. Content should support the task.**

The primary purposes of assessment are to develop higher-level thinking skills, to increase the depth and sophistication of knowledge, and to improve

performance in realistic situations. Therefore, teachers should write assessments that work in conjunction with authentic learning tasks and provide feedback that facilitates adjustments in performance. Curricular and training priorities can evolve from the assessment of student work when it catalogs errors, provides opportunities to analyze error sources, and provides guidance and information about what to do about the errors. See Fig. 14.3 for examples of high-level tasks and possible corresponding assessment strategies.

Fig. 14.3. Learning tasks and assessments.

Learning Tasks

- respond to abusive and unhappy customer

- discover regulatory violation within stock transactions

- create engineering solution for building a wooden bridge across a defined span for a minimum weight

- solve mathematical problems using rate, time, real
and distance formulae

- work collaboratively in group problem-solving situation

- access and interpret information for decision-to
making task

- compare brothers fighting for North and South in U.S. Civil War

Assessment Strategies

- videotape and review role playing experience

- use simulated materials to identify specific example

- use model wooden materials to create a scale model and test using stress-generating tools

- present contextualized problem using

 or videodisc-based situations

- observe, videotape, and analyze group member performances

- learners create database and crate links

 relate ideas

- write diary of one of the brothers to describe daily life and activities

---

For example, if an assessment in a history course is created to measure students' abilities to make comparisons, a learning task may ask students to investigate the different experiences of two brothers during the Civil War—one fighting for the North and the other for the South. Thus, the assessment would use content to look at a quality (the ability to compare). The students' task could be to write a diary from the perspective of one of the brothers. The question might be, "How were these two sons' experiences similar and different?" The students' responses would have to reflect the comparison task and be measured against specific competencies associated with comparing. Did the student compare the two brothers' experiences and perspectives? Were specific characteristics of the experiences and perspectives used in comparing the two brothers described? Did the student accurately identify the similarities and differences between the two brothers and their experiences or perspectives? Priorities regarding improving the qualities of performance could then be established and feedback provided to facilitate performance adjustments.

A second example may deal with teaching stock exchange examiners to discover and substantiate rule violations among stock traders. A simulated set of documents could be created through which the learners would search for a violation and evidence to substantiate it. The focus of the learning environment would be on the abilities to discover and to substantiate. The assessment would ask: Did the learners identify the correct violation? Could they relate the violation

Fig. 14.4. Civil War diary assignment.

Traditional Test Objectives	Assessment Objectives
• Knowledge of Civil War people • Knowledge of dates and events • Explanation of causes	• Examine ability to make comparisons • Draw comparisons between North and South • Logical thinking • Compare and contrast topics such as weather, food, equipment • Discuss important factors: beliefs, reasons for fighting, life in the army, effects of the war on home lives, changes in society, operations of the army

to specific federal rules? Did their substantiation of the violation include appropriate evidence?

Note that in both examples the focus of the assessment is on the kinds of tasks and abilities needed to perform in a variety of circumstances. The content — the Civil War and stock trading violations — is present, but it is taught within the context of the higher-level thinking skills.

14.2 Assessments should be valid and reliable.

Validity Confidence in assessment requires certain degrees of validity. For our purposes here, *validity* means that the assessment tools we use measure constructs we want to measure and that the results of the assessment are interpreted in an appropriate manner. This is true for all parties concerned with the educational process. In performance assessment this requires specifying exemplary performances and agreeing to descriptors for selected exemplars (Wiggins, 1992). In the above U.S. Civil War illustration, if the students are asked to make a comparison, their products should be held accountable for comparing the brothers and not for factual knowledge of the Civil War. For example, see Figure 14.4 for a comparison of sample test and assessment standards for the Civil War Diary assignment.

The elements examined within the desired competencies and the criteria for each of those elements should be prespecified. For example, in the comparison competency, the learning task should ask the student to accurately identify important similarities and differences between the two brothers based on prespecified characteristics — the fact that they live in two different places and the effect that these two different places has had on their lives. Determining competency criteria (in this case, ability to make comparisons) prior to the assignment of the task will increase the validity of the measure. See Fig. 14.5 for a more detailed set of elements and criteria.

Fig. 14.5. Civil War performance elements and criteria.

Comparison	• Chooses appropriate objects to compare • Identifies characteristics for comparison • Identifies similarities and differences between objects
Classification	• Chooses significant objects to classify • Identifies appropriate categories and associated rules for sorting objects • Accurately sorts objects into identified categories
Supporting Claims	• Identifies claims that require support • Provides sufficient or appropriate evidence for the claim • Specifies qualifications or restrictions regarding the claim
Systems and Error Analysis	• Identifies and articulates important errors in information or in processes • Correctly describes the effects the errors have on the information or processes • Specifies how to correct the errors
Induction and Deduction	• Identifies facts or instances from which to construct general principles • Interprets information from which inductions are made • Correctly draws conclusions from the selected information or observation
Decision Making	• Identifies significant alternatives to be considered • Establishes relevant criteria for assessing the alternatives • Correctly shows the extent to which each alternative includes each criterion • Makes an appropriate decision based on decision criteria
Investigation	• Correctly identifies known definitions, historical facts, and implications regarding the object or subject under investigation • Identifies conceptual conflicts and uncertainties regarding the object or subject • Designs, develops, and defends a credible resolution to conflicts and uncertainties
Problem Solving	• Accurately frames the problem by identifying sources of difficulty, trouble, annoyance, or perplexity • Identifies feasible solutions for overcoming the sources to the problem • Accurately implements and defends a problem solution
Invention	• Identifies a process, product, or improvement to satisfy an unmet need • Lists standards and criteria the invention will meet • Designs and develops a new process, product, or improvement

Reliability Quality assessment also requires *reliability*. Reliable assessments can answer to the following questions:

- Can the assessment produce repeatable results over many trials?

- Does the assessment use different kinds of evidence about the student's ability in comparison to the desired outcome rather than a single indication?

- Do these multiple bits of evidence agree with each other?

- Would different judges of the performance and products arrive at similar conclusions regarding the learner's strengths and weaknesses?

Establishing reliability of performance and product assessments requires multiple student performances and products based on the same competency. To demonstrate the students' true abilities to make comparisons, several learning tasks would need to be administered to show consistency of performance. In the Civil War example, students would have to produce multiple performances and products that demonstrate their ability to make comparisons, such as creating a diary, participating in a debate, creating a database, or making a presentation. However, all of these are not needed in this particular example. Remember, that the content serves as a means to an end, not as the end in and of itself. If the ability to make comparisons is something that we want to develop in our students, then we may look at one example in the Civil War case, another in a language arts subject, and still another in a biology task. For the school student, assessments are part of a long-term growth over years rather than a single activity in one subject area.

In the stock trading examiner example, learners may be required to work through several progressively difficult sample cases and finally assist an experienced examiner in a real case. A number of performance examples are more reliable and therefore more representative of a student's true ability.

Establishing the reliability of performance measures themselves requires that the people examining the performances or products arrive at similar or near similar results. To achieve reliability of the performance measures, teachers should establish such interrater reliability of the measures.

14.3 Create assessments that evoke desired performances through knowledge acquisition within a specific content field and are compared to realistic established criteria.

Effective assessments evoke both a desired performance and require interaction with a content field. Learners should be able to demonstrate their knowledge of content through the learning task. In the example regarding the two brothers and the Civil War, students are asked to make a comparison within the context of the Civil War. The evoked performance is "comparing," and the identified content is the Civil War.

Contextualize and Benchmark

Learning tasks should be contextualized and benchmarked to provide direction in learning. Contextualized and benchmarked assessments assist learning by eliciting performances from students that facilitate movement from crude to sophisticated understandings of content essentials (Wiggins, 1992).

A *contextualized task* is an authentic simulation or experience. Pilots in training gain contextualized experience in sophisticated flight simulators. Customer service representatives gain contextualized experience in practicing with actual customer questions or in complex simulations.

Benchmarking is the process of comparing learner performance to exit-level standards. The questions asked are: What are the minimum established exit standards? How is the beginner doing in comparison to the professional? How is the novice pilot doing in comparison to the expert pilot? Assessment informs the beginners and the beginners' instructors how they compare to the professional or the desired on-the-job performance level. Assessments measure progress along this knowledge acquisition continuum.

Two things, then, are necessary to contextualize assessment. First, to place an assessment in context, teachers should first design the instruction so that it requires an authentic performance from learners in which they are presented with an integrated and multifaceted problem that requires interaction with the desired content in order for the task to be done well. In a science assessment, for example, the assessment task could be based on the investigation of some invention to show the ability of the student to define the invention, to understand the invention from a historical perspective, and to demonstrate the implication of the invention in daily life now and in the future. An assessment task such as this would be an integrated, multifaceted performance that requires a desired content.

Second, it is also critical to inform learners what the established benchmarks are and that those benchmarks represent authentic behavior and expectations, not abstracted or decontextualized behaviors. Assessment standards should be completely open and not a mystery to learners. For example, to benchmark an assessment, teachers may design assessment tasks by selecting exemplars. The exemplars should be shown to the learners so they are aware of the desired performance. From the exemplars students can see the direction in which learning is to head and can use the exemplars as a form of self-assessment during the learning process.

14.4 Assessment design is part of the front-end analysis.

A common architectural aphorism is that "form must follow function." A similar aphorism from instructional design is "analysis before action." Like the architect, the instructional designer must address the "ground to be covered" and make the design fit the site and the needs of the client. The instructional designer's role is to create authentic, contextualized assessments embedded in learning tasks that evoke continuous improvement in performance and understanding to the satisfaction of the clients—both teachers and students. The more the tasks and assessments fit both the environment and the goals of the client, the better the design.

To do this, the first task is to determine what is to be learned. The designer's role is to determine the instructional priorities and how these priorities are to be translated into performance and assessments. For example, what performances or situations should all students encounter and be expected to master (Wiggins, 1992)?

The second task is to determine the instructional strategies and tactics the students will use and the products that will result from them. As stated earlier, the learning task should evoke performance and require interaction with content.

The third task is to establish the means of assessing progress toward the learning goal and the methods of keeping track of learning progress. What are the standards, criteria, and measures to be used? What are suitable benchmarks? When should these assessments take place? Whose responsibility will they be? Assessments designed with these guidelines have a stronger chance of being embedded in the instruction than of becoming a separate episode in the learning process.

LIFELONG LEARNING COMPETENCIES AND ASSESSMENT

What competencies are important to assess? What kinds of essential learning and achievements should be mastered and therefore assessed? Whereas the preceding section covered general guidelines for the development of assessments, this section focuses on six competency areas to which designers of REALs should attend: domain knowledge, reasoning skills, information accessing, communication skills, self-regulation, and social regulation. These areas are fundamental to learning in all domains and help to put the focus of learning on learning skills rather than content.

14.5 Assess content domain knowledge by collecting evidence of knowledge coherence.

Certainly, content domain knowledge is a major piece of the competency pie. Most learning events in schools today are geared toward developing competencies in particular knowledge domains, mostly declarative knowledge. In varying degrees of importance, students learn facts, processes, concepts, and principles about the domains. Discrete bits of knowledge, no matter how advanced or abstract, however, are not indicative of true domain knowledge, which demonstrates coherence, that is, integration and structure. Assessments should require students to show the connectedness of facts, concepts, processes, and principles (Shepard, 1989).

For example, a science assessment might ask a student to design an experiment or demonstration to illustrate a specific scientific concept and its implications for everyday life. Developing such an experiment or exhibit will force connectedness of facts, concepts, processes, and principles.

In another example, investigators for a stock exchange board may be asked to connect federal rules with examples of violation by brokers. To do this, the learner must understand the rules, and laws, and identify potential examples of evidence of violations.

This ability to connect pieces of information is what leads to the next principle, reasoning skills.

14.6 Assess reasoning skills by asking students to apply cognitive operations.

The higher-order thinking movement has for many years encouraged teachers to provide opportunities for learners to develop reasoning skills: analysis, synthesis, application, evaluation, innovation, and so on. Authentic problems are about more than applying facts, although good factual recall often facilitates reasoning. A student must also analyze situations, synthesize information about the problem or idea, apply innovative solutions or improvements, and evaluate the results of effort.

A short list of cognitive reasoning skills includes comparison; classification; supporting claims; systems and error analysis; supported induction and deduction; decision making; investigation; problem solving; and invention (Marzano, 1992). Learning tasks and assessments can be structured around these cognitive operations to stimulate complex reasoning and the application of knowledge. See Fig. 14.5 for examples of assessments related to each area.

An example regarding induction and deduction would be a learning task and subsequent assessment that asks a student to observe some event or entity in nature over a period of time and then to draw some generalizations regarding the event or entity from the observed data. The student's representation of the knowledge gathered from the observations would be judged on specific criteria related to supported induction. Do the generalizations identify specific and important points? Can the student rationally and logically explain the observed phenomenon? Did the student accurately interpret the information from which the inductions were made? Did the student draw accurate conclusions from the observations? Answers to these questions reflect the student's ability to apply higher-order cognitive operations.

14.7 Assess information accessing skills by asking students to seek out information from a variety of sources and modalities.

In the information age, being able to access information is a particularly important skill. Learners need to know how to find information from print-based, electronic-based, and multimedia sources. Finding information is a problem-solving activity, so learners need to have a variety of strategies on hand for overcoming dead ends and empty searches.

The two fundamental information accessing skills are reading and listening, which have many subcompetencies including the ability to determine when additional information is useful or necessary, to retrieve information from various resources, to assess the value of information, and to interpret and synthesize information (Marzano, 1992). Assessment can focus on any or all of the various subcompetencies and can be designed to measure a student's ability to perform detailed assessment of information needs. Do students know what information is needed? Do students have a basic idea of what sources to begin searching? Is the student able to distinguish between relevant and irrelevant information? What tasks will show a student's ability to search for and acquire information? How can a student's ability to judge the value of gathered information be measured?

14.8   Assess communication skills by encouraging learners to express thought as language through written, oral, and multimedia reporting.

Learners need to know how to communicate their ideas to others. Having an idea or knowing something unknown by others is not enough. Ideas need to be shared, and students need to know how to communicate their ideas and knowledge effectively. In learning environments with an emphasis on cooperative or collaborative effort this is especially true.

Assessments designed to have learners express thought as language through written, oral, and multimedia reporting also assess students' abilities to communicate to

1. diverse audiences through a variety of strategies affecting the tone, style, and message by carefully studying the needs, knowledge, and interests of the audience;

2. serve a variety of purposes through skillful use of a variety of communication strategies to inform, entertain, or persuade by clearly and effectively communicating a thematic idea, feeling or belief; and

3. present effectively through a given medium including speaking, writing, and audiovisual media in various formats including debates, panel discussions, essays, and videotaped documentaries (Marzano, 1992).

14.9   Assess self-reflection skills by providing students with complex learning tasks which push students beyond current levels of understanding and ability.

Self-reflection is a metacognitive process that learners use to direct and monitor their own learning and performance (Honebein, Duffy, & Fishman, 1993). Can learners reflect on and monitor their own behavior and efforts? When designing assessments to reveal students' metacognitive self-reflection skills, designers should attend to student behaviors that illustrate their abilities and efforts to get at different perspectives, deliberate over choices before acting, and persevere through difficult situations.

Assessment measures designed to assess self-reflection skills should measure students' abilities to (Marzano, 1992):

• consider all perspectives and options that would be beneficial to the performance or product,

• push the limits and persevere in difficult situations,

• establish clear goals and manage progress through achieving them,

• recognize problems and obstacles and know where to get help to overcome them,

• recognize errors and use them to guide learning rather than hide them or feel ashamed of them,

- examine learning strategies and accept successful ones and reject unsuccessful ones, and

- generate and pursue personal standards of performance.

14.10 Assess social regulation skills by measuring cooperation and collaboration skills.

Another competency area getting more attention is social regulation: Can the learner work in a cooperative and collaborative manner? The role of cooperation and collaboration is well articulated within education (Marzano, 1992). Cooperative and collaborative learning environments have been shown to have positive effects on achievement (Johnson & Johnson, 1987; Slavin, 1983).

Specific competencies associated with cooperative and collaborative skills are the ability to

- work toward the achievement of group goals,

- contribute toward group maintenance,

- communicate interpersonally, and

- self-assess and monitor one's own behavior.

Generative learning environments such as REALs are a means of fostering cooperative and collaborative activities. Providing students with learning and assessment tasks that require them to solve complex problems forces cooperative and collaborative behavior as learner's generate plans, identify knowledge requirements, test their plans, and revise them as needed to solve problems (Hannafin, 1992).

Assessment of collaborative skills can be done by gathering data through a four-point scaled rubric addressing each of the cooperative and collaborative criteria. See an example of a rubric in Figure 14.6.

Social regulation skills are not necessarily specific competencies. Rather, people have tendencies or propensities for these cooperative/collaborative behaviors. Assessing their presence in student performances or products requires good and careful judgment on the part of the teacher.

CONCLUSION

Hypermedia-supported REALs are particularly well suited for most of the above competencies; accessing information, for example, would be particularly difficult in an unmediated environment. Learning is a complex endeavor. Assessment of domain knowledge, reasoning skills, information accessing communication skills, self-regulation, and social-regulation is an important part of the designer's role.

Learning environments designed to include hypermedia support for learning must consider forms of assessment that will also contribute to student learning progress. Performance-based assessment for rich environments for active learning is such a form of assessment. Properly designed performance-based assessments

Fig. 14.6. Rubric for assessing cooperative skills.

Contribution to Group Achievement

1.1 How did the student contribute to the achievement of
the group goal?   1   2   3   4

1.2 Did the student contribute to the development of group goals?   1   2   3   4

1.3 Did the student help identify roles, strategies, and plans
for those goals?   1   2   3   4

1.4 Did the student elicit commitment from other group members?   1   2   3   4

Interpersonal Communication Skills

2.1 How did the student demonstrate effective interpersonal
communication skills?   1   2   3   4

2.2 Did the student participate in group interactions?   1   2   3   4

2.3 Did the student encourage other members of the group
to participate?   1   2   3   4

2.4 Is there evidence of the student's ability to express ideas
clearly, precisely, and accurately?   1   2   3   4

2.5 Did the student facilitate efforts to insure understanding of
all group members?   1   2   3   4

Group Participation

3.1 Did the student contribute to a positive group atmosphere?   1   2   3   4

3.2 Did the student contribute to an atmosphere in which individual
differences are considered a group strength?   1   2   3   4

3.3 Did the student respect and show interest in all group members?   1   2   3   4

3.4 Did the student seek and provide constructive feedback to and
from other group members?   1   2   3   4

3.5 Did the student provide leadership by guiding the group
toward consensus?   1   2   3   4

Individual Behavior within Group

4.1 How did the student reflect on and monitor his or her own behavior? 1   2   3   4

4.2 Is there evidence that the student is able to assess individual
strengths and weaknesses?   1   2   3   4

4.3 Did the student assume the appropriate responsibility for change
when necessary?   1   2   3   4

4.4 Does the student know when to speak and when to listen in the
group process?   1   2   3   4

make the learning more meaningful. Students required to show evidence of learning attach more meaning to learning. Demands for performance also encourage self-regulation. This self-regulated learning occurring in a performance-based environment also promotes active knowledge construction. It is important for designers of these rich environments for active learning to provide assessments that reflect the learning they require and contribute to the supportive structure of the learning environment.

REFERENCES

Berliner, D. C. (1992). Redesigning classroom activities for the future. *Educational Technology, 10,* 7-14.

Bruder, I. (1993). Alternative assessment: Putting technology to the test. *Electronic Learning, 1,* 22-29.

Grabinger, R. S., & Dunlap, J. C. (1995). Rich environments for active learning: A definition. *ALT-J, 3*(2), 3-23.

Hannifin, M. J. (1992). Emerging technologies, ISD, and learning environments: Critical perspectives. *Educational Theory Research and Development, 40*(1), 49-63.

Honebein, C., Duffy, T., M., & Fishman, B. J. (1993). Constructivism and the design of learning environments: Context and authentic activities for learning. In T. M. Duffy, J. Lowych, & D. Jonassen (Eds.). *Designing environments for constructive learning* Hillsdale NJ: Springer-Verlag.

Frederiksen, J. R., & Collins, A. (1989). A systems approach to educational testing. *Educational Researcher, 18*(9), 27-32.

Johnson, D. W., & Johnson, R. T. (1987). *Learning together and alone* (2nd ed.) Englewood Cliffs NJ: Prentice-Hall.

Linn, R. L., Baker, E. L., & Dunbar, S. B. (1991). Complex, performance-based assessment: Expectations and validation criteria. *Educational Researcher, 20*(8), 15-21.

Marzano, R. (1992). Toward a comprehensive model of assessment. Aurora CO: Mid-continent Regional Educational Laboratory (McREL).

Performances and Exhibitions: The Demonstration of Mastery. In HORACE, published at Brown University by the Coalition of Essential Schools, *6*(3).

Principles and goals for mathematics assessment. (Spring 1992). In State Education Leader which was taken from For Good Measure, the National Summit report by the Mathematical Sciences Education board.

Resnick, L. (1992). Principles for educational improvement. *State Education Leader, 11*(1).

Shavelson, R. J. and GE Baxter, J. Pine (May, 1992). Research News and Comment: Performance assessments, political rhetoric and measurement reality. *Educational Researcher,* 22-27.

Shepard, L. A. (April, 1989). Why we need better assessments. *Educational Leadership, 46*(7), 4-9.

Slavin, R. E. (1983). *Cooperative learning.* New York: Longman.

Wiggins, G. E. (Winter, 1988). Rational numbers: Toward grading and scoring that help rather than harm learning. *American Educator, 12*(4), 20-47.

Wiggins, G. E. (May, 1989? A true test: Toward more authentic and equitable assessment. *Phi Delta Kappan, 70*(9), 703-714.

Wiggins, GE (May, 1991). Creating tests worth taking. *Educational Leadership, 49*(8), 26-33.

Wiggins, GE (September, 1992). *Designing effective & authentic assessment tasks: Guideline, principles & tools.* Center on Learning Assessment & School Structure.

INDEX

Aa

accessing information, 258
accompanying documentation, 180
advance organizer, 50
analogies, 55
anchored instruction, 229, 233
apprenticeship learning model, 233
argumentation space, 60
assessment and context, 258
assessments, 256
assimilation bias, 125, 126
associative links, 96, 111
audible feedback for links, 92
audience analysis, 117
audit trails, 211

Bb

balance in screen design, 141, 143
benchmarking, 264
book mill, 16
browsing, 7, 8, 10, 58
button size, 92

Cc

card x of y strategy, 108, 112
center justification, 150
change in cursor type, 92
check and balance, 176
clg (command language grammar), 56
coaching, 243

cognitive flexibility theory, 122, 134
cognitive guiding questions, 51
cognitive load, 199
cognitive modeling, 38
cognitive overhead, 129
cognitive tools, 2
coherence models, 55
collaboration, 247
collaborative group roles, 219
collaborative learning, 37, 218, 229, 248
collaborative working environments, 36
commenting computer code, 179
communication metaphor, 13, 22
computer as tool, 132
concept learning, 189
concept maps, 6
consistent internal margins, 142
content space, 60
context sensitive online help, 125
contextual links, 95
control buttons, 92
cooperative learning, 218
cost overruns, 195
cursor, 167
customer feedback, 184

Dd

descriptive variables, 179
designer-constructed nodes, 78

determining multimedia outcomes, 190
determining nodes, 79
development support, 194
didactic embeddedness, 38
diminishing resources, 195
direct interface, 129
directionality, links, 90
directive cues, 155
documentation, 181
documented procedures, 178

Ee

elaboration, 48
elaboration theory, 48
elaborative links, 98, 112
ergonomic factors, 117
error messages, 126
evaluation questions, 207
evaluation, 187
evolution, 174
existing knowledge, 230
exploration metaphor, 13, 23
exploration, 240
exploring, 58
external maintenance needs, 175

Ff

feedback, 134, 167
field support, 178
focus group, 191
font portability, 145
fonts, 145
forgiveness feature, 167
forgiveness, 201
formative assessments, 257
formative evaluation, 184, 187, 207
free hypertext browsing, 37
front-end evaluation, 187
full justification, 150
functional areas, 150

Gg

generative learning, 228
glossary, 168
goal setting, 213
granularity, 64–66
graphic devices, 137, 144, 154
grouping, 92

Hh

harmony, 141, 143
HCI design, 116
headings, 153
help screens, 171
hierarchical charts, 111
hierarchical organization, 204
higher-level thinking, 258
hints, 242
holistic learning, 8
human factors, 62
human-computer interaction, 53
human-computer interface design, 116
hypercube lattice, 203
hypermedia, benefits, 2
hypermedia, definition, 7
hypermedia, risks and costs, 20
hypertext, 34
hypertext, definition, 4
hypertext in traditional classroom learning, 42
hypertext jumps, 57
hypertext user interfaces, 52, 53

Ii

icons, 90
indentation, 154
information resources, 15
informative interfaces, 202
instructional evaluation criteria, 189
instructional text, definition, 138
intentional learning, 212, 223
interactivity indicators, 92, 167
interface evaluation, 199
interface forgiveness, 201
interface metaphor, 200
interface transparency, 199, 200
internal maintenance needs, 175
interviewing learners, 207
interviews, 207
intuitive interface, 129
iterative interface refinement, 53

Jj

justification, 150

Kk

knowledge engineering, 38
knowledge integration, 189
knowledge maps, 207

Ll

labeling, 90
Layers of Necessity, 197
leading, 142
learner control, 45–46
learning experiences, 191
learning outcomes, 189, 191
learning plan, 216
learning support links, 101
learning tool attributes, 51
learning tool, 46
left justification, 150
left/right arrows, 108
legibility, definition, 138
level x of y strategy, 112
line length, 149
linear content organization, 204
link visibility, 92
links, labeling, 90
literary machines, 40
locus of control, 38, 131
lower case, 147

Mm

macroorganization of nodes, 79
maintenance procedures, 176
managing learning, 216
maps, 111
media, characteristics, 3
media, definition, 2
menu bar, 162
metacognitive awareness, 220
metaphor, 55, 119, 129, 163, 200
microorganization of nodes, 79
modular code, 182
modular code, advantages, 182
modularizing, 77
multimedia integration, 202
multimedia, definition, 5

Nn

naming variables, 179
navigation assistance, 37
navigation elements, 161
navigation tools, 161, 163
navigation, 8
new media, 1
new releases, 178
node construction, 78
node of origination, 90
node organization, 79
node size, 83
nodes, 77

Oo

observation, 207
one-way link, 90
online help, 119
orientation reflex, 21
overrun tolerance, 195
overt activity, 239

Pp

paragraph spacing, 154
patterns of use, 121
planning space, 60
preliminary instruction, 161
prioritizing goals, 215
problem analysis, 118
problem-solving outcomes, 189
procedures, 176
product evaluation, 188
product evolution, 174
product, definition, 173
production bias, 121, 122
program help links, 104
program maps, 163
program operation links, 102
program tracking links, 101
program-defined links, 89
progressive turnover, 120
project management skills, 216
Project Xanadu, 39
prototype, 198
pull-down menus, 162

Qq

questioning, 213, 214
questions, 242
quitting a program, 168

Rr

REALs, 212, 228, 257
recognizability, 140
reflection, 249
relational links, 96
reliability, assessments, 263
resource metaphor, 13, 20, 21
rhetorical space, 60
right justification, 150

Ss

safe climate for learning, 222
sans serif, 145
scaffolding, 215, 242
scanning, 58
screen location of links, 92
scrolling fields, 83
seamless content, 203
seamless organization, 202
seamless technologies, 202
seamlessness, 202
searching, 58
self-assessment, 215
self-directed learning strategies, 196
self-reflection, 267
sequential links, 95, 96, 108
serendipity effect, 19
serendipity, 19
serif, 145
setting goals, 111
shells, 78
simplicity, 141
social development, 61
social regulation skills, 268
Socratic dialogue techniques, 50
software patch, 179
space between lines, 149
student expectations, 192
support links, 100, 106
system metaphor, 201

Tt

table of contents, 161,162
task orientation, 204
teacher's role, 241
teacher/student relationship, 41
techno-love, 188
technocentric, 188
tests, 255, 256, 258
text elements, 137

title screen, 158
topical organization, 204
transparency, interface design, 115, 128-131
two-way link, 90
type size, 146-147

Uu

upper case, 147
user attitudes, 120
user orientation, 158
user support features, 168
user training, 196
user-constructed nodes, 78

Vv

validity, assessments, 261
visibility, buttons 92,
visibility, text, 139
visual effects, 167
visual feedback for links, 92
visual interest, 144

Ww-Zz

wandering, 58
webs, 111
white space, 142
windows, 130
work-around document, 179
Xanalogical storage, 39
zone of proximal development, 212